THE
SINGAPORE HOUSE
and
RESIDENTIAL LIFE
1819–1939

THE
SINGAPORE HOUSE
and
RESIDENTIAL LIFE
1819–1939

NORMAN EDWARDS

TALISMAN

REMEMBERING
PROFESSOR NORMAN
EDWARDS, 1931–2018

Originally published by Oxford University Press in 1991 in paperback

First Hardback edition published in 2017
First Paperback edition in 2019

Talisman Publishing Pte Ltd
52 Genting Lane #06-05
Ruby Land Complex 1
Singapore 349560
talisman@apdsing.com
www.talismanpublishing.com

ISBN 978-981-14-0845-8

Editor Kim Inglis
Designers Norreha Sayuti, Foo Chee Ying
Studio Manager Janice Ng
Publisher Ian Pringle

Page 1 *Malay* kampong *house.*

Page 2 *An early view of the first clubhouse of the Teutonia Club, circa 1880s. It was built around 1862 near the junction of Orchard and Scotts roads.*

Right *Portrait of the famous Ah Hoh Kay, more often known as Whampoa, with his grandchildren.*

CONTENTS

PART 3

DOMESTIC LIFE AND THE INTERIOR

PART 4

STYLE AND FORM

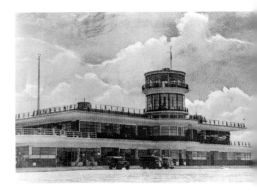

Preface

꘎꘎꘎

When approached by Talisman Publishing in Singapore a year or so back to republish *The Singapore House & Residential Life 1819–1939*, originally published by Oxford University Press, I was more than delighted to cooperate and to write this short preface to the relaunched edition. The Singapore house is not just a building; it is a cultural phenomenon. Culture means ordinary everyday values—attitudes, beliefs, ideas and heritage. These apply to the cultural landscape of which the house forms a part and is particularly applicable to a fast-growing metropolis like Singapore that has changed immeasurably in recent years.

People who know this fascinating country are full of admiration for its fiscal and economic achievements, but many residents and visitors are unaware of the rich landscape and heritage upon which the island and city were formed.

This newly presented edition addresses the House's unique nature in the context of its colonial past, but with an enhanced design and layout that honours the text I completed some three decades ago. Landscape also comes to mind in the nature of the lush, richly textured character of this new volume and the illustrations newly released and so generously permitted. Page by page, the past resonates in this book with its tinted period illustrations and, I hope, a better introduction to the history of architecture in the city-state.

In my home town of Richmond, Surrey, WH Smith, the stationer and British High Street label, sits alongside global brands such as Costa Coffee, McDonalds, Tesco and Next. It is selling off vast stocks of large format illustrated books at £5 per copy. These non-fiction volumes are of high quality, of seemingly erudite scholarship and robust intellectual content. Skilfully crafted, they include intelligently designed illustrations on white gloss paper. Their pages grab you. One feels the urge to read on, to see, to understand more. The real value of these books is probably nearer £80 per volume.

Today few people seem to read. They prefer one click on a smartphone—as if speed is a virtue—and the job is done. Even in the case of the first edition of *The Singapore House 1819–1939*, now 30 years since publication, if I ever manage to get

Overleaf View from Government Hill of the Singapore River and Chinatown, 1824. Original sketch by Edmond de la Touanne; coloured lithograph.

Page 12-13 A view of Clarke Quay and the Read Bridge, officially opened in 1889. Note the Fort Canning lighthouse in the distance, erected in 1903 which dates the photograph around the early 1900s.

Page 14 Detail from a print of the early settlement, 1852. The artist was Charles Walter Kinlock. St Andrew's Church is at centre and the Raffles Institution is in foreground on right.

any one of my four adult children to bother 'reading' it, it's a case of a fast look at a handful of the pictures, a comment such as "interesting"—and I have the book, to ponder, back in hand.

Around the corner from WH Smith is Waterstones, an eminent book retailer that, in the current climate, is hanging in there. At one time it was bought by WH Smith, then passed into ownership of the HMV Group, and now, following "poor sets of results", has been sold on to the present owner, Russian billionaire Alexander Mamut, with James Daunt as Managing Director to give the new group name credibility.

The business of these chains is monetary: to compete financially, to keep ahead in the marketplace. The business also depends on the type of books sold—on the one hand, literary, informed, of high intellectual content; on the other, entertaining, as in the case of the original launching of the HMV group as an "entertainment retailer". Both book types sell, however many, for however long.

One imagines the weaving and ducking of book retailers, juggling stocks of books of different types according to snap changes in the unpredictable demand for books of different titles in bookshops in different locations. The retailer is also in demand in regard to the matter of "brands" in whatever form, from the importance given to the Waterstones' apostrophe, to the substantial brand value of its letter "W", to commercial concessions such as coffee, to the rapid insertion of those with front-of-house educated accents.

What all this means for the book industry is anybody's guess, but for this book I invite you to accompany me on a journey. No rush. Leave behind those 21st-century habits. Armed now with understanding, join me in a ramble through the streets of Singapore, including its older detached houses and their lingering memories of former times, and, whilst relishing these, see whether book reading can be pleasurable again.

Norman Edwards
June 2016

Introduction

This book addresses the subject of the Singapore detached house in terms of its evolution from the time of first settlement to the outbreak of World War II. It does not include the urban terrace-house which, although an important component in the life of the colony, is seen as a separate subject.

The term 'detached house' calls for some clarification. It refers to both one- and two-storey separate houses, each on its own piece of ground. It includes the palatial residences of the British colonial administrators and the wealthy Chinese *towkays* at one extreme and the more modest bungalow of the less privileged members of middle-class society at the other.

The meaning of the word 'bungalow' is itself significant in terms of what follows, and deserves some discussion. The definition given in Webster's dictionary is 'a thatched or tiled house or cottage, of a single story, usually surrounded by a veranda', which describes it in physical terms and as one particular form of the detached house in general. This meaning—a form of shelter or construction—is certainly a common one, but it is too simple. The word has had, as well, a variety of social, cultural, political and economic meanings to different societies at different times.

The concept of the bungalow, including its compound or private garden setting, came originally from India as a result of the English colonial experience there in the 18th and 19th centuries. In England, the concept was embraced as a part of the romantic ideal and as a vehicle for all sorts of post-industrial social and political aspirations by the rising middle classes and, in the process, modified. It was then diffused to the British colonies, including Singapore, as the basic residential unit of the colonial community. The story of its subsequent evolution in Singapore is one bound up with the multi-cultural nature of this society and the social, economic, and political transformations that took place up to the time of World War II.

It is in terms of this perspective that this book has been written. Although the interest is architectural, it is not exclusively so. The house is also seen as a social and cultural phenomenon and, as such, as an inseparable part of the Singaporean suburban settlement. Stated generally, people live in landscapes of which the house is a part. The intention has been to take a realistic view of the Singapore house rather than one which portrays it simply in terms of its aesthetic character and, in particular, as an example of 'high art' at the expense of the ordinary, vernacular bungalow.

The book is thus written in four parts. Part I describes the emergence of the detached house in Singapore as an ingredient of the first settlement and as a product of external cultural and architectural influences, and its development in the form of the plantation villa up to the 1870s. The book then moves to the suburban house during the period 1880 to 1940. Part II portrays the physical and social process of suburbanization in Singapore echoing developments in England and India. Part III describes the house in terms of domestic life and attitudes and general social and other changes. And finally, Part IV looks at it in architectural terms: physically and stylistically.

It is hoped that, in terms of this perspective, the work will go some way to illustrate the nature and character of the pre-World War II Singapore house and to show how and in what way it developed its own identity. ❖

Origins

England

S een as a cultural as much as a physical phenomenon, the pre-World War II house was merely one ingredient of the colonial environment. A large part of the ideology underlying the form of this environment sprang from the experience that the new settlers had had of life in their home country, England, and in colonial India. Ideas and attitudes developed there were transferred to Singapore and gave shape to the early settlement and, in due course, to the form of the colonial suburb made up of its individual detached houses.

At the time the new settlement was beginning to take shape in the 1830s, England was a land of towns and small villages and large areas of countryside, mostly agricultural. During the next 100 years, however, the rise of industrial capitalism spawned a new breed of middle-class urbanites in vastly increased numbers. The Industrial Revolution had brought unparalleled opportunities for upward social mobility linked to the demand for new jobs, particularly in finance, manufacturing, engineering and the civil service. Physically, this was manifested in the expansion of the towns and cities into the countryside in a vast unplanned sprawl. By the end of the century, England had become a nation of suburban dwellers.

The factors underlying this development were complex. The new middle classes had a different set of aspirations and a new view of their social position. Both of these were tied to their residential expectations. The lifestyle of the upper-class, rural-based 'landed gentry', including the ownership of a country villa estate, now became the ideal. This was despite the fact that the earning capacity of the new middle-class employee was often little more than that of his former working-class compatriot.

These aspirations of the new bourgeoisie were fuelled by the new 'garden city' ideology. Prompted by the worst environmental excesses of the Industrial Revolution, the new movement sought a marriage of town and country. The virtues of this new ideal were displayed in a series of model estates such as Port Sunlight and Hampstead Garden suburb and, later, complete new towns such as Letchworth and Welwyn. Each house was detached on its own lot within an overall country garden setting. Underlying this image was a commitment to fresh air, health, space and privacy. There was also a new view of the countryside. Whereas previously it had been seen as a place of agricultural production, now it was seen as the setting for a new suburban rustic lifestyle. Roses above the door and a gun above the fireplace were now to be desired.

Opposite Salvation Army Social Campaign by William Booth from 1890. Such initiatives were very prevalent in England—and they influenced the aspirations of those in the new settlement in Singapore.

Lodging House in Field Lane, England, 1848.

Such ideals were largely a product of the reaction to slum conditions in the urban centres. Overcrowding, high rates of child mortality, poor sanitation, the prevalence of endemic disease, and the exploitation of the urban proletariat by a wealthy landlord and factory-owner class all contributed to the flight from the cities, of those who could afford it, in quest of new ideals in the country.

Central to these ideals, too, was the importance given to family life and leisure. The family was seen as a microcosm of an ordered, dutiful Christian society. Such a view was mainly in reaction to perceived lax moral attitudes associated with life in the slums. The new code of family behaviour was often quite rigid, partly a reflection of the insecurity of those from working-class backgrounds seeking a higher position in society.

The home then had to fulfil these many functions: to comfort and purify, to give relief and privacy from the cares of the world, to rear its members in an appropriate set of Christian values, and, above all, to proclaim by its ordered arrangements, polite behaviour, cleanliness, tidiness and distinctive taste that its members belonged to a class of substance, culture and respectability. The house itself was to be a visible expression of these values.[1]

1 J Burnett, *A Social History of Housing, 1815–1970*, London, Methuen, 1980

Domestic life embraced more members of the household than those of the immediate family. Families were often large for two reasons. The numbers of relatives, including offspring, was often high and thus, for practical reasons, servants were needed. Servants were also desired as a means of signifying social status. However, by the 1920s and 1930s, changing patterns of employment, involving an expanded middle class, meant a larger proportion on lower incomes. This was tied to a gradual reduction in the size of the household: fewer servants and a tendency towards the nuclear family of parents and one, two or three children.

The emphasis given to family life was partly due to the separation of domestic life from work. Though initially this meant fewer hours at home for the breadwinner, by the turn of the century, working hours had become shorter and the opportunities for recreation greater. The ownership of one's own allotment gave a fillip to the traditional popular pastime of gardening. The English climate, however, also encouraged indoor activities. Parlour games were popular, as was the piano, and after 1900 a spate of technical inventions, including the gramophone and the wireless, soon led to less active forms of indoor entertainment.

Apart from family activities, recreation became increasingly the responsibility of commercial and municipal organizations. By the 1920s, the cinema became the most popular form of entertainment. There were also clubs, music halls, libraries and museums. Pubs—usually known as 'hotels' to preserve an appropriate air of respectability—though mainly a working-class institution, were also popular in the suburbs, notwithstanding the middle-class emphasis on temperance and the value given to family life.

In upper-class suburban areas, an increase in the number of tennis clubs was paralleled by an even greater number of tennis courts in private back gardens. Tennis clubs were only slightly less snobbish than golf clubs, which also grew in number, as did clubs of other types. Cycling, indebted to the invention of the pneumatic tyre in 1890, coincided with the new desire to see and enjoy the countryside. If the countryside itself was disappearing under the pressure of the new population invasion, there were seaside resorts to visit. The amount of time spent in such leisure activities was qualified by the attention given to formal Christian worship reflected in large Sunday congregations and a large number of churches to accommodate them. To be seen at church was expected, and was a measure of one's commitment to the values of suburban society.

So, too, the ownership of a private bungalow on its own allotment was a perfect vehicle for signalling one's position in the social hierarchy. Status and the desire for privacy went hand in hand. The mere putting of distance between the suburbs and the urban core fulfilled both goals. This was reinforced by the concern for the right 'tone' of exclusivity. Whole estates were often enclosed to keep out the hoi-polloi and were named after well-known families or aristocratic dynasties, as were the streets of which they consisted. Along these streets, usually referred to as 'roads', 'groves', 'crescents', 'ways' and 'avenues', the houses were well hidden behind high walls or hedges and further removed from the street by front gardens. To the world outside, penetration of these hallowed sanctuaries, controlled as they were by their *nouveau riche* inhabitants, almost took on the status of a mystical act.

Such attitudes, and many of the other aspects of the new English suburban ideology, would be echoed in the nature and form of the detached suburban house in Singapore, when it began to appear in the second half of the 19th century.

Colonial India

Suburban England, though, was not the only significant external cultural influence on the character of the Singapore house. The other source was the residential compound of the British settlers in India. It was from the ranks of the new English middle-class suburbanites that most of the colonial officials sent out to manage affairs in India were drawn. Contact with India, however, somewhat changed their view of the world. From being a socially mobile class aspiring to the norms of a landed aristocracy, they became members of a special group on the edge of a less advanced foreign world. From being part of a society based on an urban-industrial economy, they were now members of a community on the fringe of a rural-based agricultural economy. The effect of this for the new settlers was a certain tension between the sense of operating from within a vacuum on the one hand and pressures to interact on the other. In other British colonies, involvement with the indigenous population was only slight. But in India, the influence of the native culture on colonial society, and vice versa, was more pronounced. To a lesser extent, this was also true of Singapore. Both colonies were witness to an interchange of ideas between the local and British communities which resulted in something unique in colonial society and in the character of its environment.

Despite this, the British were unlikely to relate too closely to native ways. Certainly in India, their position as rulers demanded a certain aloofness, and at worst, a belief in their racial superiority. Lurking behind this façade, there was also the threat of being too absorbed into a strong native culture: the fear of 'going native'. The effect of this was a certain conservatism and a concern for order and conformity. This and their passion for privacy, an important component of the English suburban middle-class ideology, ensured their security.

For the members of the Indian colonial community, being distant from the native population was matched by increasing disengagement from their British peers back home. This and the conservative view resulted in a certain homogeneity in behaviour and lifestyle. The same routines prevailed from generation to generation, resulting in something of British India's characteristic timeless quality. Such setting of their ways was reinforced by the lack of new blood. This was less the case in Singapore, where there was considerable turnover and more contact with Britain, as the new settlers usually returned after three or more years to be replaced by new recruits. Many of these were single men. Being resistant to marriage outside their own society, the majority wanted to return to marry and bring back their new brides fresh from England.

The belief in order and conformity was all-pervading, certainly in India. A prerequisite for effective administration, it extended from the unreasonable promulgation of rules and public manuals of instruction to a concern for puritanical self-righteousness in public and in private. Emphasis on polite behaviour, cleanliness, Christian virtue and family duty were no less important than the projection of these values abroad, just as they had been in English suburban society. Such ideals were fundamental to the shape of the colonial suburban settlement. In India, this generally took the form of the civil and military station. Although this was not a characteristic form of the suburban settlement in Singapore, many of the attitudes it embodied were passed on.

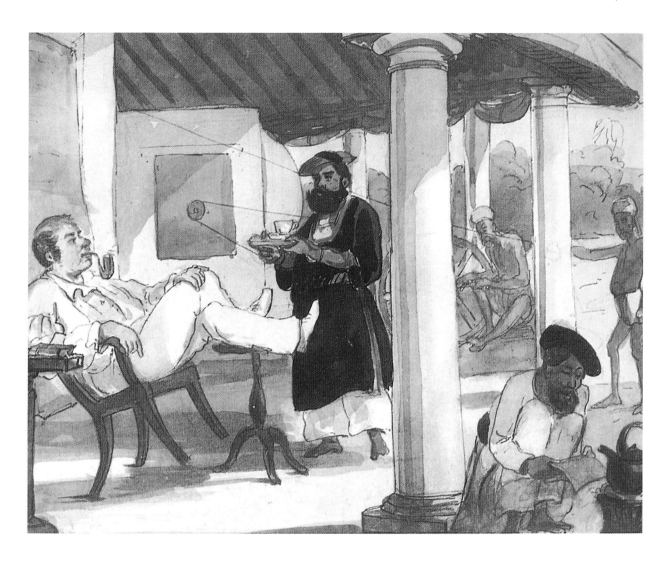

Typically, the civil and military portions were in two distinct sections. The two key elements in the military portion were the 'maidan' and the 'lines'.

European man and servants, India, 1859.

In the beginning, the military encampment had been organized in defensive lines well away from the enemy, with a clear field of fire, referred to as the 'maidan' or parade ground. The need to maintain distance between the military lines and the enemy persisted even when the need for military preparedness had disappeared. What was formerly the enemy now became the native bazaar. The need for maximum space beyond the confines of the native quarter and the British settlement was not only the fear of physical or cultural contamination. It was in response to the need to upgrade the standard of Indian urban life through the avoidance of encroachments, to minimize overcrowdedness, and to improve sanitary conditions through the provision of more light and air; values highly prized in suburban England.

Between the military and civil portions of the station, various components representative of English suburban life acted as the station's community focus: the theatre assembly rooms, the racquets' court, the public hospital, a public bath, a bandstand. Beyond, there was a park or small botanical garden on the other side of which were the residences of civil or government officials set in their own generous compounds.

The residences of government officials in India were grand edifices. This home of Lord Macaulay in Calcutta later became the Bengal Club, the original facade of which is pictured here.

The informal, open character of this area was in marked contrast to the geometrical order of the military portion. It was also in sharp contrast to the native town. This, and the distance separating them, reflected the wish to be well removed from the congestion and other perceived evils of the indigenous quarter, including lack of cleanliness, imagined or real.

The concern for a healthy, spacious environment and the value placed on privacy, Christian conduct, and English connections is apparent in this description of early 19th-century Bangalore:

"Bangalore was in a healthy situation, comparatively free from malarial mosquitoes, on high ground, with plenty of room for development. There was already a walled city and a fort there, but in the British military tradition of developing a separate area for barracks, cantonments etc. apart from the 'native' population, the new town was planned a few miles further East, on land assigned to the British by the Maharajah of Mysore. It was spaciously laid out, with wide streets, parks, Christian churches in the Classical style: and the streets and houses were given nostalgic British names: Cambridge Road, Alexandra Street, Burnside, Clovelly, etc." [2]

A key element in this description is the detached bungalow on its own piece of ground. The idea of the English suburban house was in turn very much part of the cultural transfer accompanying colonization. In its move to India and Singapore, however, it underwent some transformation.

---

2 Janet Pott, *Old Bungalows in Bangalore, South India*, London, published by the author, 1977, page 9

In India, as in Singapore, houses were often huge, as were the grounds on which they stood. Compounds were commonly five acres or more; in rural districts in India, they could be anything up to 15 acres. This was due partly to the fact that, as in Singapore, ownership of land was not initially subject to competition in the market: within the political system of colonialism, it was there almost for the taking. Large estates were important in signifying social and political status and were one of the major compensations for a life spent in exile. The cheap manpower needed to maintain and operate such large complexes was also available. A typical Indian residence would have ten to 15 servants including maids, *amahs*, a cook and cook's assistants, gardeners, drivers, a guard and a tailor.

Large houses and gardens were also a reflection of the value placed on social life, including garden parties, receptions, games and tournaments. The English fetish for such sporting pastimes as tennis, badminton and golf was accommodated not only in clubs but in private compounds; as in England, private putting-greens were popular and courts were almost as common as flower-beds.

Social and other forms of public life also necessitated privately owned forms of transport. As with the Indian élite, members of the colonial community were carried, at first in hand- or horse-drawn carriages such as the palanquin or the gharry and later by car. Space on site was therefore necessary for the storage, maintenance, and movement of such vehicles, in the form of stables, carriage houses, garages, and driveways.

Apart from such functional requirements, the compound was valued in other ways. The cultivation of an English-style garden in the more suburban settlements along 'romantic' lines or in picturesque vein was one means of establishing identity with England and with colonial society and separation from the indigenous culture.

Such values and ideas, attitudes and images were to be highly significant for the colonial residential environment in Singapore. ❖

A bungalow for English residents in India in the 19th century invariably boasted a large garden, as well as a veranda with overhangs to protect from sun and rain.

Architectural Influences

❖✻❖

Architecturally, the genesis of the Singapore colonial house before World War II lay in influences from a number of different sources, from the West and from within the Asian region. Probably the most significant of these influences was the crude native dwelling of 18th-century Bengali India, which was adopted and modified by the British colonial administrators.

This simple rectangular hut was of two types. One had a crescent-shaped thatched roof generously overhanging the walls and supported on wooden posts to form a veranda. The other was roofed at two levels: an upper pitched tile or thatched roof and a lower veranda roof. Although there is some uncertainty as to which of the two types was the one adopted by the British when they first settled in that part of India, this structure became the European residential prototype in rural areas. Simply erected, cool and comfortable, and well protected from the monsoon rains, it was an appropriate solution to the sudden demand for mass housing from the increased population of new colonial officials, planters and the military.

Romantic images of the bungalow filtered through to England during the years of industrialization and urbanization of the late 1700s and early 1800s. Set as it was in the

Village in a clearing in the Sundarbans in Bengal displaying the conical roof style; sketch by Frederic Peter Layard, 1839–1890.

Typical dak *bungalow or government-owned resthouse (1868) in the village of Narkanda in the district of Shimla in the Indian state of Himachal Pradesh.*

countryside and the hill stations of colonial India, the bungalow appeared to the British as a positive alternative to the slum terrace-house and the associations it held of environmental degradation and social exploitation of lower, working-class industrial Britain. If it were not possible to escape to India, the bungalow idea could be imported and adapted.

At first, bungalows—no longer strictly like the Indian colonial version, but in any case, simple, single-storey structures, and more importantly connoting images of rusticity—were built in England in the form of seaside developments. By the early 1900s, the bungalow had become the medium for widespread suburbanization and the solution to the housing requirements of the middle classes. In parallel with these developments, the idea of the bungalow was diffused outwards to the British colonies, including Singapore, and to other parts of the world, such as North America. In the process, it became a vehicle for different political intentions, social ideals, and cultural values.

In the case of Singapore, the social and cultural climate was an unusually cosmopolitan one. At the time of the British landing in Singapore in 1819, the population consisted mainly of Malay fishermen, with a small number of Chinese. By the 1830s, working-class Chinese, attracted mainly from southern China by the economic opportunities in Malaya, dominated Singapore's population. Although this trend progressed and the predominant culture was Chinese, other ethnic groups continued to arrive, so that by the early 1900s there were altogether 48 different ethnic groups and 54 spoken languages or dialects. On top of this was the cultural, social, and political influence of the British colonial administration.

The implications of this for the detached house, once suburbanization began in the 1880s, were that apart from the British and other European administrative and business élite, only the wealthier members of other ethnic communities could afford one. For the rest, other than for the Malays, life took place in the terrace-houses of the urban centre.

A Malay house on stilts in a village in the Straits Settlements, circa 1890.

The Malays continued in their vernacular tradition of *kampong* life and, with few exceptions, did not identify with Western middle-class aspirations such as the ownership of a suburban bungalow. The Malay hut—consisting as it did of a timber frame, wickerwork, atap or bark walling, and an atap roof—was not to prove an appropriate model for the European lifestyle even if some of its characteristics, such as its open, raised main floor and its spacious *serambi* or veranda and well-ventilated interior, were to be emulated. European requirements included a more permanent, durable mode of building which was less vulnerable to the risk of fire, attack by termites, and the effects of weather.

The main influences on the Singapore house were to be Western and mainly, if not exclusively, English and Anglo-Indian. Early European influences included those associated with the emigration of Chinese from the southern part of China to Malaya in the mid-19th century. There were two aspects to this.

The character of buildings erected by the Europeans who had established trading rights in southern China was a product of changes associated with the Confucian revival, beginning in the Sung period. Amongst these changes was the development of a more tolerant attitude towards foreign religious beliefs by the Chinese regime. Architecturally, this was reflected in a mixture of Confucian, Buddhist, Muslim and Italian architectural modes: the last of these included a stylistic mixture of semi-rococco European and Chinese motifs.

The establishment of the 'Treaty Ports' and the transfer of Hong Kong to the British also precipitated significant political, ideological and other artistic changes. Even the traditional belief of the Chinese in their own cultural superiority was put to question. An outcome of this transformation was the appearance of houses in a variety of Western styles emanating from those countries most active in economic intervention in the region: Germany, Russia and Britain. The amalgamation of these styles, all of which drew upon classical idioms, became known as the 'compradoric style'.

Other Western influences on Malayan life and culture, and thus on the Singapore house, were more direct and preceded the colonial intrusion into the mainland Chinese ports by some 300 years. First came the Portuguese, who penetrated the Malayan peninsula via Malacca in 1511 and built stone fortifications, churches and residences in a unique Mediterranean version of the classical style. They were followed by the Dutch, who brought a more elegant, highly developed interpretation of classicism in their public and residential buildings and interiors. This style appealed greatly to the Malayan Peranakan people or Babas, the name loosely referring to the progeny of marriages between Chinese males and Malay females. More generally, it was the Chinese who were most exposed to the influence of Dutch culture because Malacca was then the centre of Chinese civilization in Malaya. However, as influences on the form of the Singapore house, all of these were minor compared to those from Britain and colonial India.

The British view of the bungalow as a modest romantic retreat was certainly one thing, but there was another equally significant interpretation of the Indian colonial house. This was the grand Regency town residence in the Palladian manner, adapted, through the use of verandas, wide overhangs and high ceilings, to tropical conditions. Simultaneously, the British aristocracy had transformed the simple pyramidal roofed bungalow into something much more dignified, resulting in a unique interpretation of the Palladian style.

The popularity of Palladianism in English high society at that time was due, amongst other things, to the proliferation of pattern books within the ranks of the master builders, craftsmen and artisans. The Palladian style had thus in varying ways entered the architectural bloodstream, not only of England, but also of other European countries, and in turn was diffused to their respective colonial realms in Asia.

Watercolour by German artist, Justinian Ganz, of a Palladian-style European house in Madras. 1834.

Georgian-style mansion called Suffolk Park in Penang (circa 1805). During the 1810s and 1820s, the mansion served as a meeting place for critical political discussions, including, most notably, discussions with Stamford Raffles regarding the founding of Singapore.

If Palladianism in Malaya began with the Portuguese and continued with the Dutch, it flourished under the rule of the British, whose arrival in Penang in the 18th century coincided with the emergence of Georgian and Regency architecture in England. Its entry into Malaya by way of colonial India was a result of the arrival of the British East India colonists there, an event which in due course gave rise to the term 'Anglo-Indian', referring to the Palladian style of Georgian architecture as it evolved in colonial India during the 18th century. In India, as well as in the Straits Settlements of Malaya, the style was universally preferred by the British élite, who associated the concepts of Renaissance humanism upon which it was based with their own ideals of rank, prestige and elegance.

With these as the principal background influences on the emergence of a new set of middle- and upper middle-class residential aspirations for Malayan colonial society, what of local, regional influences? The form of the Malay house has been mentioned. The Chinese, who came to Malaya and who were soon to comprise three-quarters of the Singaporean population, had their own traditional attitudes to residential form.

These emanated from a deep-seated belief in the harmony between man and nature and between inside and outside space. The congruence of individual and social man and the notion of the family as a microcosm of society were two aspects of the Chinese concept of unity. Cosmic forces, the symbolism of natural features and of correct orientation were also profoundly significant. Within the universe, the Chinese house was seen primarily as a refuge from the world outside. It was also a symbol of respect for social and family order. It was the centre of Chinese life.

Spatially, this was manifested in the residential compound of courtyards, pavilions and enclosing walls. These elements were ordered by a strict formal regularity and concern for axial symmetry. The internal organization of spaces reflected the balance between four essential functions: shelter; private worship; work; and the mutual interaction between domestic, public and ceremonial activities. Unlike the grand architectural traditions of the imperial structures of northern China, however, these houses were part of an unselfconscious process of vernacular building based on models handed down through previous generations.

In the movement of the southern Chinese to that part of Asia to the south—called the Nanyang, or 'South Seas'—these beliefs and forms were transferred, initially with relatively little change, as a result of their contact with other cultures. In Malaya it was only Peranakan society—or more generally the so-called Straits Chinese, the descendants of Chinese-Malay marriages—who assimilated certain Malay as well as European cultural customs.

The typical Peranakan terrace-house, for example, had many of the characteristics of the southern Chinese house, including courtyards, ancestral hall and screens, all within an enclosing wall, but at a reduced scale. However, it was narrower and deeper than its mainland predecessor. It also reflected a unique lifestyle in its furnishings and decoration.

In due course, the wealthiest members of Peranakan society also aspired to the ownership of a European-style detached residence. Like the British themselves, they became enamoured with the pomp and grandeur of the Greek and Roman motifs and other classical idioms of the modified Palladian style after it came to Malaya in the late 1700s. A number of the Anglo-Indian-style grand mansions which were built by successful Chinese merchants in Penang, like those of the British, reflect these tendencies. Houses such as these would also be characteristic of the new colony in Singapore when it was founded shortly afterwards. ❖

Many early Chinese homes in Singapore were built in European style, but there were exceptions. This home was one of them! Built in 1882 by early pioneer, Tan Yeok Nee, it reflects the oriental desire for harmony between man and nature.

The First Settlement

In England, the suburban exodus was just beginning when Raffles established Singapore as a British settlement in 1819. Earlier, life for Raffles had been conducted against the background of late 18th-century Georgian London. In Singapore, the settlement that quickly took shape under his direction reflected this experience, including his work with the London office of the East India Company and his later achievements as Assistant Secretary to the Company in Penang. The form of the settlement was also a product of attitudes developed through the British colonial experience in India, inasmuch as Singapore was administered by the East India Company office in Calcutta.

In London, John Nash's famous Palladian Regency plan for the improvement of the West End had been published in 1812. The order and conformity of Regency London with its well-regulated rows of terrace-houses and garden squares were soon, however, to be submerged by the spirit of romanticism, including the urge to escape to the suburbs.

A view of Singapore from Government Hill, 1850s.

Nash's scheme represented the first effective state control of the development of London and must have had some bearing on the Regency flavour of the early settlement in Singapore

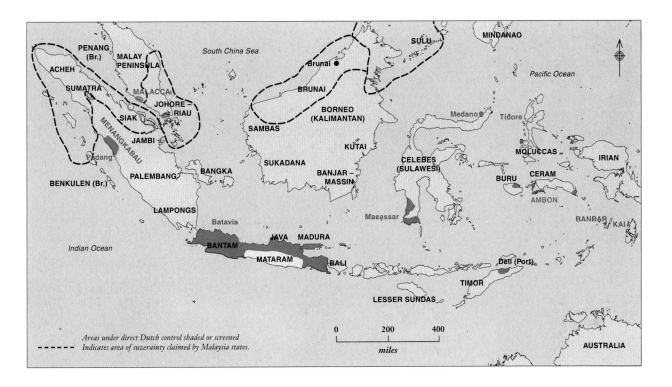

Areas under direct Dutch control shaded or screened
Indicates area of suzerainty claimed by Malaysia states.

following Raffles' directives. Penang, the other British station from where Raffles directed, in absence, the development of the early Singaporean settlement, also embodied Georgian and Palladian themes in its architecture and layout.

Map of the Malay World, 19th century.

But there was another equally significant influence on the physical character of the new settlement: the late 18th-and early 19th-century British Indian rural settlement or cantonment. These, together with the associated belief in order and regularity of the British administration, clearly gave physical shape to Raffles' plan for the new colony.

The historical circumstances leading to the establishment of the colony had included, over several centuries, the rise and fall of Singapore as a trading port in favour of Malacca, which was occupied by the Portuguese and then by the Dutch in the 16th and 17th centuries. Prompted by Raffles, the British were determined to undermine the authority of the Dutch in the region by establishing Singapore as a main base in addition to the existing British stations at Bencoolen on the Sumatran coast and Penang to the north. These stations were considered too far from the main routes of the Spice Trade and Raffles sought a more commanding site 'inside the gates' of the Dutch East India Empire.

Raffles' first task on landing was to seek an agreement with the Malay Sultan and his chief minister, the Temenggong Abdul Rahman, on trading rights in exchange for satisfactory cash considerations. This accomplished, he immediately issued directions for the layout of the settlement and, leaving its implementation to his newly appointed Resident, Colonel William Farquhar, left for Penang. Meanwhile, news of the landing of the British force had already attracted immigrants from other parts of the Archipelago, who came eager to take advantage of the new work opportunities.

The decisions necessary to accommodate this influx reflected policies adopted in laying out the British Indian settlements, modified to local circumstances. Unlike the flat, open landscape setting of the British Indian settlements, the amount of space available along the shoreline was restricted in depth by rising ground and uncleared jungle and at either end by rivers and marshlands. Under the terms of the Treaty, the settlement was physically defined by Tanjong Katong and the Rochore River in the north, Tanjong in the south, and inland as far as the range of a cannon shot.

Physical compactness was desirable in any case at this early stage, for it was necessary to act expediently, to put up temporary buildings and establish the main areas and road-ways in anticipation of further clearance and reclamation at a later date. At the same time, decisions made now would have long-term implications for the future shape of the colony.

In handing his instructions to Farquhar, Raffles allocated the area to the north of the Singapore River for the official cantonment; the Temenggong's camp was also on this side. Stretching further northward was the European town. Further to the north again was the Sultan's private compound in the area known as Kampung Glam. The Chinese quarter was disposed to the opposite, swampy side of the river and a bridge was to be built to connect the two sides. The commercial section was to be along the east coast.

Between 1819 and 1822, developments were left entirely in Farquhar's hands. Meanwhile, the population had grown from 500 to 10,000 as immigrants from all parts of the region poured in. They included Malays and Indonesians, Bugis seamen from the Celebes Islands, Chinese whose ranks now swelled to bursting point, Armenians, Arabs and Indians.

All of these nationalities had to be accommodated in designated areas and new ones established. Europeans at this stage were small in number. Apart from the officials working directly for the East India Company, most of these Europeans were representatives of the large Calcutta trading companies who hastened to take advantage of the opportunities for free trade. Others were reluctant to move in until land grants were issued. This in turn awaited confirmation that the East India Company would keep Singapore as a permanent possession in the face of strident Dutch opposition.

Farquhar's hand, meanwhile, was being forced by the merchants, who clamoured for land grants on which to build warehouses and offices, not where Raffles had allocated them on the shallow, sandy area of the east coast but on the northern bank of the Singapore River. Under pressure, Farquhar yielded, but subject to the condition that the buildings erected here may have to be demolished and the merchants relocated.

The decision to allow this change to original instructions infuriated Raffles, who on his third visit in 1822 made moves to dismiss Farquhar and to set up various committees to advise on the planning of future developments. Advice was also given by one Mr Coleman, 'by profession an architect'. George Drumgoolde Coleman was soon to influence developments in a more obvious way by erecting many of the earlier, more important permanent buildings.

The new planning proposals were outlined in a memorandum and a 'Master Plan' compiled with summary promptness by Lieutenant Jackson in 1822. The essence of this plan was that the former cantonment was to be enlarged and confirmed as the Government quarter, the European town consolidated and extended, a public esplanade

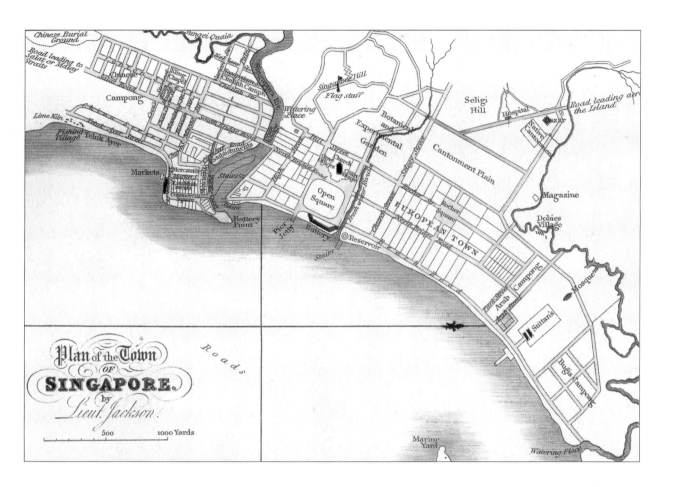

delineated along the waterfront, the various ethnic communities further segregated, and areas nominated for religious worship, commerce, education and a botanical garden. The plan also specified house sizes, street dimensions and materials.

Plan of the new town of Singapore by Lieutenant Jackson, 1823.

The execution of the plan, however, posed several problems. One was the removal of the Temenggong's camp from its position in the proposed Government quarter. This Raffles achieved with tact and diplomacy, including a gift of 5,000 Spanish dollars and 200 acres of land for the Temenggong's new settlement at Telok Blangah. Another difficulty was the lack of room for expansion of the merchants' territory which now occupied both banks of the river and part of the Government quarter. It was decided to move all of the merchants to a new area on the present site of Raffles' Place.

The basis for many of these decisions lay in Raffles' experience in England and his knowledge of colonial India. At this stage, the layout of the colony was still essentially that of a military camp and the new immigrants merely camp followers. The key element of the plan was still the cantonment, including the lines and parade ground for the troops and adjacent space for the officers' bungalows, all within the shadow of the fort and the residence of the 'chief authority'.

These represented the main components of the Indian military cantonment or camp. In India the cantonment was typically dispersed over a wide area of flat plain to enable rapid deployment of troops and artillery, whereas in Singapore the lack of space and orientation of defence lines toward the sea suggested a tighter, more restricted configuration. Even

Possibly the earliest surviving view of Singapore town, this sketch by Lieutenant Philip Jackson entitled 'View of Singapore from the Sea' dates from 1823. It shows a cluster of houses, including the Land Office and Post Office, on the northern side of the Singapore River. The house at the top is the bungalow Raffles built on Government Hill.

so, as in British India, considerations of health, safety, and fear of native contamination all suggested proper separation of the European community from the Chinese and native quarter: "… it will be necessary to allot sufficient space in a convenient and proper situation for officers' bungalows."[1]

But the health, safety, and convenience of the native residents were also on Raffles' mind, just as it had become an aspect of concern to the British administration in India: "In those quarters of the town occupied principally by the native inhabitants, the houses have been built without order or regularity and the streets and lanes have been formed without attention to the health, convenience or safety of the inhabitants."[2] It was a situation unworthy of an important centre of the future Empire. In the spirit of this new mood, Raffles decreed that "… proper measures be taken for securing to each individual the indisputable possession of the spot he may be permitted to occupy."[3]

As to planning matters, Raffles placed great stress in all his ordinances on the widths of roads and dimensions of the shops and warehouse properties bordering them. This must have been prompted not only by practical matters such as the efficient movement of people and vehicles, the risk of fire, convenient surveillance and considerations of climate, but also by images held of the ordered regularity of Georgian London. All of this served to reinforce the uniform appearance of the predominantly built-up commercial part of town,

1 Raffles to Farquhar, 25 June 1819, Straits Settlements Records, L10, National Library, Singapore
2 Sten Nilsson, *European Architecture in India 1750–1850*, London, Faber & Faber, 1968, page 68
3 Raffles to Farquhar, *op cit*

in contrast to the more spacious and rather more suburban, albeit Regency, character of the European town. This had been set out: "… as far eastwards as practicable, including as much ground as can possibly be acquired in that direction."[4] Within this regular layout, the Europeans were permitted to erect their own villas where they pleased and this in due course took place. As in Calcutta, "… there was only a small number of Europeans and each of them demanded attention and space for himself."[5] This had considerable visual significance: "… it adds greatly to the superb appearance that the houses are detached from each other and insulated in great space."[6]

Furthermore, in keeping with contemporary changes to the waterfronts of several British Indian towns—Calcutta, Madras and Tranquebar, for example—the European villas were to be given full prominence facing the waterfront as a sign of the concentration of wealth and power in British hands. As in these towns, the reservation of the area along the waterfront as a public esplanade in front of the European town would reinforce its visual impact, particularly in an age of sea travel and associative imagery. The actual building of the villas for the rich European merchants in the Palladian manner would await the granting of full sovereignty to the East India Company, but meanwhile the stage had been set. ❖

Raffles' ordinances for the layout of the new town included the parade ground that was central to every cantonment in colonial India. Here we see the Court House and the Padang *in the 1860s.*

4 Raffles to Farquhar, *op cit*
5 Nilsson, *op cit*, page 66
6 *Ibid*

Classicism

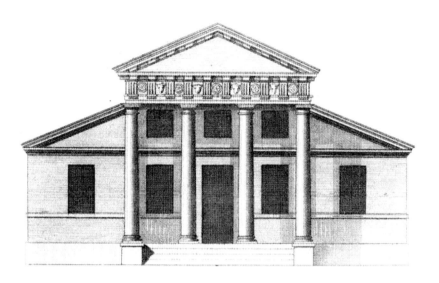

Drawing of a villa with a superimposed portico, from Book IV of Palladio's I Quattro Libri dell'Architettura.

It was fortunate that the sudden need for proper, substantial buildings coincided with the arrival in the colony of an eminently well-qualified and talented architect, George Drumgoolde Coleman. In most cases during these early years—and for some time to come—the design of both private and public buildings would fall to engineers and draughtsmen. Most of them lacked proper architectural training and therefore depended on the reproduction of ideas and images from buildings already in existence, particularly from architectural pattern books brought from England,

By that time in England, architectural patronage had begun to move from that of the well-travelled and well-informed dilettante aristocrat to that of the wealthy Victorian industrialist or merchant whose primary motif was to declare his wealth rather than, as before, to communicate good taste. Architects were therefore required to accommodate these ambitions in the form of a variety of available styles, often chosen at whim. Decisions on style were as much to do with the client as his architect. The effect of this, in any event, was to encourage the study of historical styles through travel or through the use of pattern books and architectural encyclopaedia, which now began to appear in larger numbers.

The use of architectural publications and the tendency to architectural plagiarism, however, were not exclusive to the post-Georgian era. The neo-Palladian buildings and fashions of Regency England, too, had been a product of such methods. The proliferation of pattern books and the arrival of younger draughtsmen from Europe also facilitated the transfer of

Palladian and other classical ideas to India and their embodiment in the major residences and public buildings there from the 1700s.

Coleman, for example, studied architecture in the Georgian city of Dublin and travelled extensively through Europe studying Roman, Renaissance and other architectural remains and generally becoming well versed in the classical vocabulary, before moving to Calcutta. There he became in great demand as the architect *par excellence* for rich merchants' residences. Following further experiences in Batavia, including the design of a cathedral which did not materialize, he came to Singapore in 1822.

His reputation having preceded him, Coleman was commissioned from the moment of arrival to advise on the design of what in effect became Singapore's first Government House, Raffles' first residence. This was not a major commission, for it was Raffles' wish that this be a modest building. It was of Malayan character, of wood and atap, long and low with large verandas, well ventilated and protected from sun and rain. It was set well above the plain on top of Bukit Larangan—later Government Hill—to catch the sea breezes. This exercise must have served to reinforce in Coleman's mind the way in which the form of vernacular buildings, such as the Malay hut, like the Indian bungalow, came from an appropriate response to climate.

From the following year, Coleman was engaged as architect for many of the houses to be put up in the European town as well as a number of public buildings. The stylistic connections between these houses and Coleman's work in Calcutta had their roots in the classical architecture of Georgian England and colonial India and also the Anglo-Indian bungalow.

The main elevation of Chiswick House designed in neo-Palladian style by Lord Burlington, and completed in 1729.

The bungalow, based as it was on the rectangular native Bengali hut, had been adapted to European needs by the enclosure of the four corners (or the two sides) of the surrounding veranda for use as bedrooms or bathrooms. The main central room was kept open front to back to allow through ventilation and, notwithstanding the veranda overhang, some light from outside. Above, the roof was in two sections: a high pyramidal portion supported on the walls of the main space and a second, lower pitched roof over the veranda.

The adaptation of such basic vernacular building forms by the early colonial officials in the rural areas of India may have sufficed for a time, but as colonial society began to develop its own hierarchy and as the administrative revenue-collecting arms of the East India Company were consolidated, more elaborate arrangements were necessary. Already by the late 1700s, the typical layout of a country residence, such as those at Bangalore, was that of a large, lofty, centrally placed drawing-room and a dining-room of equally generous proportions behind. The two rooms were linked through a wide rectangular or arched opening in symmetrical fashion and flanked on either side by large bedrooms. These were each equipped, on the outside walls, with interconnected bathrooms and dressing-rooms following Georgian precedents of a century before.

Often, a large, high-columned Palladian-style porch, an essential Regency feature, had been added axially at the front as an entrance and waiting space for carriages and, in the case of the larger houses, elephants. In many such country residences, the porch opened out on to a wide, deep, columned veranda, often semicircular in form, in the Regency manner; this acted as a reception and informal entertaining area.

Inspired by Windsor Castle, Banglore Palace was built in Tudor style in 1887. Complete with fortified towers, Gothic windows, battlements and turrets, it was built for a maharajah.

Sketch of a two-storey Georgian-style house with fanlight detail below the roof. Such architectural drawings would have been readily available to architects in the early settlement in 'pattern books'.

By now the double pyramidal roof form had gained an extra dimension through the addition of clerestory windows to light the central dining-room or drawing-room.

Such houses were generally on one floor, but in the case of the more substantial mansions, particularly in urban areas, they were usually of two storeys. In this case, the basic layout of main rooms was transferred to the upper-floor level, with the lower floor typically consisting of an inner hall bordered by service rooms and veranda, coachmen's and harness rooms and store-rooms.

In both one- and two-storey houses, the external wall was often carried up in the form of balustrading in the spirit of English Regency architecture, in which case the pitched roof was partly hidden. More commonly it was flat. While such Regency-style residential palazzos may have had their porticoes and columned porches, they responded less to the tropical climate than did the bungalow with its wide overhanging roof and generous verandas.

Nonetheless, with their high ceilings, *punkahs*, spacious rooms and wide internal doorways, they could be made comfortable enough. For the present, considerations of what was fashionable and appropriate to a British ruling oligarchy were more important, and the staid architectural vocabulary of neo-classicism was rather seen to be the language of authority, power, and privilege than that of the thatched roof and open veranda. To this end, great heed was paid by the designers of these buildings to the classical pattern books such as Colen Campbell's *Vitruvius Britanicus*, which had provided the impetus for the introduction of Palladianism into England in the early 1700s, and the subsequent translation of Palladio's *I Quattro Libri dell'Architettura*.

Such books were bound to have been part of George Coleman's collection, which included a spate of later pattern books, including John Loudon's extensive publications of the 1830s. With such reference material at hand, an eager, rich clientele and 200 convict labourers at his disposal, Coleman set to work.

One of his first important commissions was a large private residence for John Argyle Maxwell, a prominent merchant of the day and Honorary Secretary of the Raffles Institution Board of Engineers, to which Coleman also belonged. The land on which the house was built was provided through an oversight by John Crawfurd, Farquhar's successor as Resident, as it ran counter to Raffles' directive that land in this area on the north side of the Singapore River be reserved only for public purposes. On completion of the house in 1827, Maxwell applied for a statutory grant and, because of the earlier misunderstanding, the whole matter was referred to the office in Calcutta who replied in conciliatory vein that, since Maxwell had invested so much in the building, it would be unreasonable to deprive him of the advantage to which he may be entitled through the possession of this valuable lot. In this spirit, Maxwell promptly offered the house back to the government.

From that time on, the building became the colony's Court House and thereafter served a variety of other public purposes, each of which involved numerous renovations and remodelling. At one point it even served as Singapore's Parliament House, but as a shadow of its former self.

Early drawings depict a two-storey rectangular building with pedimented porches on all four sides and surmounted by a tower flanked by a pair of cupolas on the river frontage. These and the strong piers comprising the portico on this side were possibly more English than

An archive image of the Court House circa 1860; it was originally built as a private residence. Reproduced from an album of photographs of Singapore in the former Colonial Office Library in London.

Italian in origin. In other respects, there was the influence of Palladio and his English devotees in the porches, porticoes and the ground-floor rustication and in the elevation to the first floor of all principal rooms. Access to these was gained by means of a curved stair within the main entrance portico.

As to the style of the building, THH Hancock, the senior PWD architect involved in remodelling the building in 1954, had this to say:

"The Court House, stuccoed in two colours, with its studiously proportional Roman Doric colonnade, had a bold Italian air. The piazza treatment of the ground floor evidently was based by Coleman on a Palladian motif. The portico and pediment of his design are reminiscent of Palladio's Villa Malcontenta of 1551. Much else in the composition and, in particular, the river elevation with Ionic columns and cupolas, suggests [sic] influences from English sources. The central tower was possibly designed as a look-out towards the roads to watch the arrival of shipping. Coleman's design, distinguished for its restraint, illustrates his ability to invest even the simplest of designs with an elegant distinction."[1]

The Maxwell residence set the tone for many of the European residences to follow, but there was another equally important precedent, Coleman's own house, built in 1829. Whereas the Maxwell house echoed Calcutta and Madras and had the flavour of such monumental edifices as the great country house of Barrackpore, Coleman's own house was rather a noble version of the Anglo-Indian bungalow. As distinct from the columned portico of the Maxwell House which was characteristically a distinct and highly important element, in the Coleman house it was part of the main body of the building in the form of a grand veranda, but in classical vein.

Early views show a square, symmetrical building of generous size surmounted by a hipped, tiled roof with an attic. Set in a large compound, it included stables and servants' quarters with separate outhouses at the rear. Externally, the building appeared in the form of an arcade of flat Doric pilasters, paired at the front and single at the sides, on a deep plinth. Between the pilasters were arched windows and openings with deep verandas at the front and back. The tropical character was carried through in the use of louvres and timber Venetian shutters in the window openings to minimize glare and encourage through ventilation.

Internally, the ground floor included an entrance porch linking the long veranda-like portico to an inner hall surrounded on all sides by subsidiary rooms, including an office, study, cloakrooms, harness and coachman's room, wine and other stores, and a service veranda.

In orthodox Palladian manner, twin staircases, symmetrically juxtaposed, led from the entrance porch to an entrance hall on the first floor above. From here, access was gained to a large lounge room and thence to a central dining-room. These two rooms were flanked on both sides by bedrooms and bathrooms, with deep verandas at the front over the entrance porch as well as at the back, very much in the manner of Indian colonial houses of the time. Throughout, high ceilings accommodated *punkah* fans.

1 THH Hancock, 'The Assembly House', *Quarterly Journal, Institute of Architects of Malaya*, Vol 4, No 1, 1955, p 35

Panoramic view of the
new settlement taken
from St Andrew's
Church spire, 1863.

As in the Maxwell House, Coleman followed certain Palladian precedents in putting the dining-room on the upper floor and making it a lofty space, lit through semi-circular windows between the two levels of pyramidal roofs above. Here a deeply coved ceiling, a moulded entablature and plaster wall-panelling were all reminiscent of the work of the Adam brothers of the late Georgian period in England. While perhaps not as refined in its execution as that of English Regency houses, the interior none the less reflected the widespread influence of late Georgian and Regency pattern books such as William Pain's *The Builders Pocket-treasure Or, Palladio Delineated and Explained* of 1793.

Other houses designed by Coleman, such as that for the lawyer, David Napier, of 1826—his first important commission—and the Caldwell house of 1843, later to form part of the Convent of the Holy Infant Jesus, were stately Regency villas set in spacious gardens. In form, the Caldwell house responded only partly to tropical conditions. It was a simple rectangular box with

a Georgian-style curved bay at the front but without a porch or veranda. In this it was similar to many of the British colonial residences in India, such as Aildeen in the Tollygunge area in Calcutta.

Internally, the house had a central drawing-dining room opening right through the house, with bedrooms on either side. Bathrooms, servants' rooms, stables, store-rooms and the kitchen, as in most of these houses, were disposed in a separate wing at the rear.

The Caldwell House and the Maxwell House were characteristic of other houses built in the European quarter up to the 1840s. But Coleman's own house was also significant in representing the change toward a more appropriate response to tropical conditions. By the 1840s, there were more houses with pitched, overhanging roofs and deep upper-floor verandas. As in Penang, these houses were still Palladian, but now more tropical in character. Partly this was due to the influence of the traditional Malay way of building. This would become more evident in the character of the country villas in the years to follow. ❖

Plantation Villas

※

With the change in the colony from its military origins to a centre of free trade, the European quarter would also change. Until the 1830s, it had the ambience of a Regency town formally built around its open square which Raffles had put at its centre. There were 20 or 30 dignified Palladian-style mansions in their garden settings; the atmosphere was elegant and the pace of life leisurely.

A new phase began with the arrival of the British schooner *Royalist* in 1836. This, and the despatch of a shipping fleet from Singapore to China in anticipation of new opportunities in the trade of opium and the founding of Hong Kong, signalled Singapore's new role as the key entrepôt in trade between India and other international ports of call.

In the centre, property values began to rise as thousands of immigrants and dozens of new firms clamoured for space. A large house previously costing $10,000 was now valued at double the price. The purchase of Napier's Palladian-style house in Beach Road for $3,000 was therefore an absolute bargain, thanks to the rumour that it was haunted by ghosts.

An 1837 view from the seafront of the Padang *with St Andrew's Church and Government Hill behind; in the early days the settlement had the ambience of a Regency town.*

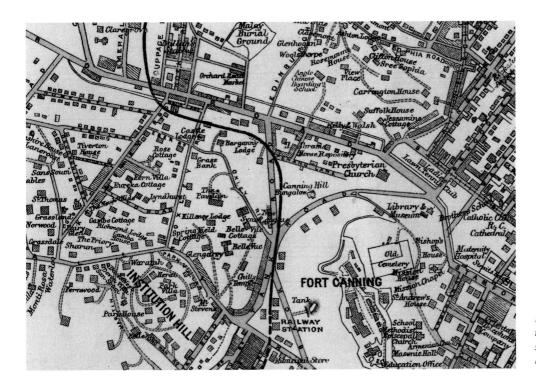

Detail from an 1846 map of Singapore, showing some early house names in Tanglin.

For the rich Europeans, it was not the rise in house prices so much as the increase in congestion which prompted a few to seek a quieter, more spacious environment further inland. A number of large villas began to appear in choice country hilltop locations. Many of these were residences for the owners and managers of nutmeg plantations which were established partly as a response to the availability of cheap Chinese manpower to work them. These and gambier and pepper farms attracted settlement in the Tanglin area west of the town, where the land was higher, the roads better and, in the case of gambier and pepper, there was the timber necessary for their processing. This area was in any case a more attractive environment than the area to the north and a number of rich merchants preferred to live here, quite apart from the value of the area agriculturally.

William Cuppage, who was one of the first to build, chose Emerald Hill in the Tanglin area as the site for his estate and built Erin Lodge there in 1837. On the other side, Charles Prinsep built a house for his manager at the centre of a very large estate stretching to the north and as far as the centre of the town. This estate became the site for the present Government House, built in 1869. A number of houses were built as company houses for managers. Broadfields, for example, was put up by Paterson Simons & Company in the late 1830s. In 1840 a house was built for Charles Carnie of Dyce & Company at the centre of a 67-acre plantation on the hill named after him, Carnie Hill, later known as Cairnhill.

One of the largest estates was that of Dr Thomas Oxley. Oxley had bought the land, 173 acres of uncleared jungle, from the East India Company in 1837 and had it cleared for his nutmeg plantation a few years later. The property stretched from Clemenceau Road and River Valley Road as far as Grange Road to the west. The house that Oxley erected there in 1842, Killiney House, was characteristic of other plantation villas of the time.

Killiney House, later re-named Belle Vue, was essentially a more straightforward, functional version of the Anglo-Palladian model that Coleman had begun to adapt to Singaporean conditions, but it went further in this direction. Like other plantation houses, it followed the form of Coleman's houses, in particular that of his own house of 1829, but any architectural affectations that these earlier houses may have had were now set aside for the practical considerations of country living. These included the elevation of the body of the house on piers to exploit the breeze and the view, to avoid the penetration of termites, and to provide storage space beneath. This characteristic of the plantation house was undoubtedly inspired as much by the traditionally Malay form of building as by Coleman's own house, Palladian trimmings were eschewed and the brick piers and arches which had been introduced by Coleman to support the upper floor, although still with Tuscan capitals and bases, were now more simple. The custom of using Madras *chunam*—an extremely hard-wearing plaster applied to the walls—was now more than ever an advantage, as the quality of brickwork that could be achieved, particularly in these relatively inaccessible locations, was usually poor.

As in other plantation houses, the rooms of Killiney House were large and the ceilings high, and there were *punkahs* to provide additional ventilation to that induced through large, shuttered openings. These in turn led on to deep timber verandas which were

Built around 1840, Killiney House (later re-named Belle Vue) was located in Oxley Rise.

View of Tyersall from Bot. Garden

shielded by hanging rattan or 'chick' blinds. In the Anglo-Palladian tradition of Coleman's houses, rooms were usually arranged symmetrically. Bedrooms were placed on either side of two or three large central rooms interconnected through large arched openings. Whatever names these rooms were given, they were equivalent to the Palladian drawing-room and dining-room.

Increasingly, the kitchen, servants' rooms, and stables were located in a separate outhouse at the rear rather than below, on the ground floor. This arrangement was particularly suitable on sloping sites, as was often the case, in that the outhouse could be set close to the level of the main living area of the house. The elevation of the house provided additional space for the storage of vehicles, equipment and produce, and for use as a games or children's play area or for offices. This area was formed of rough concrete and paved with Malacca floor tiles whereas the upper floor had exposed, polished, wide timber boarding.

Like other plantation houses, Killiney House had a roof of simple, hipped form with a projecting gable over the front entrance porch, a precedent well established in the houses of the 1830s and 1840s. In general, roofs were clad either in atap, following the Malay custom, or—and this became more general—in Chinese semicircular clay pantiles which were economical and readily available, even if they were not entirely efficient. To improve their waterproofing qualities, the tiles were lapped several times, which also provided better insulation, but at the same time increased the weight of the roof.

In 1847 Dr Oxley built a second, larger house called the Pavilion, at the highest point of the estate, and from this time on lived in one or the other, renting out the one he was not using, until his retirement.

View of the house known as Tyersall (1892), owned by the Sultan of Johore, as seen from the adjacent Botanic Gardens.

By the late 1840s, there were 20 or so such estates, mostly cultivating nutmeg, all owned by Europeans including WW Kerr, Joaquim d'Almeida, Dr Oxley, Charles Prinsep, T Hewetson, and other important persons in business and the professions. Guthrie and Kerr were amongst those who moved farther afield to Telok Blangah, near the Temenggong's vast holdings which had been allocated by Raffles in 1823. This area was later to become increasingly desirable, both for its elevated position overlooking the waterfront and because of the prosperity generated in the area by an expansion in the Temenggong's personal fortunes as a result of the virtual monopoly that he held of the trade in gutta-percha.

Meanwhile, others followed the example of these earlier pioneers in moving even further afield, clearing away yet more jungle and establishing plantations on hilltops to the north, east and south. By 1862, J Moniot, the Surveyor-General of the time, was able to list 70 plantations within a two- to three-mile radius of town, mostly in the area of River Valley Road, Orchard Road and Tanglin Road, which were the most popular locations. The names given to these large estates reflected the interest of the majority of the owners, who were British, in maintaining psychological connections with the British countryside: Mount Sophia, Mount Emily, Mount Cardine, Osborne House, Raeburn, Everton, Spottiswood Park, Mount Victoria and Hodins Field.

Charles Walker Kinlock's 'A sketch from Cummings Bukit' (1852) shows the Tanglin area in the 1850s with a typical plantation bungalow, a pepper plantation in the foreground and nutmegs behind on right.

Despite these developments, Singapore in the 1860s looked much the same in its general configuration as in the 1840s. It was still contained within an area defined by the Rochore River to the north and about two miles to the south along the coast to Telok Ayer and inland for a mile or two. From the town centre, roads radiated outwards. To the north-west, Bukit Timah Road, bordered by a market garden area between nutmeg plantations, ran to Toa Payoh. To the west, Orchard Road, reaching to the gambier and pepper plantations of the Tanglin forests, passed through the nutmeg plantations of Claymore

Bendemeer House, the residence of Whampoa; built in 1855.

and River Valley. To the east, Geylang Road ran towards Paya Lebar, Geylang and Siglap through flat agricultural land. And to the north-east, Serangoon Road penetrated to the Rochore and Kallang districts of ginger plantations and agricultural holdings, the whole area dotted with detached country houses.

Of these houses, one of the more interesting was that owned by the legendary and eccentric Hoo Ah Kay, a wealthy Chinese merchant. Hoo, commonly known as Whampoa, bought a large property about two and a half miles from the town in an area containing a neglected nutmeg plantation in 1840. The property occupied an area of about 400 acres.

The first house on the site was a large wooden bungalow which Whampoa replaced by an even larger brick house, to become known as Bendemeer, in 1855. This was a building of elegant appearance and in other respects typical of many plantation villas, with the living accommodation on two floors: the dining-room below and lounge above, flanked by bedrooms on either side, with bathrooms at the rear. To the front was the usual carriage porch with an open sitting-veranda above. The kitchen, stables and servants' quarters were in separate outbuildings at the rear connected by a covered passage to the main building.

The quality which made Whampoa's house especially interesting was its theatricality, its eclecticism, in the way the house was furnished, in its ornamental detailing, and in the landscaping. The property became the setting for regular parties and a popular showpiece.

Whampoa had developed the grounds, which overlooked the river named after him, into something quite fanciful. There was a large orchard and ornamental gardens which included

Panglima Prang, the residence of Tan Kim Seng, a Chinese businessman, 1890s.

miniature rockeries, artificial ponds, paths bordered by coloured shrubs, a menagerie, a lotus lake, and curious dwarf bamboos and plants trimmed into the shapes of animals. In the house itself there were Chinese, Malay as well as European influences in the furnishings, the finely fretted and turned timber balusters, the moulded brick and stucco pilasters and piers, the slender timber and cast iron columns, and the full-length glazed and louvred windows. A large, elaborately decorated dining-room was added in 1867 and completed in time for a lavish dinner party for Admiral Keppel, with whom Whampoa had close contacts through his shipping activities, which included the importation of ice from America.

In all of this and in the ebullience of Whampoa himself, there was a foretaste of other equally effervescent Chinese men of wealth and of the visual rhetoric of their houses as well as a characteristically Chinese attitude to landscape.

An example of this was the house known as Panglima Prang, built about five years after Bendemeer. Panglima Prang, a name signifying the nautical interests of its owner—the words literally mean 'Admiral of War'—sat on River Valley Road on the edge of the Tanglin area, overlooking the Singapore River. Much of the area on the opposite side of River Valley Road, which had formed part of Dr Oxley's estate, had been subdivided and sold off in lots in the early 1850s, and by 1858 about 20 houses had been built, an early sign of the suburban expansion which would follow some 20 years later.

Like Bendemeer, Panglima Prang was built by a prominent Chinese merchant, Tan Kim Seng, for his own use. As in the case of Bendemeer, the house was, architecturally, another example of the Palladian mode adapted to tropical conditions.

In form, it was a simple rectangular structure similar in its symmetrical layout to that of Bendemeer and other country houses, but on one floor. This was raised on square, plastered brick plinths supporting well-proportioned Doric columns carrying large timber beams which bore the roof timbers of a hipped Chinese-tile roof. Behind the columns there was a full-length veranda with the usual projecting porch in the middle, but roofed in this case, somewhat awkwardly, with a gable roof running parallel rather than at right angles to the main façade. The general effect, however, was one of satisfying proportions, elegance and restraint.

Unlike Hoo Ah Kay, Tan Kim Seng was from a Peranakan family and this was reflected in the way the house was furnished. In contrast to the restrained appearance of the house externally, the interior consisted of a mixture of styles in the furniture, decorative appurtenances and artefacts. Following the Peranakan custom, the central area into which one entered was arranged very formally, with traditional Chinese furniture and family portraits prominently displayed. Behind this was a second room which acted as the Ancestral Hall, complete with an ancestral table at which family offerings were made. Here, too, there were portraits brought from the family ancestral home in Malacca, paintings of Western origin, plaques, and, in the best British colonial tradition, two deer heads mounted as trophies and flanked by rifles. Although the display of sporting weapons was not uncommon in Peranakan interiors, the rifles in this case had additional significance in that Tan Kim Seng was particularly interested in the defence of the colony, had donated guns to the colonial government, and indeed fancied his house in its elevated position overlooking the river as some sort of fort!

Tan's emulation of European ways carried through into the furniture and fittings which included Victorian chairs and cabinets, Empire-style chandeliers, and mirrors in gilded and mosaic frames. Like Bendemeer, all of this reflected a lifestyle quite different from, indeed remarkably more Victorian than that of the well-to-do English and other Europeans, even though the houses occupied by them were from the same Anglo-Palladian mould. It was a lifestyle that was soon to disappear as a result of pressure to sell off these large estates to property speculators and private buyers. These developments were hastened by the sudden appearance of a mysterious disease which wiped out most of the nutmeg plantations in 1862, after which cultivation immediately ceased.

Subdivision of the land, now fallow, quickly followed and the sale of smaller lots attracted the building of dozens of suburban villas.

Within the more fashionable Tanglin area, the community life engendered by these developments was given expression in the establishment of the Tanglin Club in 1865. Four years later, the erection of the new Government House in large grounds off Orchard Road further encouraged the building of suburban villas nearby in Claymore and Tanglin. The suburban character of these villas, their architectural styles and the picturesque quality of their garden settings represented quite a change from the more formal, urban Regency character of the original European town. By the 1880s, the change would be of such an order that T J Keughran, after an absence of several years, could say:

"I found new streets of houses had sprung up where in many places there had been vacant ground…. When however, I approached the suburbs, pretty rural villas confronted me at every turn, surrounded by neatly kept flower pots…. The style of architecture of these buildings betoken new tastes in the owners and doubtless too, new and more varied assortment of occupants."[1] ❖

1 T J Keughran, *Picturesque and Busy Singapore*, Singapore, 1887, page 2

Early Suburbanization,
1880–1900

The gradual increase in the number of new bungalows in the western area of Tanglin which had taken place by the 1880s was matched by similar changes in other directions. New houses had sprung up in clusters and along the major roads leading into the countryside and up and down the coast. Here the land was flatter and the environment, for those privileged enough to live there, was more desirable than further inland, other than for the elevated wooded area of the Tanglin Hills west of the town centre. These developments reflected the level of economic prosperity that had been reached in the colony by the last quarter of the 19th century.

Economic and Social Developments

By then Singapore had begun to experience a substantial increase in trading activity. Despite a world slump in 1893, its trade would multiply by a factor of eight by the beginning of World War I in 1914. Already, by the middle of the 1870s, it had secured an important place as South East Asia's major entrepôt for the import of Western manufactured goods and the export of raw materials. This was due both to its strategic position on the East-West Straits of Malacca trade route to the Far East and as an essential link in the chain of British ports and coaling stations from Gibraltar to Hong Kong and Australia. Its position was reinforced by the displacement of sail by steam, which reduced the time of the voyage from Europe from months to weeks, and the opening of the Suez Canal, which shortened the trip still further. Its economic role also began to extend beyond trans-shipment to the processing of raw materials.

To support this burgeoning economy, the colony steadily built up the necessary infrastructure, including port facilities and communication links and the formation of new companies and banks. New wharves, warehouses and workers' quarters were erected on reclaimed land at Tanjong Pagar. The tramway system, which had been introduced in 1867 and taken over by the Tanjong Pagar Dock Company six years later, continued, albeit at some financial loss, to operate as a means of carrying freight from the port to the town centre. New buildings were constructed for the Hongkong and Shanghai Banking Corporation and

Opposite *Hong Lim Green, built with a $3,000 donation by Chinese businessman Cheang Hong Lim, in front of the old Central Police Station, 1888.*

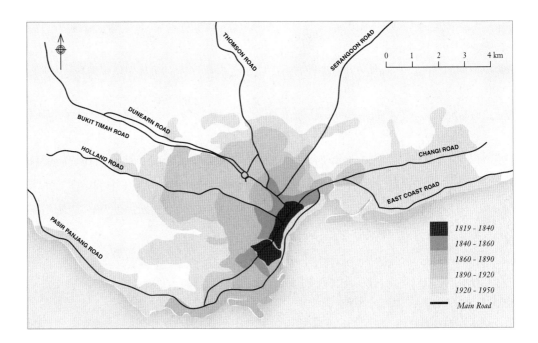

Map illustrating the growth of Singapore, 1819–1950.

the Chartered Bank and new premises erected for the Ellenborough Market and a second market on reclaimed land at Telok Ayer. The inauguration of a regular postal service and the introduction of the telephone began to put commercial transactions on a more reliable footing.

A key factor in the colony's economic development was its human resources. The relatively small size of the European community was in inverse proportion to its political influence and its significance for the colony's economy, which depended on Chinese manpower in large quantities. The years 1875–1900 saw ever-increasing waves of immigration. Between 1878 and 1888, the Chinese population jumped from 34,000 to 103,000, and despite the effects of the 1893 slump, by the turn of the century it was almost 164,000 or nearly three-quarters of the total population.

The bulk of this large influx settled in or near the town centre, which, by the 1880s, had already become highly congested with vehicles of all descriptions. Even the introduction of a second tramway system in 1882 from New Harbour to Rochore provided only partial relief. The pressure on the town centre was to some extent alleviated by the government's action in levelling the coastal hills and in draining the marshes in Telok Ayer to accommodate an extension of the urban area towards the east.

Living conditions in the centre were nevertheless described as grim by the 1896 Commission of Enquiry. Singapore's mortality rate was higher than that of Hong Kong, Ceylon or India. The town area was rife with endemic diseases—a result of poverty, overcrowding and malnutrition. The mass of the population had no medical facilities.

Decentralization

For those who had the means and the opportunity, there was no choice but to move well outside the town centre, like the plantation owners had done 20 to 30 years before. By the early 1880s, suburban development had begun through a process of scattered infilling in the interstices between the former villa estates.

This took place to the west on either side of River Valley Road and Orchard Road within the Tanglin area, north over the former market gardens and coconut plantations between Serangoon Road and Thomson Road, and south toward Tanjong Pagar and along the coast at Telok Blangah. Expansion towards the east, other than for a number of Malay and Indian *kampongs*, was inhibited by swamplands surrounding the mouth of the Rochore River.

Malay *kampongs* now covered much of the swampland and riverside area stretching from lower Serangoon Road to the coast. This was because of the opportunities here for fishing and other waterside activities and the fact of rising land values in the centre, which forced the poorer Malays to move further out. It was due also to a consolidation of decisions, made much earlier by Raffles, by the colonial government.

Control of the development of suburban and rural land was transferred from the municipality to the government by ordinance in 1887, leaving the town area the responsibility of the Municipal Council. By then, much of the territory north of the Rochore River basin between Geylang Road and Upper Serangoon Road was occupied by Chinese vegetable farmers housed in makeshift villages. This was also the case south-east of the town beyond Pearl's Hill, where Chinese agricultural holdings occupied the whole of the area south of the Singapore River and Alexandra Road to the pineapple plantations of Mount Faber and other high ground overlooking Telok Blangah.

Although there was a definite pattern in the attraction of different areas to particular ethnic groups, there was now also considerable intermingling. Within the Tanglin area, for example, a number of wealthier Chinese, and, to a lesser extent, other races, were beginning to move into this essentially European preserve. Mount Elizabeth was becoming popular with the Straits Chinese, as was much of the land along River Valley Road. Closer to the town centre, Waterloo and Queen Streets and nearby streets were becoming increasingly popular locations for Jews, Eurasians and Chinese. Europeans, for their part, were spilling over into the increasingly cosmopolitan area along and on either side of Serangoon Road to the north.

Typical Malay kampong, *late 19th century.*

The Northern Suburbs

Unlike the Tanglin area where the houses were set in large, self-contained wooded compounds arranged informally in the manner of the English romantic garden, the houses to the north of Bukit Timah Road were aligned along the main roads and a network of new streets occupying the area between Serangoon Road and Thomson Road. This arrangement was economical in terms of land subdivision, and, in any case, the rest of the land was marshy. Perhaps as well there was the fact that for the Chinese, who occupied many of these houses and for whom wealth was the single key to social standing, the notion of public display was important: their new houses were therefore to be visible.

Other houses, for instance those erected as early speculative 'country bungalows' on the edge of open countryside on Balestier Road, were addressed more particularly to Europeans, especially the English, to whom the ideal of life in a bungalow in the country would naturally appeal. As it turned out, a number of these houses were occupied as 'messes' by single English employees who were less eligible or had less need for a large, Tanglin-style residential compound.

The proximity here of the two communities, the English and Chinese, was further signalled by the presence of the Swiss Rifling Club and the Protestant and Roman Catholic Cemetery immediately next to the grounds of the Chinese Club on Newton Road.

Ethnic groups, however, were even more mixed nearer Serangoon Road. On the network of short streets extending along the western side of Serangoon Road itself, Eurasians (Anglo-Indians and Anglo-Chinese), Indians, Arabs and Chinese lived cheek-by-jowl in modest-sized timber bungalows. On the Kallang side, the emergence of several streets of detached houses for Indian Muslims in the newly settled area of Kampong Kapur further signified the tendency of the various races to live with their own kind but at the same time to rub shoulders with other

A single-storey house raised from the ground on piles, with overhanging eaves and an open veranda resting on the plinths of the pillars is a typical example of a simple 19th-century country home in the early settlement.

Postcard depicting cattle raising in Singapore in the Serangoon area in the 19th century.

races. The cosmopolitan character of the Serangoon Road district was quite in contrast to the more culturally and socially self-conscious environment of the Tanglin area. It was also well removed from the socially rigid caste system and the class-consciousness of British India or, for that matter, the snobbishness of suburban England.

Of the various ethnic groups in the Serangoon Road area, Indians were in the majority. This was partly a product of much earlier developments, such as the establishment in the 1820s of brick kilns and lime pits and the importation of Indian convicts to work them. A later influx of Indians and other races stemmed from opportunities for cattle rearing and trading provided by an abundance of grass and water and the collapse of various commercial agricultural ventures, including sugar, nutmeg, coconut and rice, in the area nearby. A key figure in the area was one Mr Belilios, 'Merchant, Rochor Road', a Venetian Jew from Calcutta and an importer of cattle and sheep. Cattle was in considerable demand as a form of transport until the early 1900s and as a source of milk and meat. Mr Belilios had as a neighbour a Mr Landau, 'Pineapple Planter and Preserver'. Pineapple skins were used as fodder for the cattle. Other industries such as rattan and wheat-grinding factories, also made their appearance.

Later, in the 1890s, the British employed Indians in the construction of the grandstand at the old racecourse, on the western side of Serangoon Road. The racecourse had been there since the 1840s. It helped further to attract both Europeans and Chinese who, while having less interest than the English in equestrian sports, had a reputation for inveterate gambling.

Thus, by the turn of the century, the area had attracted not only a range of racial communities but a variety of buildings to accommodate them. The more successful immigrants put up compound houses and bungalows in addition to atap houses and shophouses. The less well-to-do lived in rented rooms over shops and stables. Physically and socially, this was all quite in contrast to the Tanglin area immediately opposite, on the other side of Bukit Timah Road.

Tanglin

Unlike the socially heterogeneous character of the Serangoon Road district, the Tanglin area reflected the reality that Singapore was mainly an English and, to an increasing extent, a Chinese, preserve. The British held the monopoly of political power, provided protection, justice and administration. Singapore's economy was mainly dominated by Western firms whose employees lived in comfort and style in spacious residences in very large gardens.

Much of the real prosperity, however, lay with a handful of wealthy Chinese merchants and *towkays*, a number of whom were beginning to make their presence felt within the Tanglin area, if not within the ranks of Chinese society. By now, a large detached house in its own garden was not purely the prerogative of the Europeans. As the Europeans represented only two per cent of the population, it was inevitable that, in Singapore as a whole, the larger number of new houses being put up during the late 1800s would be owned by non-Europeans. However, a large part of the Tanglin area west of the Scotts Road–Kim Seng Road artery was still exclusively European in flavour. To the visitor from outside, the prosperous, English appearance of the Tanglin suburb seemed to epitomize the character of the colony in general. This impression was not changed by the knowledge that more and more Chinese were buying and building houses in the area, particularly nearer to the town centre, on Mount Elizabeth and in the district stretching from Orchard Road to River Valley Road.

Orange Grove (1893), the house of Alexander Leathes Donaldson, a lawyer at Donaldson & Burkinshaw. In common with houses at the time, this home had deep overhanging eaves and the all important encircling veranda.

On Mount Elizabeth and other nearby hills, the houses that had already appeared by the 1880s were large, originating as they did in the gradual subdivision into six- and eight-acre lots of these former hilltop sites in the 1860s and 1870s. The houses on Mount Elizabeth were typical in having English names such as Glyndherst, Maldern and Mapledurham. Near these houses, others of similar size and character had since appeared, some built by Straits Chinese *towkays*, many of whom also had an ancestral home at Telok Ayer. For these rich merchants, the ownership of a traditional terrace-house in the town and a mansion of Anglo-Indian-cum-Malayan derivation on Mount Elizabeth was perfectly consistent with the Straits Chinese culture as an amalgam of European, Malayan and Chinese ways.

Next to Mount Elizabeth on Cairnhill, Cairnhill House stood as it had done since its erection as a plantation villa in the 1840s. On Emerald Hill, Erin Lodge and Fern Cottage, which had been built by Cuppage in the 1850s, were still unaltered, but the whole of Emerald Hill was sold in 1890 to one Edwin Kock and thereafter it became an orchard. Like Cuppage's former nutmeg plantation, it failed, and by the turn of the century, the land and its three houses became the property of one or two rich Chinese businessmen who were to exploit its potential value by subdividing it into smaller lots in the manner of the Killiney Road area on the opposite side of Orchard Road.

This area south of Orchard Road, formerly a part of the plantation of Thomas Oxley and subdivided by him in the 1850s, was now home to numerous Chinese families for whom the ownership of a modern-style bungalow, however small, was a matter of some importance. Some of the houses here were at least as impressive in their size and style as the more substantial of the European-owned houses elsewhere in the Tanglin area, but the majority were of modest size, though by today's standards hardly small: few were below 200 square metres in area.

Partly because of the flatness of the ground here and partly because the area was more accessible to the town centre via Orchard Road and River Valley Road than the rest of the Tanglin area, the competition for space was keener, the land prices higher and the subdivisions smaller. Allotments were nevertheless of the order of one to two acres, large by current standards. The compounds in the hillier parts of Tanglin further west, however, were huge—about six or seven and up to 10 acres—as in much of British India.

Bordering the Killiney–Devonshire Road area on the slopes of Mount Oxley, there had been little change since the erection by Oxley of Killiney House in the 1840s and the subsequent addition of a number of equally grand villas during the 1860s and 1870s. Killiney House, renamed Belle Vue, was bought and altered by Sir Manasseh Meyer, one of several Jews prominent in the business and political life of the colony at the time. Jewish businessmen were no less significant for the development of land and property than Arabian families such as the Alsagoffs.

A number of Chinese, such as Tan Yeok Nee, were also involved in property speculation. Tan, a prominent Teochew merchant of the day, was somewhat of an exception in building a large house for his own use in traditional mainland Chinese style, complete with curved roofs of traditional Chinese form, external wooden carvings and granite pillars, on the eastern side of Oxley Hill in about 1885. Tan's house was one of a small number of houses built on traditional Chinese lines before the turn of the century, beginning with Tan Seng Pok's house on Hill Street in 1869. Almost entirely, the Chinese, in the building of their new houses, turned for inspiration to the houses of their European overlords rather than to the Chinese mainland.

In style and panache the Tan Yeok Nee residence was rivalled by houses built from the 1860s by other members of the Chinese élite, including Panglima Prang on River Valley Road with its resplendent, eclectic interior. Panglima Prang was but part of a large swathe of land on River Valley Road which was already, by the 1860s, in Chinese ownership.

Overlooking River Valley Road, Institution Hill was an exception to the general pattern at this time in having been completely laid out and built as a residential estate sometime during the 1880s; the more common pattern then was that of houses added one by one. The estate on Nassim Hill was another exception to the rule. Built at about the same time, this included the addition of Mayfield and Burn Brae together with half a dozen other large houses in a single estate which included a much earlier house, Belvedere.

The appearance several years apart of Cree Hall, Balaclava, and Glencaird as separate houses off Stevens Road to the north of Nassim Hill was more typical. Although these were all of the same class, being substantial buildings in large grounds, and linked by a common access road, in appearance they were quite unalike. Cree Hall, with its

Cree Hall, built in the late 1870s, was placed as was usual at the time in substantial grounds.

dignified portico of fluted Doric columns set on high pedestals and its simple, broad hipped roof, was, if anything, reminiscent of Panglima Prang. Balaclava was more typical of the conventional mid-19th-century plantation villa with its encircling timber veranda, raised, full height, on Tuscan piers of rudimentary form. Glencaird, the last of the three, by contrast, with its pointed tower and asymmetrical entrance arrangement, was more evocative of the mood of romanticism that had already begun to take hold by the 1890s.

Elsewhere in the Tanglin area, two-storey houses such as Grassdale on River Valley Road and Spring Grove on Grange Road were more representative of the style of upper-class residential buildings of the time. So, too, beyond the Tanglin area on Balestier Road, was Bin Chan House, later known as Sun Yat Sen Villa. Such houses were of symmetrical form, with a central projecting porch of rectangular or pentagonal shape, a hipped roof, and, more often than not, pseudo-Renaissance features such as rusticated walling on the ground floor. They came from the Palladian-style villas of Coleman and other Anglo-Indian sources but were now becoming more stylistically self-conscious. Architecturally, as well as socially and culturally, such houses were representative of the formative years leading to the turn of the century and the beginning of the next era of suburban expansion. ❖

Glencaird (1897) had a pointed tower above the stair hall which was a typical Victorian feature.

Progress and Consolidation, 1900–1920

❦

Economic and Social Developments

At the turn of the century, there were two events which secured the wealth of the Malay Peninsula and Singapore as its principal commercial outlet and port. One was the invention of the motor car and the beginning of assembly-line production of the Model-T Ford car. The other was the development of a process involving the use of tin for the canning of food. The burgeoning of the rubber plantations and the growth of tin mining coincided with the failure of the Malayan coffee crop in 1897 due to disease and the emergence of Brazil as a competitor in the world coffee market. These developments secured the fortunes of the Straits Tin Company and that of the rubber industry, which was also in debt to Henry Ridley, the then Superintendent of the Singapore Botanic Gardens, who invented a foolproof method of tapping rubber.

By 1903, Singapore had become the world's seventh largest port. This was despite the grossly inadequate, cramped and congested conditions of its port facilities, including the use of ox-carts to move goods to and from the docks. The reluctance of the Tanjong Pagar Dock Company to take action prompted the government to nationalize the company, leading to major improvements between 1905 and 1910.

Meanwhile, international events led to a severe slump in trade in 1908. This resulted in serious financial and commercial difficulties for the colony. It took until 1911 for trade to revive, but the next three years until the beginning of World War I constituted a period of unprecedented prosperity. This was only temporarily curtailed by the war, and by 1919 the economy was again running high. The exhilaration of this post-war period was, however, short-lived, and by 1920 there was another major recession. The effects of this would be felt for the following several years.

The fluctuations of economic fortune of the colony during these years were of profound concern to both the European and Chinese communities, but in different ways. The major banks—The Chartered Bank of India, the Australia and China Bank, the HongKong and Shanghai Banking Corporation and the Mercantile Bank of India—and other financial institutions were controlled by the English, but the Chinese, whose fortunes were steadily expanding, ran most of the businesses. As in previous years, the accumulation of wealth was mainly in Chinese hands.

Carriages and rickshaws on Cavenagh Bridge around 1906; after the invention of the motor car, scenes such as this were not seen again.

The predominantly male Chinese population, which had doubled its size between 1881 and 1901, increased steadily until the war, when it constituted more than three-quarters of the population. The revival of prosperity in 1911 was at least partly sustained by a massive influx of Chinese immigrants in that year due to famines and floods on the mainland. Mainland Chinese increasingly outnumbered the Straits Chinese. By 1910, the proportion of Straits-born Chinese had fallen to one-quarter of the population. The influence of the Straits Chinese, however, was proportionately higher because of their position as the traditional leaders, commercially and professionally, and their closer relationship to the English colonial hierarchy and way of life.

More generally, the Chinese and the English were socially segregated, a situation at least partly due to the division of the education system into two streams—Chinese and English. The Straits Chinese and the mainland-born Chinese were also divided. This was accentuated by the growing commitment of the Chinese colonial community to either the Manchu Royalist regime or the opposing revolutionary movements led by Sun Yat Sen. The outcome was a virtual identity crisis amongst the Chinese, which was partly relieved by their unification in the face of competition with foreign business interests.

The continued arrival of ethnic groups other than the Chinese served to boost the island's population and contributed to Singapore's reputation as the most cosmopolitan city in South East Asia. Amongst the many different races, the Malays, from different parts of the archipelago, were numerically second only to the Chinese, and they were followed by the Indians, mostly mainland-born. Eurasians of diverse backgrounds, principally of Dutch and Portuguese extraction, but also of Anglo-Indian and Anglo-Chinese lineage, steadily increased to fill the ranks of subordinate posts in commercial and government offices. Of the remaining races, the Arabs, which included prestigious family names such as the Alkaffs, the Alsagoffs and the Aljunieds, as well as the Jews, were most likely to succeed to senior positions in the world of business and thus to acquire the trappings of European status, including the acquisition of a bungalow in the suburbs.

Urban–Suburban Developments

At the opposite end of the social scale, the majority of the population still lived in conditions of extreme squalor in the centre of town. An outbreak of cholera in 1905 claimed 759 lives but the very high mortality rate was due mainly to malaria. Prostitution was rife at least until 1914, when it was legally forbidden, and the illicit sale of opium was sufficiently prevalent to account for half of Singapore's revenue. Actions to alleviate such conditions were part of an overall strategy which included a second Commission of Enquiry in 1909 and the passing of an ordinance in 1913 to give more control to the government. It also precipitated a range of municipal improvements. New water reservoirs were constructed at Thomson Road and Pearl's Hill, the Kallang River Extension Scheme was undertaken, and the first section of Singapore's piped sewerage system was put in hand. Night-soil collection was taken over by the government and two new public hospitals were erected at Moulmein Road. By 1912 the infant mortality rate had begun to decline. Other physical improvements included the introduction of gas lighting, which was soon superseded by electric lighting in the central area. Already, by 1906, electric lights and fans had replaced oil-lamps and hand-operated *punkahs* in private houses.

Such commitments in the public sector were matched by a newfound confidence in the community, reflected in an impressive array of new buildings. These included the new Raffles Hotel, the Adelphi Hotel and the Hotel de l'Europe; the new John Little Emporium and the Chartered Bank in Raffles Place; the Chased-el-Synagogue, St Joseph's Church, Wesley Church, and the Convent of the Holy Infant Jesus; a new Government Printing Office and Central Fire Station as well as new, larger, and more permanent markets in Buffalo and Serangoon Roads.

If these improvements belied the poverty of the town, they were also in sharp contrast to the confusion and chaos resulting from traffic congestion. The situation was hardly improved by a rickshaw strike which paralysed the town in 1901. By 1910 the density of horse-drawn vehicles had reached a peak. (The introduction of motor transport provided further opportunity, for those who could afford it, to move further from the centre, but added to the congestion and further deteriorated the already inferior road system. For the rest of the population, public transport was quite inadequate. It consisted mainly of rickshaws and two lines of trams, initially horse-drawn, then electrified in 1906, running from Keppel Harbour to Geylang and to the north along Serangoon Road.) "The fact of the tramway running into the country at Geylang and Serangoon'," said one observer in 1908, "should tend to encourage building operations in these districts."[1]

Horse-drawn taxis ply their trade in front of the John Little & Co department store on Raffles Square, 1900.

1 A Wright and H A Cartwright (eds), *Twentieth Century Impressions of British Malaya: Its History, People, Industries and Resources*, London, Lloyds Greater Britain Publishing Company Ltd, 1908

Hotel de l'Europe, Singapore.

Top *Old postcard depicting the grandeur of the Hotel de l'Europe which was built in 1905.*

Above *Raffles Hotel, built in 1899, brought new higher standards of hospitality to Singapore.*

Development to the North and East

Undoubtedly suburban development in these areas—and indeed generally—would have been more rapid but for the recession in that year and in the several years following, and the interruption caused by World War I. Compared to the post-war period of grand public and private residential estates, these were years of incidental building activity, mostly in the form of piecemeal additions: a house or two here and there or, at the most, a new street of half a dozen houses. Overall, fewer new houses were built than in the preceding 16 years from 1884 to 1900. As before, most new houses were put up by better-off Chinese, particularly Straits Chinese. Indeed, with the Chinese now forming a relatively much larger proportion of the population and more wealth passing into certain Chinese pockets, the percentage of newly built Chinese-owned bungalows jumped from 38 to 46 per cent.

Conversely, the proportion of new houses owned by Europeans and Eurasians dropped slightly. Within the European camp, more houses were now being built by companies for their senior managers. Most were in the Tanglin area. For those next in the social scale who could afford the luxury of a detached house, it was necessary to look toward the freehold land areas to the north-east, where the ground was flatter and the subdivisions smaller and cheaper.

Here, Chinese, Indian, and Eurasian small businessmen and white-collar employees built modest detached houses interspersed with others of more substantial size. The smaller houses were mostly in timber and elevated on piers to avoid rising damp and the effects of periodic flooding along the major routes, Serangoon Road and Geylang Road, and adjacent side streets. On Serangoon Road, most of the houses were to the north of Syed Alwi Road: below this, rows of two-storey shophouses, built and occupied mainly by South Indian retailers, had begun to appear by 1910. These and the continuing presence of Indian Muslims in Kampong Kapur on the eastern side of Serangoon Road further consolidated this area as Indian territory, a fact signalled by the turrets and spires of the Abdul Gaffoor Mosque. As a landmark for the area, this building vied with the two watch-towers for this section of Serangoon Road, the Kandang Kerbau Police Station and the Rumah Miskin Police Station.

The lower part of Serangoon Road, however, was not exclusively Indian. Other races were present, but they tended to be more mixed further to the north and east. Eurasians in their timber bungalows, with their tiled hipped roofs and projecting porches, tended to predominate on Upper Serangoon Road and on bordering streets which were now gradually being formed here and on either side of Geylang Road. Eurasian-owned houses were interspersed with those owned by Chinese. East of Serangoon Road, along the southern edge of the mangrove swamps forming the Rochore River basin, were the Malays of Kampong Boyan, Kampong Bugis and Kampong Kapang, and beyond, the remnants of Chinese farming communities in their atap-roofed huts.

By the early 1920s, the swamps, formerly a source of water for agricultural activity and cattle raising, still extended inland as far as Serangoon Road and at its bottom end, from Syed Alwi Road to the north east for a distance of nearly two miles. Even though much of this flooded area had been partially drained between 1900 and 1910, by the early 1920s there was still virtually no new building between Serangoon Road and Geylang Road, other than for an assortment of elevated atap-roofed dwellings on Lavender Road which had been erected much earlier. An interesting exception to this was Bendemeer.

Opposite *Detail of Map of Singapore, 1905, showing the area that later became known as Little India. From the 1900s onwards it became more and more occupied by South Indians.*

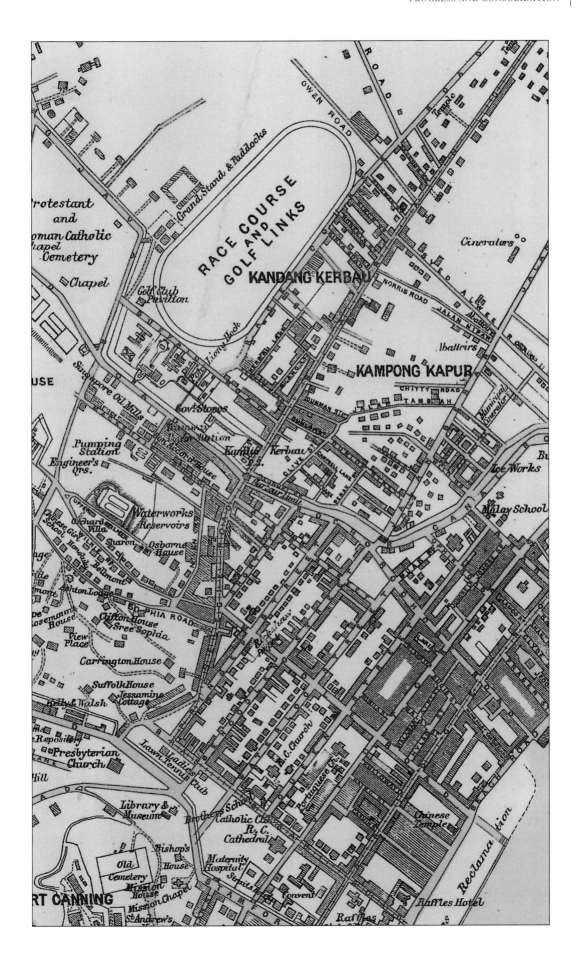

A house in Tanjong Katong, circa 1900. The area became popular as a seaside destination for those with the means.

Apart from tentative municipal attempts at drainage, the deterrent to suburban expansion posed by the extensive areas of swampland was gradually circumvented by the formation of new roads, partly on reclaimed land. In addition to the construction of a new road branching off Geylang Road and leading, across the swamps, eastwards along the coast, there were changes resulting from reclamation further inland, to the west of Serangoon Road. These included the formation of Moulmein Road, the construction of the new Tan Tock Seng Hospital following its removal much earlier from Pearl's Hill to Balestier Road, and a network of short streets in the former paddock area behind the racecourse grandstand. By 1920, the formation of these streets had given rise to several detached timber houses.

However, in general, residential building was confined to the major arteries. On Geylang Road, following the newly formed tramway route, 30 to 40 new houses for well-to-do and less privileged Chinese, Eurasians and others had sprung up on either side and on adjacent newly formed laneways or *lorong*.

Much of this development had been forced to leapfrog the area of swamps and an assemblage of sawmills, ricemills, tanneries and a new gasworks bordering Kampong Bugis and the mouth of the Rochore River. Tanjong Rhu, on the opposite shore of the Kallang Basin, had also become partly industrial, consisting as it did of boatsheds and boat-repair workshops. This environment changed abruptly into one of higher-class residential building at Tanjong Katong immediately to the east.

Apart from several large mansions, this beachside area was steadily becoming a weekend retreat for the Straits Chinese, one or two rich Malays and the occasional European civil servant. Rather in the spirit of the English seaside villa holiday resorts, these villas, however, were more substantial: well spaced, elaborate, of generous, wide proportions on terraces extending to the water's edge. The relaxed semi-rural environment of this waterside area had also begun to attract a number of public facilities, such as the Singapore Swimming Club and the Grove Hotel, mainly to cater for the recreational needs of the European upper set.

The Tanglin Area

Many of the richer Europeans and Chinese had access to a second house facing the sea while maintaining a permanent home in the Tanglin area. Like these waterside suburbs, the atmosphere of Tanglin was still semi-rural. But unlike the flat, sandy terrain and less dense vegetation of coconut palms along the coast, Tanglin was hilly and well wooded, despite the steady increase here in the volume of house-building. Over 100 new houses were built between 1900 and 1920, about the same number as in the preceding 20-year period. The majority were put up before the 1908 recession and the remainder in the years immediately following the war.

By 1920 the less developed portions, Mount Alma and Nassim Hill, had attracted a number of large villas, but not exclusively for Europeans. Many of the new residents were Chinese, with a sprinkling of well-to-do Malays and Indians. Of the European houses, several were built by prominent banks and other mercantile companies for their senior executives and managers.

The area of Cluny Road skirting the Botanic Gardens—which, like the Tanglin Barracks, had acted as a barrier to further private building in this direction—was more especially European territory. Here three private estates had been established by 1920. On their western edge, Gallop Road was one of a number of new roads built in the Tanglin area before the war; others included Nathan and Chatsworth Roads. Shortly after, Holt Road, off Nathan Road, saw several of the first of the very fine so-called Black-and-White houses erected for the managers of private British firms. Chatsworth Road gave access from Grange Road to the new estate of Tanglin Hill, whose houses featured evocative Scottish names such as Telcarne, Roseneath, Invery, Strathmore and Auchen Cairn. Auchen Cairn, which was the earliest of the group, having been built in the late 1800s, was demolished in about 1920.

A mess house built in 1920 on Cable Road for one of the early trading houses, McAlister & Co. Designed by Swan & Maclaren, it is a classic post-World War I Black-and-White residence.

The European flavour of Tanglin is seen here in the Tanglin Hill House, built in 1926 by the manager of the French Banque Indosuez.

A conspicuous addition to the area south of Chatsworth Road was the architecturally eclectic grand mansion Mount Echo, set in a large estate at the corner of Tanglin Road and Jervois Road. Built sometime just after 1920, this house in fact replaced an equally impressive one which appears to have been built in about 1870. Originally occupying an estate of about 25 acres, the earlier property had been bought in 1882 by the HongKong and Shanghai Banking Corporation, which had opened its first branch in Singapore five years earlier. Poised in stately fashion on elevated ground above Tanglin Road, Mount Echo was approached by a long winding driveway which led in another direction to a second house of comparable status, Matteran.

Mount Echo was merely one of a number of company houses erected during this period, the majority in the Jervois–Chatsworth–Tanglin Road area. More than half the houses built here were for the senior executives of large companies or banks. All of them appeared during the short period of optimism from 1919 to 1920.

However, with the changes toward greater social mobility and economic uncertainty, not all of the new houses were as grand as Mount Echo or those of Tanglin Hill. Speculative bungalow developments were now beginning to appear on the hallowed ground of several former Tanglin estates. By 1920, Jervois Road gave access to two such developments on the more elevated northern side of the road, for marshy ground precluded extensive building opposite, despite the recent construction of a drainage canal discharging into the Singapore River.

The presence of swamps further north between Nassim Hill and Mount Victoria and Goodwood Park also inhibited building. But apart from these low-lying flooded areas and the large public reserves—the Botanic Gardens, Tanglin Barracks and the Chinese Burial Ground below Mount Elizabeth—most of the Tanglin area was now occupied by residential properties, though at very low densities. Compounds were still of the order of five to six acres compared to one to one and a half acres in the Kallang–Geylang area and as small as a quarter of an acre in the Selegie Road area bordering the town centre.

Larger properties, however, continued to appear. Some of the European élite were now looking to the higher ground of Bukit Tungul on the opposite, northern side of Bukit Timah Road, where several large villas—Mount Rosie, Chancery House, Greenhill, Westmore and Wrexham—had by 1920 made their appearance. Closer to and overlooking Bukit Timah Road another fine residence, Dunearn, had also been built, although its atmosphere was somewhat marred by the addition of new residential development on the newly formed Barker Road which now encircled it.

On the slopes below Bukit Tungul, several other new private roads also gave access to the grounds of Braemar, Brothey and Gilstead. The tranquil environment of these properties was shortly to be disturbed by the construction of a railway track and the Newton Railway Station next to Bukit Timah Road nearby. On Newton Road itself, several Chinese families were left with less appealing subdivisions on which to erect their single-storey bungalows.

Developments near the Centre

The majority of Chinese in the Tanglin area still preferred a location closer to town. Some were now laying claim to sites on Mount Elizabeth and Mount Sophia. Cairnhill, now reached by Cairnhill Road and Emerald Hill Road, was a desirable location, although of seven houses planned for this area by Chinese in the years before the 1908 slump, none was actually built. In the end, the only additions on Cairnhill Road were two large, two-storey villas: Mount Elizabeth and Surlingham, the latter a company house built in 1919.

Emerald Hill, which had been purchased by one Seah Boon Kang at the turn of the century and subdivided in 1901 into 38 plots of varying sizes, was now the subject of more intensive development in the form of terrace houses. As this area had the advantage of an elevated position and a location now closer than ever to the edge of the town, the change from a suburban to an urban residential environment would be the beginning of an inevitable trend near the centre.

More typically, the Chinese continued the pattern of the previous period in building houses of diverse styles, mainly on the peripheral busier roads, Scotts Road, Kampong Java—which attracted most new buildings—and Cavenagh Road. Although both large and small houses were found in all areas, most of those in Kampong Java—on flat ground extending into Toa Payoh to the north—were more modest in size while those on Cairnhill Road tended to be larger. Equally, while different races were also interspersed, Kampong Java attracted Malays as well as Chinese, whereas Scotts Road was almost entirely a Chinese preserve.

The mixture of ethnic groups and sizes and indeed styles of houses was also characteristic of the more densely developed area bordering Orchard Road and River Valley Road. On Orange Grove Road, for example, there were three new houses, all built between 1901 and 1904. One, the smallest of all the new houses in this area, was built for a Chinese family, another of medium size was European-owned, and the third, the biggest of the entire group with over 700 square metres in area, belonged to an Indian businessman. Some streets, such as River Valley Road and Killiney Road, were predominantly Chinese enclaves, whereas Oxley Rise remained essentially European, but apart from this there was little evidence of racial segregation.

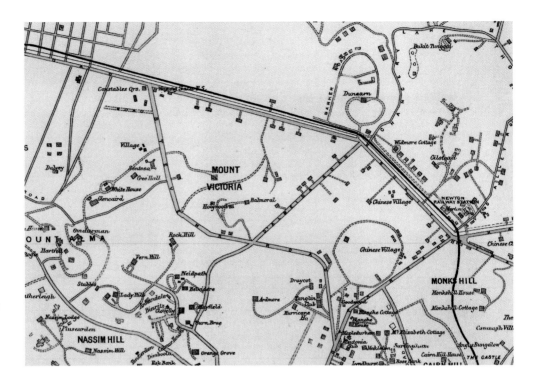

Detail from a 1903 map of Singapore shows development in the central areas of Nassim Hill, Mount Victoria and Bukit Tungul.

Developments to the South

The residents occupying the area south of the town were mainly Chinese, the majority of whom were packed into terrace houses in the town centre itself, while the more privileged minority enjoyed the comforts of a bungalow a little further out.

This former flat agricultural area, south of Alexandra Road, though extensively occupied by Chinese burial grounds, continued to attract several of the Chinese *nouveau riche*, particularly in Tiong Bahru at the foot of Pearl's Hill. Pearl's Hill itself, one of the island's highest areas and occupied much earlier by the Tan Tock Seng Hospital and then by the Civil Gaol, a public reservoir and various military facilities, prevented the extension of the town in this direction. The expansion of the town was therefore confined to the New Bridge Road–Kampong Bahru area and the South Bridge-Keppel-Tiong Bahru route parallel to the coast.

Partly for this reason, the whole area west of Pearl's Hill was still rural in character. The new bungalows which had sprung up since the 1880s sat in small clusters amidst the more vernacular Chinese villages and makeshift agricultural dwellings. By 1920, one or two new houses for Chinese owners had also been built along Havelock Road bordering the Singapore River to the north, in less appealing locations characterized by strip warehouse developments leading into areas of mangrove swamps. For the rest, a location closer to the coast on Telok Blangah or Kampong Bahru Road or one of its new offshoots was preferred.

This area, particularly the more elevated portion on the slopes of Mount Faber, which had been established much earlier as a desirable location for the well-to-do, also attracted senior personnel engaged in administering the port. By 1920, the Singapore Harbour Board had erected a number of the new Black-and-White houses to the design of the government architects' office, on Pender Road and Seah Im Road. Above Pender Road, in the spirit of the earlier spacious country villas of the 1840s, a much more substantial residence, Golden Bell, had made its appearance for Tan Boon Liat in 1909. Golden Bell echoed in its appearance the mood of eclecticism and romanticism characteristic of the years before World War I. It was in this house that Dr Sun Yat Sen stayed briefly in 1911 as Tan's guest on his triumphant way to Shanghai to become the Provisional Resident of the new Republic of China.

Other estates of less modest status, such as Spottiswood Park and Bushy Park bordering Breeze Hill, were laid out in English romantic garden-suburban vein further to the east. Such houses also accommodated senior European officials involved with the thriving port activities nearby. By 1910 new godowns had been constructed, not only on the vast area of reclaimed land in Telok Ayer Bay, but also bordering the new wharves along the whole of the Keppel Harbour shoreline. New roads had been built to serve them, a new wet dock carved out, modern machinery installed and electric power introduced. The graving dock, finished in 1913, was at the time the world's second biggest. In the context of such impressive developments and the general prosperity of those years, it is significant that by 1920, despite the interruption caused by the war, so few houses had been built in the Telok Blangah area and indeed elsewhere in the colony. In any event, it would take another three years for the real building boom to begin. ❖

Expansive view of Keppel Harbour taken from the eastern ridge of Mount Faber around 1890. A large country home is at left in the foreground.

End of an Era,
1920–1939

Social and Economic Changes

On the face of it, Singapore appeared to be relatively unaffected either by World War I or the Chinese revolution of 1911, but profound changes were beginning to take place. On the surface, the inter-war years were deceptively calm. Steadily, however, the Europeans and Asian communities drifted apart. If life for the European well-to-do and some of the richer Chinese was becoming increasingly leisurely and indulgent, that for the bulk of the population was conducted in conditions of extreme squalor. Meanwhile, the zest and vitality that had characterized the British administration in the early 1900s

Improvements in infrastructure included the addition of the Singapore trolleybus, system. Circa 1930.

had disappeared and the general attitude was now rather one of complacency, smugness and, at worst, indifference. Although British rule was firmly entrenched right up to the latter years of the 1930s, this was to be the twilight of the Empire: the end would come with World War II.

Much of the complacency on the part of the British was due to the fact that the colony's fortunes were riding high, despite the set-back resulting from the global depression of the late 1920s and early 1930s. The halcyon years immediately following the end of World War I resulted in a short-lived boom, to be followed by several years of economic hardship, but from 1923 the colony began to experience steady and spectacular growth as a result of record prices on the world market for tin, rubber and palm-oil. Apart from the depression years, the economy remained buoyant right through the 1930s although prices were never to reach the level of those attained in 1927. Despite a drop in commodity prices and capital values, the late 1930s saw a steep rise in the value of land in the centre and in bordering suburban areas.

Much of the profit received from the trade in primary products went into the pockets of a relatively small number of Chinese businessmen such as the Tiger Balm King, Aw Boon Haw, but Arab families also made substantial fortunes by trading in spices. Foreign business interests in commodity trading as well as property were also represented in the activities of organizations such as the German firm, Behn Meyer & Company.

At the same time, the prosperity of the colony saw a rapid rise in the number of small Chinese business firms, partly a product of the sudden increase in size of the Chinese population due to immigration, which reached a peak in 1927. Although the number of new arrivals dropped markedly during the depression years of the early 1930s, the new Chinese immigrants continued to overwhelm the locally born Straits Chinese. Meanwhile, the more well-to-do Straits Chinese, who had a closer relationship to the British than their mainland-born counterparts, continued to seek better educational opportunities, accentuating further the division between the working classes and the European and other privileged members of society.

For the latter group, the quality of suburban life was enhanced by the availability of a greater variety of food supplies through such outlets as the Singapore Cold Storage Company. Other new conveniences included wireless sets and motor cars, which had already grown in number by a factor of four during the war years and were to multiply several times over during the 1920s and 1930s. There were also increased opportunities for social life and leisure in clubs, hotels and in private homes or, for the less well-to-do, public entertainment in the form of amusement parks and cinema houses.

Living standards were also given a boost by a range of municipal improvements, including the extension of the sewerage system into suburban areas, the construction of water reservoirs, the establishment of the first electric power station at St James and, following the failure of the tramway system, the introduction of electrified trolleybuses in 1929 and motor buses a few years later. Already in 1923 the Johore Causeway had been opened to road traffic and the railway line, for which a new and impressive terminus was built in 1932.

Expansion to the West and East

Such improvements, however, did little to alleviate the conditions of the urban working classes. In response to this situation, the Singapore Improvement Trust was established in 1927. One of its primary objectives was to put in hand a series of slum clearance programmes. Laneways were constructed in the town centre to provide light and ventilation to the backs of the existing blocks of terrace housing. Other terrace blocks were demolished and the occupants rehoused in new, modern-style flats on land formerly occupied by Chinese squatters to the south of Alexandra Road, on the south-western side of the town. Modern flats were also built to house the British officials of the Singapore Improvement Trust on the northern side of Alexandra Road. New streets such as Kay Siang Road and Tiong Bahru were constructed to serve these developments. By the late 1930s, other modern blocks of flats were being built further west of the town centre at Queenstown and to the east at Kallang.

Suburban expansion to the south of the town consisted largely of such municipal housing developments. A number of estates of large detached houses for the British port officials and shipping company executives and others began to appear on the slopes of Telok Blangah and further west at Pasir Panjang and immediately south of the town centre on Bukit Kim Cheng. But, with the intrusion of the railway marshalling yards behind Keppel Road and further port developments along the Telok Blangah waterfront, private suburban residents—apart from those fortunate enough to reside in the fashionable area of the Tanglin Hills—preferred to live on the eastern side of town.

One reason for the move towards the east was that the amount of land available for residential building on the Telok Blangah side was limited. It was because of this that a number

The centre of Singapore with its overcrowded and insanitary shophouse streets resulted in the establishment of the Singapore Improvement Trust and a massive slum clearance programme.

Jinriksha Station, Singapore.

Haw Par Villa (1937), also known as Tiger Balm Gardens, was built on a hill in Pasir Panjang in a modern architectural language by Aw Boon Haw for his younger brother Aw Boon Par.

of large houses also began to appear along the shoreline further west at Pasir Panjang but, as at Tanjong Katong on the opposite side of town, these were mostly weekend retreats for very wealthy Chinese *towkays* and their numerous wives, children and mistresses. By the 1930s, the concentration of wealthy Chinese households along the Pasir Panjang Road, though mainly weekend residents, was such that this stretch became known as 'millionaires' row'.

Included within the ranks of the rich at Pasir Panjang were Lee Kong Chian, the rubber magnate, and Aw Boon Haw who, with his brother, established the huge Tiger Balm empire. As an expression of his success in the world of business and as a place in which to relax with his family and to entertain his friends, Aw built the palatial and highly individualistic modern-style Haw Par Villa on elevated ground overlooking the Pasir Panjang waterfront. Though facing partly west, which, as with other houses in this area was a disadvantage, the siting of Haw Par Villa was carefully determined to satisfy the requirements of good *feng shui* and thus to ensure prosperity and good fortune. *Feng shui*, traditional in China, was the art of ensuring that daily practices were in harmony with natural forces and that buildings therefore were advantageously sited in response to physical as well as cosmic forces.

For the majority who aspired to a permanent home in the suburbs, the district comprising Geylang, Siglap and Paya Lebar, east of the centre, provided most opportunity. Partly this was due to municipal intervention in the form of land reclamation, the drainage of former swamplands and the construction of public roads. The availability of freehold land at Paya Lebar and Siglap also provided a positive inducement to speculative and private residential development in this direction.

The introduction of the motor trolleybus service along Geylang Road in 1929 gave access to town for those on middle incomes who, like their wealthier counterparts, were now able to enjoy the comforts of life in a suburban house well removed from the congestion of the urban centre. Such houses and the allotments on which they were built were generally appreciably smaller than those of the Tanglin area or Telok Blangah and were likely to be occupied by middle-class Eurasian clerks, subordinates and others.

There were, however, exceptions to this. The house built for Lee Siong Kiat at Siglap, for instance, was quite grand and of two storeys whereas single-storey bungalows were rather the rule. Some larger houses appeared in areas such as Grove Estate, bordering the rich Jewish neighbourhood of Amber Road and Meyer Road along the Katong waterfront. Along here, too, various public facilities, such as the Tanjong Katong Park and bandstand, the Tanjong Rhu Club, and the rebuilt modern-style Singapore Swimming Club, had appeared by the mid-1930s, mainly to serve the needs of the wealthy upper set.

New weekend bungalows, owned and rented mainly by well-to-do Chinese and Europeans, also made their appearance here and further east as far as Tanah Merah and Changi. The rich Jewish entrepreneur, E S Manasseh, who owned the Goodwood Hotel, the former Teutonia Club, had one such bungalow at the end of Changi Road. Manasseh was typical in also having a palatial permanent Tanglin residence; it was on Nassim Road. At the back of this house, Manasseh had a racing circuit built to satisfy his passion for horse riding and racing.

Belonging as they did to the upper crust, most weekend houses were large and, like the one built at Tanjong Katong in 1921 for Madame Leong Kee, were on piers to exploit the ocean view and catch the sea breeze. Madame Leong's house was less elaborate than most, being more akin to the basic form of the earlier plantation house, whereas eclecticism was the order of the day, and by the 1930s, the vogue for modernism had begun to make its appearance. As grand as some of these houses were, the lifestyle was thoroughly informal. Only a few houses at Katong had electricity, relying instead on oil pressure-lamps. Typically, houses were set on an acre or two of ground, planted with coconut trees, stretching to the water's edge. There were jetties, tiled swimming enclosures and, occasionally, pavilions set out over the water as at Pasir Panjang.

Established in 1894, the Singapore Swimming Club was a popular draw in Katong. This view shows the modern-style clubhouse and pool in the 1930s.

Weekend house, Meyer Road in Katong, built before the 1920s.

The Tanjong Katong beachfront extended into the waterfront industrial area of Tanjong Rhu, the spit of land extending westward into the Kallang Basin, and here, until the mid-1930s, almost cheek-by-jowl with the prestigious Jewish area of Meyer Road, were located a number of Malay fishing communities in timber *kampongs*, many built on piles over the water. By the mid-1930s, however, they had all been removed to new *kampongs* set aside by the government further inland and to the east, to make way for the construction of the new Kallang Civil Airport. Already, by the late 1920s, new Malay *kampongs* had been established at Geylang Serai and, in the opposite direction, at Pasir Panjang and beyond. Here the Malays continued to live in their leisurely way as they had always done, their lives little affected by general social and environmental changes.

Other Malay communities, such as Kampong Kapur bordering Serangoon Road, had also been cleared away and their occupants moved to new settlement areas to the east. By the early 1930s, the area formerly occupied by Kampong Kapur had been invaded by Chinese retailers and completely built up with rows of shophouses. In general, though, the area bordering Serangoon Road continued to be mainly an Indian preserve. However, those Eurasians and Chinese who could afford to do so, continued to move into areas bordering Upper Serangoon Road, where they built modest single-storey timber houses. These were mostly raised off the ground because of the propensity of the area to flooding, despite the fact that most of the former mangrove swamps south of Lavender Road had by now been drained and the area developed, partly for new bungalow developments and partly in the form of public recreational facilities,

Early Singapore was a country of contrasts. Scenes such as the above, where kampong *houses on stilts whose owners continued to live fairly traditional lifestyles, lay cheek-by-jowl with modern developments.*

including the New World Amusement Park and the Jalan Besar Stadium. Such facilities were in keeping with the general character of the area extending on to the opposite, western side of Serangoon Road, consisting as it did of the Balestier Plain Recreational Ground and the Farrer Park Racecourse.

This was quite in contrast to the intense urban shophouse character of lower Serangoon Road and Selegie Road to the south, which had become more than ever working-class Indian territory. It was also in contrast to the upper-middle income, suburban character of Upper Serangoon Road and streets such as Owen and Rangoon Roads running off it.

Once beyond the urban area, Serangoon Road, like other streets penetrating to the north and east such as Geylang Road and East Coast Road, was narrow, passing between groves of coconut palms and other vegetation. Life for the residents of these areas was relatively relaxed, despite an increasing number of horses and carriages, rickshaws and motor cars passing through. The diverse social and rural suburban character of the whole area was largely a reflection of the fact that it was changing rapidly and, in the process, attracting a variety of residents of different races and incomes. At one extreme there were the wealthy Arabs of Balestier Road and the Jews of Tanjong Katong in their substantial brick mansions, and at the other, the rather poorer Chinese and Eurasians of Paya Lebar in their timber bungalows and, nearby, the Malays in the timber and atap-roofed huts of their native *kampongs*.

The Government Estates

The character of this area to the north was quite in contrast to the established, genteel quality of the suburb of Tanglin, west of the town centre. Houses typical of the Tanglin area were now being built as far south as Alexandra Road, to the north-east up to Thomson Road, and well beyond Bukit Timah Road to encompass much of the hilly countryside to the north.

This area was still exclusively upper-class and English in flavour and characterized by houses of substantial dimensions set in large gardens. However, with the rising number of government administrators and senior personnel of British-owned private companies and the intervention of the government on their behalf, its character began to change.

By the 1920s, a number of large residential estates had been built by the colonial government on formerly vacant or sparsely developed land north of Bukit Timah Road and south of the Grange–Napier–Holland Road artery running to the west, and there were others on remaining hilltops in between. These estates were built for civil servants, army officers and the executives of private companies.

The civil service estates were mainly to the north of Bukit Timah Road on crown land bordering Mount Pleasant, Malcolm Road and Chancery Lane. Later in the 1930s, other civil service estates were laid out on high ground, reached by Pender Road, overlooking the waterfront at Telok Blangah, at Seton Close off Tanglin Road, Adam Park and elsewhere. With the exception of Mount Pleasant, these estates were made up of the Black-and-White houses.

Designed as they were by the architects of the Public Works Department, the Black-and-White houses were a sensible and original interpretation of the 19th-century plantation house in Tudoresque black-painted half-timbering on walls of white stucco over timber lathing. The Tudor references appear to have come from the mock Tudor style of the planned garden suburbs and new towns of late 19th-century England, probably by way of the Indian hill stations of Poona, Ootacamund and Simla. Just as these garden suburbs and colonial outposts had been bastions of civilian rule and social superiority, so too the civil service estates of Malcolm Road and Mount Pleasant accommodated their

29 Malcolm Road (1925), one of many Black-and-White residences built to house government officers.

Police Inspectors-General and other senior colonial officers in a style appropriate to their rank. It was important that these houses and their gardens were at least as large as the biggest of those elsewhere in Tanglin and that they be seen as such. It was fitting, too, that they had the requisite number of servants, including a cook, a driver and an *amah* or two.

Black-and-White houses appeared also in the estates of Goodwood Hill off Stevens Road where lived government servants from the ranks of Magistrate and others slightly less senior. This was a good location: well elevated, within walking distance of the Tanglin Club, the centre of upper-class British social life, and a mere 10-minute ride by saloon buggy or hackney carriage to the centre of town.

In layout, Goodwood Road estate was typical of others in having winding roads following the contours and houses set, as if by accident rather than design, into the landscape of sweeping lawns and trees in 'natural' groves. But the influence of the English romantic tradition and that of the idealized country estate was not confined to Goodwood Hill or any other of government estates. Nearby, just off Stevens Road, there was Wee Garden City, one of the many small private speculative developments that sprang up in the 1920s and 1930s in different parts of the Tanglin area. There was an echo of the English garden suburb, too, in the various private company estates, such as Swiss Cottage Estate off Bukit Timah Road and Holland Park off Holland Road. These estates featured very large houses with evocative English and Scottish names such as Holmesdale and Brean Down, each set well above and away from the street and approached by long, curving driveways. Immediately behind Goodwood Hill was a house of no mean size which, like its neighbour Wee Garden City, echoed in its name, Bukit Rose, sentiments both Eastern and English.

Black-and-White houses were characteristic also of the army estates of the late 1920s, such as Ridley Park off Holland Road to the south of the Tanglin Barracks. The increased British military presence in the 1930s prompted the establishment of other army estates at Alexandra Park and Portsdown Road and for these, houses of more simple, modern design were built. The clean lines and uncluttered surfaces of such houses were echoed in others of Dutch flavour in

View of an elegant Black-and-White house and parkland built in Ridley Park in the late 1920s and early 1930s for army personnel.

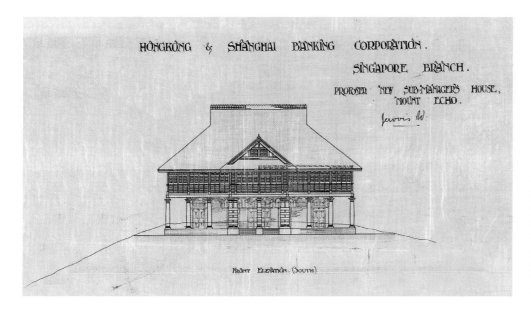

HONGKONG & SHANGHAI BANKING CORPORATION.

SINGAPORE BRANCH.

PROPOSED NEW SUB-MANAGER'S HOUSE,
MOUNT ECHO.

Jervois Rd.

FRONT ELEVATION. (SOUTH)

Drawing submitted to the Municipality by Swan & Maclaren in 1902 for the proposed Sub-Manager's house, HongKong & Shanghai Banking Corporation. that was later built on Mount Echo.

Holland Park and Dalvey Estate and other private company estates at Belmont Road and Cluny Road. Such houses, with their broad, hipped, deeply overhanging roofs, white stucco walls and sloping piers, large semicircular windows and brick-banded arched openings, though Dutch, were also symptomatic of the change toward a more forward-looking style of architecture.

This change was already making its appearance in houses of more radical form which were being built in other parts of the Tanglin area, but more commonly in the residences of wealthy Chinese in the waterfront areas of Katong and Siglap. The flat-roofed geometrically abstract style of these houses had been adopted for the municipal housing estates of the Singapore Improvement Trust but was deemed to be inappropriate for senior army, civilian or company executives, for whom a certain dignity and sense of tradition were considered important. Modern-style houses, moreover, were hardly as suitable to the Singaporean climate as the Black-and-White houses.

It was the Black-and-White house therefore that was adopted by a number of the private companies as the prototype in the building of estates for their senior personnel. Two examples were the MacAlister Trading Company Estate on Cable Road and the Firestone Rubber Company Estate at Firestone Park, both in the vicinity of the Tanglin Barracks. The presence of the Barracks enhanced the park-like setting of these estates by virtue of its own spacious, landscaped environment, which included a 16-hole golf-course extending from the edge of the Botanic Gardens on Napier Road at one end to Tanglin Road at the other.

The exclusive atmosphere of these estates or that of Sri Menanti on Jervois Road with its imposing pseudo-Renaissance-style residence for the HongKong and Shanghai Banking Corporation clearly identified their occupants as being a cut above the rest of Singaporean society. The desire to signal their position in the social hierarchy, however, applied equally to the upper middle-income residents of the many smaller, more compact estates of English vernacular-style cottages along Bukit Timah Road, Scotts Road and River Valley Road. Most of these estates and their established lifestyles were, however, shortly to disappear in the context of the political change from colonialism to independence precipitated by World War II. ❖

Recreation in the Suburbs, 1800s

❧❧❧

As in England and India, recreation in Singapore was an important part of the suburban ideal. Attitudes to recreation were brought to Singapore by the British, both directly and indirectly via India, as part of the general transfer of cultural ideas between Europe and South East Asia. In both India and Singapore, English attitudes were adopted and adapted to colonial circumstances and often extended to influence the recreational habits of the indigenous population.

For members of the ruling English society, there were opportunities for recreation to which in suburban England they may have aspired, but never achieved. A part of the English suburban dream was the supposed association between the appeal of the countryside and opportunities for recreation and leisure. As it turned out, most of the new English suburbanites, some of whom were to make up the ranks of the colonial élite, had neither the time nor the money for such pursuits. For the male breadwinner, long hours were spent in working and commuting and although the typical middle-class family may have afforded a maidservant, until the turn of the century there was little free time.

Those English suburban residents on higher incomes were better off. They could, for example, join one of the new tennis or golf clubs when these came into existence in the 1880s and the 1890s. By then, however, tennis-courts also began to appear in even modest-sized English backyards. In Singapore, ownership of a private tennis-court or membership of a club, though confined to the suburban well-to-do, was less exclusive. Even such sporting pastimes as hunting and shooting, which in 19th-century England were available only to the very rich, were at hand, as in India, for those so inclined. So, too, were such traditional upper-class pursuits as horse riding, cricket, golf or even rowing.

Women played little part in such activities. Sport was strictly a male affair, a situation partly to do with the exigencies of colonial life. Prior to the mid-19th century, sporting activities were often a palliative for boredom or loneliness and, as in India, some compensation for the sense of isolation and general cultural disorientation. For the predominantly male population, sport was also an antidote for the scarcity of women. Typical of the English colonial attitude was the belief that, as *The Straits Times* (1867) put it: "Manly exercises will prevent other evils which flesh is heir to."

Like the taking of the proverbial cold shower, sport was seen as manly, character-forming and, in the spirit of the public school imperial ethos, the hallmark of the 'decent

chap'. It was also a useful diversion for the lonely bachelor or husband in exile who, during the early years, was subjected to long weeks of waiting for word from home at a time when mail came by sailing ship. As such, it served as an alternative to family-oriented indoor forms of recreation such as parlour games, piano-playing and group singing, activities enjoyed by their English suburban counterparts as part of the new middle-class emphasis on family life.

While there were opportunities for male social interaction in group 'messes' and in other ways, these were limited by the small size of the colonial community. Before the 1850s there were only 500 Europeans, and by 1880 the number had increased to only 3,000. For many, monotony was the order of the day. The delibitating effect of the hot, humid climate, the prevalence of mosquitoes, and the current obsession of the English with health were additional factors underlying the enthusiasm for sport. "We are," said *The Straits Times* (1882), "the healthiest country in the East and attribute no small share of it to our activity and love of outdoor sports."

In the sense of spectatorship, this had been the case even since the 1830s. The New Year Regatta of the then newly formed Singapore Yacht Club, first held in 1834, had been extended in 1839 to become an event of major proportions: the social highlight of the year. A large enthusiastic crowd assembled to watch a wide variety of sporting and other outdoor activities. This event became an annual affair in which the Malays and *orang laut* (sea-gypsies) figured prominently as regular victors in the annual boat race. Involving as it did all communities, it

Founded in 1884, the Ladies Lawn Tennis Club occupied an unused area on Dhoby Green, between Stamford and Bras Basah roads.

Cricket match at Tanglin Barracks in the 1800s.

was also an occasion to openly challenge the monopoly held by the English and to compensate for the racial divisions that existed in sport and in other areas of life.

Typical of the prominence of the English in sporting activities was cricket, which first appeared on the Esplanade in the 1830s in the form of regular Sunday afternoon matches. Nearby, in Empress Place, a Five Courts building was put up in 1836; this game, somewhat resembling handball and a predecessor of squash, was played by several men using hands instead of racquets. Horse and pony riding, soon to become a daily social ritual amongst the Europeans, was also a regular event.

Horse racing, until 1843 a popular but uncoordinated activity, was put on to an organized footing with the establishment of the Singapore Sporting Club, later known as the Turf Club, in 1843. At about the same time, the area of swamp to the west of Serangoon Road was reclaimed to form Singapore's first racecourse. Within the Serangoon Road community, the breeding, training and care of horses became an important local industry, particularly amongst the Baweanese, who excelled in such activities.

Even before the construction of the grandstand, huge crowds were attracted to regular racing events. These were occasions for much social merriment and heavy betting. There were brass bands, merry-go-rounds, cake stalls and much fanfare surrounding the arrival of the Governor at opening ceremonies. This was another sporting event which brought together all races.

From 1891, the Serangoon racecourse was to serve a double purpose with the use of the track area for nine-hole golf on Sundays. Soon after, a small clubhouse was put up by the Singapore Island Club, which had been founded in 1865. Unlike racing, golf would remain an essentially European pastime. The Singapore Island Club and the Singapore Royal Golf Club, which was to follow five years later, were also exclusively European.

Racial discrimination, however, was not simply because of snobbishness on the part of the British: the Chinese, in particular, wanted it that way. The Chinese themselves had their own exclusive clubs, clans and secret societies. However, most of these groups were not established primarily for sporting activities. The main motive in the case of the Chinese was to further individual business interests. Tied to this was a need for immigrant groups to band together, which they did, often to the point of bitter inter-group rivalry. Many of the groups came out of the various support networks that had developed amongst the Chinese *sinkheh* or new Chinese immigrant labourers who had flocked to the Malay Peninsula in response to the boom in tin and rubber.

The pattern of immigrant and class divisions was extremely complicated. Some of the clubs were patronized by middle-class businessmen and these received encouragement, official and unofficial, from the colonial government. At the other extreme were the secret societies, which were illegal but nevertheless flourished.

Sectarianism applied to all races. It existed, for example, amongst the Indians and Ceylonese, though in their case not in any organized way until 1923 when, for the first time, they began to formalize their interests in the establishment of the Indian Merchants' Association and a number of sporting and other societies. In the case of the Arabs, the Jawi Peranakan (locally born Muslims of mixed Indian and Malay ancestry), and the Malays, the majority of clubs, like those of the Europeans, consisted of the better-educated and more cultured members of society.

Even amongst the European clubs, there were differences in status. The Singapore Cricket Club, for example, which was founded in 1852, was number two or three on the European executive list. The European club *par excellence* was the Singapore Club in Fullerton Square. Like the Singapore Club, the Singapore Cricket Club was conveniently located near the centre of business activity bordering Raffles Place, and was thus a convenient venue for business luncheons. Housed originally in a small pavilion at the end of the Esplanade and overlooking the playing field, it was progressively added to in the 1870s and the 1880s.

The Eurasians, though looked down upon by pure-blooded Europeans, could take comfort in the fact that, like the Chinese, they were outside the European social hierarchy. Not to be outdone, they established their own Singapore Recreational Club and built their own building to accommodate it at the opposite end of the Padang in 1884.

Some 20 years later, the Singapore Cricket Club went one step further in giving their building an entirely new façade and adding two large wings. Almost simultaneously, the Straits Chinese, who identified so much with European ways, but like the Eurasians understood perfectly well their racial position, followed suit by setting up the Singapore Chinese Recreational Club at Hong Lim Green. The ground, which was given to the Chinese community by the colonial government, was developed into a park in 1887 at a cost of $3,000 donated by one Cheong Hong Lim; a new pavilion had been built in 1885. Here in the years to follow were played all of the European games—cricket, tennis, football, hockey, athletics, and even billiards.

Of these, rugby football was the least likely to be taken seriously, being mainly a European pastime. Even for the Europeans, football carried less weight than cricket or tennis as a social activity. The exception to this was the British Army team which, from the time the game was first inaugurated in 1849, conducted regular association football matches with the Chinese and Malays on land near Tank Road. The Chinese also had a small group of enthusiasts who formed their own Tanjong Pagar Football Association in the late 1880s. Although football was more popular among the Malays, for them it was soccer rather than rugby that was preferred.

Sporting activities such as these were not confined to the suburban well-to-do, for whom sport none the less was the main form of recreation and the main vehicle for social intercourse during the 1800s. In this, the bias was both European and male. Opportunities for women, such as they were, took other forms. The doors of the German Teutonia Club, founded in 1856, were open to both sexes. So, too, were those of the Tanglin Club, which was opened nine years later. The Tanglin Club quickly became the social centre for the English upper set; other races, including the Jews, were strictly prohibited.

The 1860s saw the establishment of other clubs, some of which, like the Teutonia and the Tanglin Clubs, were open to wives and other family members. Others, like the Singapore Swimming Club and the Gymnastic Club in Scotts Road, followed the usual pattern of catering, at least implicitly, to men rather than women. A number of clubs, beginning with the Raffles Club of 1825, came into existence and faded after a few years. Some of these admitted women, for whom, in the late 1800s, there were other social outlets such as luncheon and tea parties in the tiffin houses or dinners and dances at various hotels, which also offered facilities for such diversions as card games and even skittle bowling.

The pavilion of the Singapore Cricket Club in the 1880s.

At a more serious level, a number of literary, musical and other cultural societies made their appearance in the 1880s to cater for those so inclined. Church-going was important for the British, as it was in suburban England, and this was matched by the religious devotion of the Jews, Armenians, Chinese, Indians and Muslims, for whom altogether there were over 100 places of worship. Churches catered not only to spiritual needs but also social ones, with fellowship meetings, concerts, talks and outings. The churches attracting the largest attendance were the Anglican Cathedral of St Andrews, the Presbyterian Church of England, the Methodist Episcopalian Church and the Roman Catholic Cathedral Church of the Good Shepherd, all in the vicinity of the original European settlement near the Esplanade. For the Armenians, the centre of worship was the Church of St Gregory on Hill Street, and for the Jews, the Synagogue on Waterloo Street. For those of Muhammadan persuasion, there were 23 mosques in various parts of the island. This only slightly exceeded the number of lodges, including the main lodge in Coleman Street which was extended in 1887, for the Masonic fraternity.

By the end of the 1800s, recreation was still largely tied to such formal institutions as the church, the social club, the sporting club and other associations. While these would continue to be important, social life would, however, become more informal during the next several decades. ❖

The Teutonia Club, founded in 1856, was a centre for European entertainment for many decades. At the turn of the century it moved to these imposing premises which today house the Goodwood Park Hotel.

Social Life and Leisure in the Suburbs, 1900s

With the arrival of the Edwardian era at the turn of the century, social life in Singapore, as in England, gradually became more relaxed and liberal, even if many of the old taboos, such as racial and sexual discrimination, lingered on. But even in the hitherto sacred male province of sport, the situation was changing. Up till then, women had been kept strictly to the sidelines. As in England or colonial India, the participation of women in outdoor activities, other than as spectators, had not been contemplated. The enveloping nature of female attire, crinolines, long dresses, petticoats and bonnets, in any case, ensured this. Chauvinism applied, too, in the clubs; if admitted at all, ladies were kept out of sight.

The gradual emancipation of women which would reach a climax in England with the winning of the suffragette battle in 1918 and the idealization of the liberal, outdoor housewife in the 1920s and 1930s, was, however, already in the wind. It was reflected in

Even though sport was mainly a male activity, women began to be catered to from around the turn of the century. This photo depicts a cycle race for ladies in 1898.

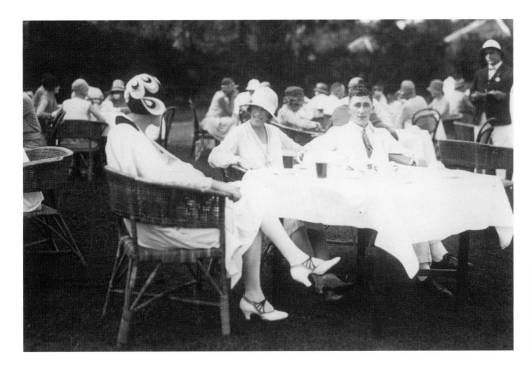

the establishment of clubs such as the Lotus Club for the female members of Indian and Ceylonese society in the 1920s. But already in 1884 it appeared in the claim by the female members of the European community for a club of their own and grounds on which to play lawn tennis, which had been growing in popularity since its official inauguration in the first Singapore championships in 1875. Despite the climate of male chauvinism, the ladies were stoutly assisted in this new move by the opposite sex; the club was launched, a building put up and seven courts laid out at Dhoby Ghaut. How the ladies, ensconced in long dresses and elevated shoes, managed to negotiate the ball is another story. In any event, the involvement of both sexes in tennis was such as to cause J D Ross to exclaim in 1898: "The amount of tennis played in Singapore is something astonishing. All this promotes social relations between the sexes."

As tennis increasingly gained social respectability, particularly for women, so did hockey, which was played on the Esplanade from 1892. Hockey, however, was less popular with women than with the male Asians and Eurasians who excelled to the point of completely dominating the various interracial matches from that time on. If hockey was a little too vigorous, the ladies could indulge in the more genteel pastime of archery or croquet which, like tennis, could be played in the privacy of one's garden.

By the turn of the century, if the frequency of private tennis-courts did not match that of the English suburb, certainly most of the Tanglin residences had their own courts and they were becoming increasingly common in other areas. Private courts were venues for social intercourse within the European community in the form of informal tennis parties, family activities and even dinner parties.

Just as tennis was one form of outdoor activity now available to members of the family other than the male breadwinner, so was cycling, which became instantly popular with the invention of the pneumatic tyre in 1890. A cycling club was formed in the same year. Although there were fewer opportunities for cycling excursions in the countryside in Singapore than in England, at least many of the roads were now sealed. Cycling was therefore much easier, particularly for ladies, assuming a little discretion in the manipulation of skirts, gears and pedals.

Trips into the countryside away from the built-up area also became feasible for those who could afford it, once the motor car started to become popular in the late 1920s. For more serious-minded enthusiasts, there was motor car racing which began with the establishment of the Singapore Automobile Club in 1907. At a more social level, the car provided access for whole families to seaside bungalows and waterfront activities such as picnics.

Seaside bungalows were not exclusively the prerogative of the rich Europeans. Many of those built in the Katong and Tanjong Rhu areas were for wealthy Straits Chinese. A number of rich Arab families also owned a second holiday house. The Alkaffs, for instance, had a house on the east coast at Siglap, another on the west coast at Pasir Panjang, and a country estate, Mount Washington, at Pender Road in Telok Blangah, which occupied 30 to 40 acres.

It was to the Alkaff family that many families owed their thanks for providing the popular picnic spot known as Alkaff Garden. Built in the 1920s between Macpherson Road and Serangoon Road, it was originally intended as a 'small' garden for the Alkaff family. It was eventually thrown open to the public free-of-charge with, however, a small levy for boat rides and fishing on the lake. The lake formed part of an imitation Japanese country setting including a miniature Mount Fuji; a quite unrelated but additionally exotic feature was the Alkaffs' pet camel. Such a characteristically 19th-century English romantic conception, devised by Arabs, was popular not only with the English and other Europeans but other ethnic communities including the Chinese and Indians.

A view of the idyllic Alkaff Garden in 1929. Thanks to the largesse of the Alkaff family, entry was free to all.

Façade of Capitol Theatre, an air-conditioned cinema built by the Namazies in 1931. This photo dates from 1947.

A less romantic aspect of Alkaff Garden was its motor-cycle track, the first in Singapore. Motor-cycling had already become popular by the 1920s but, like the motor car, only amongst those who could afford it. For the rest, there was the excitement of motor-cycle racing. This was at least accessible to a wider audience, but an even more popular form of entertainment was the cinema.

The first silent, black-and-white movies came in the 1920s, introducing a new dimension to leisure activity. Though mainly an Asiatic preoccupation in Singapore, cinema-going naturally also appealed to Europeans, although more to children than their parents, who were understandably sceptical about the risks involved, such as undesirable company and the risk of fire.

The first films were shown in large tents. Later, wooden buildings, such as the Gaiety or the Harimah Hall (which was rebuilt as the Tivoli) were erected for the purpose. Pathé films, or 'bioscope shows' as they were known, featured melodramatic episodes from the Russo-Japanese War or comedy shows such as Charlie Chaplin or Laurel and Hardy to the accompaniment of a screeching violin or an out-of-tune piano.

In the late 1920s, more substantial cinema houses were built, though none was of the impressive size of those in England which had a capacity of up to 2,000 seats, nor did they have their luxurious decor. On Beach Road there was the Alhambra which, like the Pavilion on Orchard Road, was considered a first-class cinema; at a lower price of between 10 and 75 cents a seat, were the Marlborough or the Roxy. Only the first-class cinemas would do for European audiences; the Capitol, with its Art Deco interior, built in 1931, was the most popular venue of all.

For those with upper-class pretensions, there was theatre at the Victoria Memorial Hall. This was strictly a black-tie affair. These were occasions for imperialistic airs and graces which, however, were quickly dissolved by the razzle-dazzle and jolly good humour of a Gilbert and Sullivan operetta or the raucous laughter accompanying a Victorian farce played by local amateurs. There were, on the other hand, occasional serious productions including visits by metropolitan opera companies.

Western theatre was unlikely to attract Chinese patrons other than the educated Babas who were inclined to European habits. The Babas had the best of both worlds because there was also the *Wayang Kassim* near Arab Street where Kairo Dean, the idol of the Babas, captivated audiences for many a long season during the golden era of Malay opera.

Those with more traditional Chinese inclinations could go to the Cantonese theatre in Smith Street or the *wayang*—the itinerant Chinese street operas on their makeshift stages— which made regular appearances. *Wayang* were best seen during the seventh lunar month, at the Festival of the Hungry Ghosts, when street hawkers pooled their resources and mounted lavish celebrations to the accompaniment of the high-pitched falsetto shrieks of the *wayang* actors and the burning of joss-sticks and paper money.

To European eyes, no less than to those of other races, the spectacle of such activities was sufficient entertainment in itself as was the kaleidoscope of national costumes and the cacophony of different languages. In such a multi-cultural environment, festivals were almost a weekly event. There was the Chinese New Year, which was ushered in by a gala performance of pyrotechnics including festoons of firecrackers along the riverfront, and the sights and sounds of hawkers and shops doing a brisk trade in all kinds of seasonal delicacies, such as good-luck oranges and kumquat trees.

Victoria Theatre and Victoria Memorial Hall (the latter is now known as the Victoria Concert Hall), 1905.

No. 76. A chinese theatre

Performed on makeshift and removable wooden stages, wayang *or Cantonese theatre was popular during festival times.* Circa *1905.*

Quite as colourful was the annual Chingay parade of stilt-walkers, lion and dragon dancers, acrobats, and decorated floats taking to the streets amidst the clashing of cymbals and beating of gongs and drums. The Mid-autumn or Mooncake Festival on the 15th day of the eighth lunar month offered a somewhat less raucous experience in the annual parade of children bearing their flickering, brightly coloured paper lanterns.

Within the Indian community, there was the festival of Chettiar Thaipusam with its pilgrimage of entranced penitents; and there were the Hindu festivals of Navarathi and Timithi, the Fire-walking Festival, and Deepavali, the Festival of Lights. The Muslims had their Hari Raya Puasa and the lavish celebration at the end of Ramadan, the month of fasting.

The Europeans celebrated Christmas, the Gregorian New Year and Easter, quite apart from momentous occasions such as Coronation Day (the celebration of the coronation of Edward VII in 1901), the visit by the Duke and Duchess of York in the same year, or that of the Duke of Connaught in 1906. On such occasions, the whole town was adorned with Union Jacks, bunting and streamers, and there was much flag-waving, cheering and showering of confetti upon the visiting dignitaries.

Patriotic sentiments were maintained in other ways. For the British, there was the pomp and circumstance of the Regimental Band on the Esplanade every Tuesday and Friday afternoon. Less dramatic, but just as nationalistic, were events such as the annual Agricultural Horticultural Show of the Federated Malay States, even if the representation was almost entirely European.

To add to this panorama of cultural entertainment, there were visits to the town by troupes of circus performers and groups of wandering minstrels or *boria* singing songs and ballads to the accompaniment of violins, mandolins and guitars.

A 1946 view of the Serangoon Road entrance to the New World Amusement Park. The brainchild of the entrepreneurial Shaw Brothers, it attracted clientele from all walks of life.

The heyday of the minstrels came, however, with the introduction of the cabaret and, with it, a revolution in popular entertainment in the form of the giant Amusement Park. The first of these, built in the early 1930s, the New World Amusement Park, had all the elements of the fair: hawkers, eating stalls, shops offering cheap merchandise of all descriptions, amusement sideshows, 'opera' halls catering to different ethnic groups—Teochew, Hokkien, and Malay—musical performances, and a variety of other items.

The New World was the initiative of the enterprising Shaw Brothers, who were also instrumental in bringing silent movies to Singapore. Like the cinema, the New World generated enormous enthusiasm and was cheap and thus accessible to even the lower middle-income earner. Unlike the cinema, however, it invited active participation. The most evident indication of this was the cabaret. This took place in a hall which, by colonial standards, was huge, accommodating up to 700 people dancing at one time.

The centre of attention was the cabaret girls, with whom, for a small charge, one could quickstep or do the conga to the music of a Goanese band. Dancing started at 7pm and continued until midnight. At week-ends, there were so-called Tea Dances starting at four in the afternoon. The cabaret girls, mainly local or Hong Kong Chinese, with a few Eurasians, Indians and Filipinas, were, contrary to popular opinion, mostly respectable, usually well educated, and able to speak fluent English. This, nevertheless, did not calm the fears of the elder and more conservative generation of Babas who reacted with alarm at the tendency of their younger, more liberal offspring to frequent such haunts. The New World, however, attracted not only the younger generation. Malayan royalty went there, as did British managing directors and wealthy Chinese *towkays*, along with office workers on ordinary salaries, clerks and storekeepers, members of the British armed forces, and whole families, Europeans and Asians alike.

View of the entrance to the Happy World Amusement Park, circa *1955*.

So successful was the New World venture that two more Amusement Parks, the Great World and the Happy World, were launched, with all the features of the New World and a few more besides. At the Happy World there was the 'Miss Rebut Show', a popular series of comedies based on family life, and at the Great World, bird displays, 'dragon' performances and, most successful of all, two first-rate Chinese restaurants. Not to be outdone, the New World added the Malay *ronggeng* and the *joget*, an open-air dance performance.

For those whose inclinations were less robust, there were increasing opportunities for leisure and social life in the clubs, hotels and restaurants as well as in private houses. Entertaining at home had always been an important social function for the well-to-do Europeans and Chinese, who, however, rarely entertained each other, but at this time there was a good deal of socializing outside the home as well.

European clubs such as the Tanglin Club continued to offer diversions such as bridge, chess, billiards and, of course, dining and drinking. Billiards had been first introduced into Singapore in 1829 with the founding of a club—Singapore's first—in support of that activity. The club itself did not last, although the game remained extremely popular in clubs, hotels, private houses—European as well as Chinese—and in messes, where the billiard tables were commonly housed in a separate annex, traditionally barred to women.

Men continued to have the advantage in being able to meet in private messes which were set up whenever half a dozen male companions—which is all that was needed—decided to do so. Above this figure it was necessary to apply for formal registration. Other popular mess games were poker and chess.

The popularity of chess was signalled in the opening of the Singapore Chess Club which did not have a permanent home but met once a week at the Hotel de l'Europe, conveniently located opposite the Singapore Cricket Club, and subsequently at the Adelphi Hotel and finally at the YMCA in Stamford Road.

The Hotel de l'Europe, which had been established in 1855, moved into a large and impressive new building facing the Esplanade in 1905 and this remained an important centre of European social life until the 1930s, when it was demolished for the new Law Courts building. From that time, the Raffles Hotel became the European venue, while the Grove Hotel and Sanatorium, like the Seaview Hotel at Katong, became a favourite meeting place for Sunday family outings.

By the 1930s, life for the European well-to-do had become exceedingly gracious and relaxed. Long lunches and extended afternoons at the Raffles, the Hotel Van Wijk, the Adelphi, or the Seaview were quite the done thing as were dinner dances and balls and, for the menfolk, long evenings spent in the bar which closed only at midnight or even later on Sundays. The exclusively European flavour of these occasions was evident in the rules which forbade entry to other races, as well as in the music, the food, the formal attire and, in large part, the somewhat staid atmosphere. By contrast, there were the open-air night-clubs, such as the Coronet at Pasir Panjang, or the Singapore Swimming Club, which were more lively and informal.

For the Chinese upper set, there were private clubs—exclusively male, of course—and dozens of good restaurants or 'Tang Halls', as they were known. The clubs consisted of several adjoining houses stylishly furnished and equipped with facilities for mahjong and female companionship of all kinds, from well-groomed 'sing-song' girls to high-class prostitutes. Discreet arrangements with the opposite sex were made by various public bodies and private clubs but the most popular venue for such activities and amusements of other kinds and the centre of Baba social life was the Chinese Weekly Entertainment Club.

Such then was the social scene at the end of the 1930s. The enjoyment of social life and leisure had become, for Asians and Europeans alike, almost an end in itself and indeed the atmosphere had become so carefree that little attention was being paid to the threat of war which was soon to overtake and extinguish colonial life once and for all in preparation for the next era of national independence. ❖

Right *The pavilion of the Straits Chinese Recreational Club at Hong Lim Green,* circa *1905.*

Opposite top *The Hotel de l'Europe and the Singapore Cricket Club, 1920s.*

Opposite bottom *At the opposite end of the Padang was the Singapore Recreation Club;* circa *1884.*

Social and Cultural Changes

The nature of domestic life and the reflection of this in the interior environment of the detached house in Singapore before World War II was a part of general social and cultural changes spanning more than a century: from the establishment of the European residential quarter in the first settlement, through the period of the country plantation villas and the emergence of suburbanization in the 1880s, until the twilight years of British colonization preceding the war.

For the first 60 years, the predominance of the large, Palladian-style colonial villa, the predecessor of the suburban house, reflected a lifestyle ineffably and exclusively British, but one modified by the Anglo-Indian experience. As one author put it, "In one of those peculiar cultural distortions of Empire, which gave the British dungarees and mulligatawny soup and the Indians blazers and banana custard...."[1]

Although the British were a small minority in a population which, by the turn of the century, was already nearly three-quarters Chinese, their impact on the cultural life of the colony continued to be very substantial right up to World War II. It was reflected in the widespread adoption of the European style of house, in some form or other, by the Asian *nouveau riche* as a sign of their new social and economic status. To varying degrees, it was also reflected in the transformation of their domestic habits. This was the case, despite the retention of traditional values.

Whereas English domestic life reflected a set of middle-class values which included the importance of such virtues as privacy, comfort, spaciousness, salubrity, tidiness and polite behaviour, for the Chinese, residential life, traditionally, had meant something different. For them, notions of respect for social and family order, the unity of man and nature, the family as a microcosm of society, the significance of cosmic and natural forces, harmony, and the home as a refuge from the outside world, were fundamental concepts. So, too, in personal life were such attributes as industry, honesty, hospitality, celibacy, economy, moral responsibility, family loyalty, obedience and deference to elders.

Opposite Lifestyles in the British colonies reflected middle-class values from 'home'. Here we see a tea-party set out on the lawn of a Black-and-White house in the early 1900s.

1 P Davies, *Splendours of the Raj, British Architecture in India, 1660 to 1947*, London, John Murray, 1985, page 105

Such values were intrinsic to the Chinese and had endured for generations. The capacity of the Chinese family now to incorporate much of the English ideology in form, if not in substance, was undoubtedly a measure of its capacity for pragmatism in a society in which success and social standing were signalled now through the use of Western rather than Eastern symbols.

This, however, depended on the particular Chinese subculture. The Straits Chinese through successive generations in Malaya had held fast to the Chinese way of life, but they had also succumbed to the influence of the Malayan environment and European customs. A whole new culture, reflected in quite unique forms, including the domestic interior, had grown out of the amalgam of Chinese, Malay and European ways. Certainly, in their desire to identify with their British overlords, the Straits Chinese were the first to enthusiastically embrace Western fashions internally and externally.

The capacity to identify with English ways was also true to varying degrees of the *nouveau riche* mainland-born Chinese and other ethnic communities, such as the Indians and Malays. It was certainly there in the case of the wealthy Middle Eastern Jewish and Arabic residents whose representation in lavish suburban villas was disproportionate to the rest of non-European society. Many Jews and Arabs and a number of Chinese speculated in property and the choice of Western-style villas was therefore often as much a matter of appealing to the widest market as satisfying personal and family preferences.

Beneath the surface, however, many non-European families held fast to traditional customs. The importance of ancestor worship in Chinese households, the significance of the proper placement of shrines and deities in Hindu forms of devotion, or of correct orientation in the case of the Muslims were aspects of this. For the Straits Chinese, whose religious inclinations embraced ancestor worship, Taoism, Buddhism and Christianity, the effects were more complicated.

Two portraits from the early 20th century of Peranakan family members. The first on left was taken in 1913 when it was still the norm for Babas to wear local dress. As the Straits Chinese became more influenced by the English, the men began to wear Western fashions, as seen in this photo of a bride and groom dated 30 May 1939.

As was the norm in England, in Singapore leading up to World War II, women were in charge of the domestic realm. Here we see a portrait of a fairly sophisticated Malay wife and a group of Tamil women.

The place of women in society and in the domestic hierarchy certainly affected the way houses were used, if not planned. This applied to all races, but especially the Malays and the Indians. Even for the Chinese, there was often relatively little social intercourse between man and wife. Womenfolk were expected to occupy themselves in domestic tasks such as mending, even if there were servants. The subjugation of women was most evident in the tendency for the richer Chinese *towkays*, for whom it was a matter of some pride to own a large establishment, to have several wives and mistresses.

For the Chinese, there must have been conflicts in the reconciliation of traditional beliefs in *feng shui*—the correct siting and layout of the house according to cosmic and natural forces—and the fact of orientation being determined by more mundane considerations such as municipal road layouts and land subdivisions. For the Straits Chinese, there were other adjustments. Traditionally, rooms had been arranged one behind the other and screens were placed to further subdivide spaces, extending from the front door to the back, but the layout of the Anglo-Indian residence, which many of them adopted, was quite the reverse.

The influence of Western ways applied to the middle-income employee, who at the turn of the century may have been earning $60 a month and employing a cook and an *amah*, no less than to his upper-class counterpart with six or eight servants. Quite apart from the assemblage of wives and mistresses in wealthier households, Chinese families tended to be large, irrespective of income level. Most Asian families were larger than European ones, which were usually confined to parents and children. Among the Chinese, Malays, Indians and Arabs, extended families embracing in-laws and up to three or four generations were more usual, although the houses accommodating them were not necessarily larger, even in the number of rooms.

A house on Scotts Road, built in the 1920s, shows the general trend towards smaller residences after 1920 or thereabouts.

To the English wife and mother who managed domestic affairs, albeit with the support of servants, the notion of the extended family and its gregarious internal social life was quite alien to the English ideal of order and seclusion. To her, the English middle-class concept of the nuclear family was quite superior, even if, as one unkind observer put it, "The white woman has inevitably tried to recreate England and usually Surbiton in the tropics."[2]

Many of the English houses, of course, were very much grander than those of Surbiton. Certainly this was true of those owned by British senior executives and government officers and their families, who were able to enjoy a higher standard of accommodation than was ever possible at home. For the British, the stateliness of their houses was also a means of signalling their position of social and political superiority.

The house of the British senior executive and senior civil servant was likely to be larger also because his family had come with him, even if the children had been left for most of the time in boarding school in England, whereas his junior executive employee was more likely to be a single man. In all cases, however, the usual period of contract was two to three years followed by three to six months of home leave, which meant that the domestic environment was less well established and less permanent than that of the typical Asian suburban resident. It was also less personal because most of the large executive houses were not only designed and built but also furnished by the employer organizations for use by a succession of occupants. The transient lifestyle also applied to middle-class Indians.

European-owned houses, even those of less senior officials and employees, were generally more commodious than Chinese-owned ones if judged by the size of the house in relation to number of occupants. This was largely because Europeans and Chinese had different attitudes to and requirements for space. The fact that so many houses of medium size—by colonial standards—were owned by Chinese was not necessarily a reflection of the fact that many

2 R Flower, *Raffles. The Story of Singapore*, Singapore, Croom Helm Ltd, 1984, page 168

Chinese could not afford or did not want larger houses, but rather that, culturally, the Chinese extended families were accustomed to living at closer quarters.

This was the case both inside the house, within each family, and externally, between houses. Other than for the very rich, Chinese-owned houses tended to have smaller allotments and to be built at higher densities. This was both a reflection of the traditional Chinese urban way of life and of their own particular perceptions of exterior space, which, amongst other things, included a different view of the aesthetic and symbolic value of the suburban garden.

The significance of cultural values for house sizes is suggested by the fact that, even with more and more of the colony's surplus wealth passing into particular Chinese hands, creating further opportunities for those so inclined to compete with their European counterparts in building larger houses, as a general rule this did not happen. Allowing, of course, for exceptions, Chinese houses in all parts of the colony were on average generally no bigger, and often smaller, than European ones.

Overall, there was a trend for new houses, whatever the race of their owners, to increase markedly in size during the boom years of 1880 to 1900. Even allowing for the dampening effect of the depression years of the early 1890s, by the turn of the century houses were three to four times bigger than they had been in the early 1880s. Thereafter, with a greater proportion of Chinese as well as Europeans and other races progressively moving into the ranks of the middle classes and, like their counterparts in England of nearly a century earlier, being able to acquire a bungalow, however modest, in the suburbs, the average size steadily decreased.

Even for the rich—certainly for the European élite—the opportunities for grand living supported by an abundance of servants began to diminish from the late 1920s. As servants were reduced in number, so houses became more compact; there were fewer people under one roof and the need to reduce housework was more evident. The trend towards smaller houses was also due to the subdivision of land into smaller allotments as the population increased in relation to the available supply of serviced land. This went hand in hand with the general trend towards austerity in domestic life during the depression years of the 1930s.

Even so, the average floor area of European-owned houses in 1939 was undoubtedly a good deal larger than that of the typical English suburban bungalow of the same year—a reflection of the higher standard of residential life enjoyed by the colonial expatriates in comparison with their former colleagues who increasingly, as a result of rising land prices, were being forced to live cheek-by-jowl amidst the seemingly endless sprawl of suburban London.

If houses became smaller and servants fewer, there was some compensation in technological advances which made life a little easier or more comfortable. The introduction of the car was not the least of these. There were improvements also in forms of public transport. Although electric lighting and fans first replaced oil-lamps and *punkahs* in 1906, it was not until the mid-1930s that, with the extension of the electric supply system into the suburbs, they became common in private houses. By the 1920s, sewerage, first introduced in 1913 and then delayed by the war, had generally replaced the old night-soil system. Kerosene refrigerators began to replace ice chests in private kitchens. And, if life was a little more stringent, it was at least made more entertaining by the arrival of the wireless set, the gramophone and the recorded music of Victor Silvester, *keroncong* music and the BBC news. ❖

The Plan

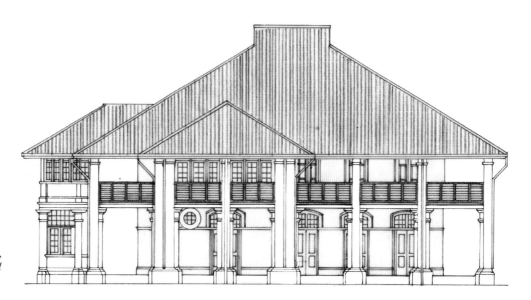

*Elevation of Inverturret,
designed by RAJ Bidwell
in 1906.*

As with all buildings, the relationship between the form of the Singaporean house and the life within it before World War II—including activities, meanings and values—was a two-way process. On the one hand, private or family activities and priorities such as the need for an additional dining-room or the accommodation of servants, or the meaning attached to the separation of visitors from the family, influenced and gave rise to an arrangement of rooms and spaces reflecting those requirements. On the other hand, the provision of a particular form of house as a result of broader cultural, economic or other factors, including, for example, the value given to ideas about status or fashion, would usually lead to adaptations in private, family behaviour. The house, in other words, can be seen both from the point of view of the family and general social and cultural life of the time, and in terms of its formal spatial characteristics as reflected in its physical layout, or plan. These are two views of the same phenomenon: an evolutionary, cultural process which, in the case of the house in Singapore, began with the Georgian Palladian residence of 18th-century England.

This form of house, modified as it was by the British in India, emulated by the architect, GD Coleman, during the early years of the settlement, and adapted to colonial life and the tropical climate in the plantation villas of the mid-1800s, was to continue as the dominant influence on houses, large and small, well into the 1900s. As far as the layout was concerned, there was still the same symmetrical arrangement of bedrooms on the upper floor and the drawing-room (or equivalent area) and dining-room symmetrically disposed below in front of the more private family rooms at the rear. In single-storey houses or bungalows, as in colonial India, the bedrooms were arranged symmetrically on either side of two or more interconnected spaces—equivalent to the traditional drawing-room—in the middle.

As in India and in the plantation villa, the front of the house usually had a veranda, with a central projecting porch which, in two-storey houses, had a semi-enclosed living-room or veranda over an open vehicular entrance porch below. More often than not, there was also a veranda at the rear of the house equivalent to that at the front, but it was just as common for the veranda to enclose the house on four sides. This was more usually the case with larger houses on wider allotments, but the more common trend, as land became further subdivided, was towards narrower and deeper layouts, to the point where the space occupied by the central drawing- and dining-room in the middle was reduced to a mere passage, though usually wide enough for informal family use. In this case, the drawing-room—or whatever name it may have been given—and the dining-room and other rooms for social and family use were placed at the front of the house and at the back, facing on to their respective open verandas. To the rear, as in colonial India, the kitchen, service rooms and stables, and servants' accommodation were housed in a separate outbuilding linked to the main body of the house by a covered passage.

This symmetrical arrangement, in some form or other, was prevalent right up to the 1920s. At best, in the hands of a competent architectural firm such as Swan & Maclaren, the plan was well composed and the rooms of good proportion, but very often, the houses built for those of lesser rank had little to commend them in purely architectural terms, whether in plan or in elevation, and were certainly nothing of the calibre of the earlier plantation houses or those by Coleman.

Ground-floor and first-floor plans of Inverturret, showing the almost continuous veranda and balconies that encircled the house.

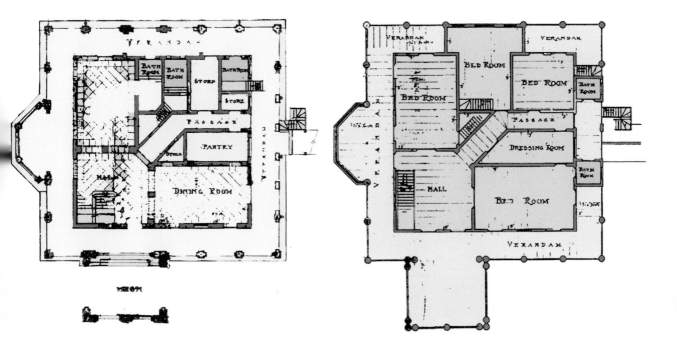

A single-storey bungalow raised from the ground on piles, with over-hanging eaves and open veranda resting on the plinths of the pillars is typical of a simple country abode in the late 19th century.

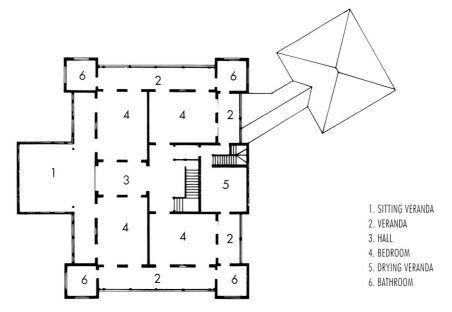

First-floor plan of a house for an electrician (1908). On the first floor the 'sitting veranda' was placed above the porte-cochère, while other verandas encouraged ventilation and gave inhabitants further cool places to sit.

1. SITTING VERANDA
2. VERANDA
3. HALL
4. BEDROOM
5. DRYING VERANDA
6. BATHROOM

By the turn of the century, however, there were more houses of superior quality than before, a situation reflected in the floor plan of a 'House of an Electrician' on Telok Blangah Road (see above). This example was also typical of the trend towards houses of wider, shallower proportions and, at the same time, towards greater architectural formality, as for instance in the importance given now to the entrance hall and the celebration of the main staircase within it. Prior to this, two stairs were common: one recessed on the side of the entrance hall and another at the rear of the house for the domestic staff, as part of the practice of segregating servants strictly within their own domain, following precedents established in England and India a century or so earlier.

Numerous two-storey houses of this type were built during the years of renewed economic prosperity before 1908 in response to the demand from newly formed English firms and others. The house built for the prominent Jewish businessman E S Manasseh on Lady Hill in 1903 was of this kind, though rather more commodious than most. Manasseh's house, however, was not exceptional in having a billiard room, an entrance hall of generous size and proportion, and dining-room arranged *en suite*, in the manner of many 18th-century English country houses. In this there was an echo of the Georgian habit of the proper reception of guests, if not in the hall—or saloon as it had been earlier called—then in a reception room to one side, from which the guests then retired, in sequence, to dine and thence, in the case of male company, to port and cigars or to a game of billiards. Billiard-tables in England had been a feature of the grandest English country houses since the 17th century, but it was not until the late 1800s that a special room was set aside for this purpose.

The symmetrical floor plan remained popular despite the trend towards greater architectural experimentation. The adoption of the symmetrical classical house form, as in British India, signified social prestige and political power. The appearance of other plan forms reflected both the mood of romanticism, and the emergence of the professional architect and the tendency to plagiarism, assisted by the general transfer of ideas from Europe.

A residence for a European family, from circa 1920 shows a more compact form.

The British themselves could afford, even before the turn of the century, to be less conventional by adopting more picturesque compositions, including those inspired by the Arts and Crafts Movement. Within the European community, the 1903 house of John Somerville on Cluny Road (see right) was not altogether an exception for its time in following the Victorian inclination for more asymmetrical arrangements, yet being at the same time thoroughly tropical, with its deep, long veranda wrapping around the corner, on to which one entered from beneath the *porte-cochère*, set, in picturesque vein, away from the house at an angle of 45°. This form quickly became *à la mode* with some of the European community and, once established as a common type, was adopted by other communities.

The overwhelming interest in European house forms by non-Europeans left little room for references to their own indigenous dwellings. More Chinese, it could be expected, might have built detached houses in the manner of the traditional courtyard house of the southern Chinese mainland, yet with few exceptions, such as that of Tan Yeok Nee of 1885, or Cheong Quee Tiam's of 1898—which, being nearer the centre of town, was in any case more of a town house than a suburban residence—this did not happen.

From 1908 until after the war, the trend was towards a greater variety of architectural configurations as the mood of romanticism and eclecticism began to take hold. At the same time, the vicissitudes of economic fortune and the growing pressure on land meant greater economy in planning. With the revival of trade after the war, many houses, still of formal symmetrical layout, again made their appearance, but being more compact and shallower,

A 1920s house on Balmoral Road shows a variety of influences: on stilts with wooden tracery beneath the eaves in the Malay style; yet with a grand front veranda and symmetrical arrangement of rooms in the European style.

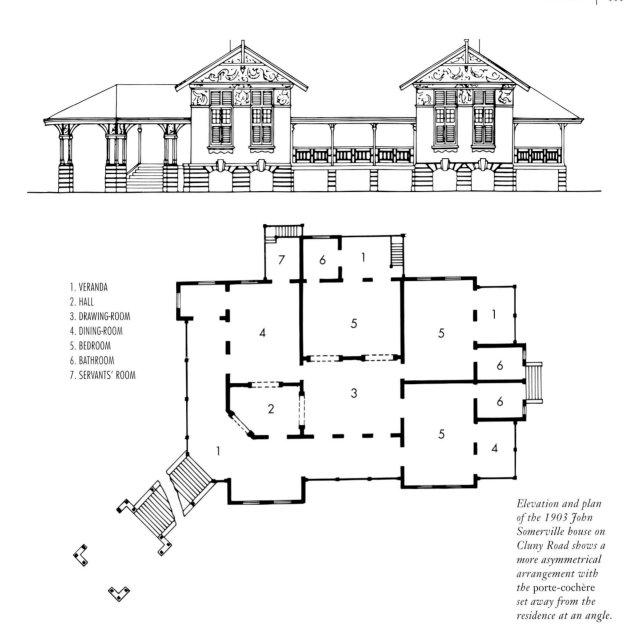

1. VERANDA
2. HALL
3. DRAWING-ROOM
4. DINING-ROOM
5. BEDROOM
6. BATHROOM
7. SERVANTS' ROOM

Elevation and plan of the 1903 John Somerville house on Cluny Road shows a more asymmetrical arrangement with the porte-cochère *set away from the residence at an angle.*

often without verandas and having only one or two family or reception rooms rather than three or four, they had become altogether more English and suburban rather than tropical and colonial in flavour.

This tendency was to continue right into the 1930s and with it came a change towards the less pretentious Arts and Crafts and other 'vernacular' form of bungalow designs then fashionable in England. Although the grand colonial-style mansions of former days, with their deep verandas, imposing entrance porches, and spacious, formally arranged interiors, continued to be built by the upper set, the main trend was now towards houses of more modest dimensions—and more quaint imagery. The conditions which gave rise to these developments included an increase in the number of middle-class suburban dwellers, a world-wide economic recession and, associated with this, a change from a leisurely lifestyle on open verandas attended by an abundance of servants, to one that was more inward-looking, austere and, in the case of the non-Europeans, focused on the immediate family than on larger numbers of relatives.

The implications of this for the internal layout of the house were that, as in English bungalows of the time, it was less spread out than previously, with fewer interconnecting passages or even none at all, and rooms opening directly from one to the other. With the reduction in the number of servants and advances in domestic equipment, the kitchen was, for the first time, brought into the main body of the house. As a result, it had a much closer relationship to the family eating area and to the formal dining-room. For the Chinese, who had always favoured a somewhat deeper arrangement of rooms, including the placement of the family rooms and even the main dining-room further to the rear and well away from the entrance, this was less of a departure than it was for the Europeans. Indeed, in Chinese-owned houses, it was now just as much a matter of the dining-room moving further back towards the kitchen as vice versa.

The bathroom was also removed from its previous position as an external appendage to each bedroom, where it had been set at a lower level to facilitate night-soil removal. Where previously there had been a bathroom to every bedroom, now commonly there was only one for the house as a whole. Instead of the former method of bathing with water poured from a Shanghai jar replenished regularly by servants, there was piped water connected to built-in sanitary fixtures. Verandas were reduced in size or even eliminated. Porches were also smaller, although if present in the better middle-class houses, were used as a covered entrance for the car where the family could afford one.

Economy in construction, including savings in the cost of land, and the need for efficiency in housekeeping were not the only reasons for compactness. There was also the desire for verticality rather than horizontality in architectural expression. All of these factors had their effect of the arrangement of outbuildings. The detached outhouse, which had always been an essential element in houses, was still there, but closer to the main house and more a part of its architectural character.

Paradoxically, the outhouse had become relatively more important in the sense that it was at least as large as before, having taken on a somewhat different role, whereas the house proper was smaller. By this time, the outhouse began to include rooms for use by the family, for relatives, or for letting out, whereas previously it was strictly the servants' domain. Occasionally it was on two floors, in which case the upper floor was used mainly for family purposes. By the early 1930s, it was often used by servants and even members of the family for income-generating purposes, such as tailoring or sewing.

Despite these developments, there were still those who could afford to build on a more lavish scale. With this, and with the recovery of the economy towards the mid-1930s, many of the larger houses that began to appear were in a variety of styles as the new owners and their architects became more than ever influenced by foreign ideas. These were no longer confined to Europe or the Indian subcontinent. Awareness now of fashions in America and of other solutions to the need for residential accommodation even closer to home, such as those of the Dutch in Indonesia, meant a greater variety of architectural styles. The result was that the design of these houses came even less from a considered response to the local climate. The fact that they could just as well have appeared in other parts of the world reflected also the continued cosmopolitanism of colonial life.

These circumstances were mirrored in a variety of plan forms. At one extreme, there were the more conventional layouts adopted in the new housing estates. At the other, there were cross-shaped, U-shaped, or extended, rambling configurations inspired by later Arts and Crafts designers or by the work of such avant-garde architects as Frank Lloyd Wright. There were also the more functionally ordered asymmetrical arrangements of the Modern Movement, although many of the plans of buildings in that style were indistinguishable from more conventional layouts, except for the rounded corners.

Such developments, however, were ephemeral, coming as they did from the fashions of the moment. At a less superficial level, some aspects, such as the relationship of the house to its setting and the way it was approached from the street, had not changed at all. ❖

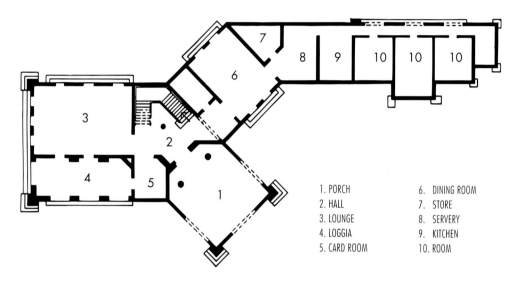

1. PORCH   6. DINING ROOM
2. HALL   7. STORE
3. LOUNGE   8. SERVERY
4. LOGGIA   9. KITCHEN
5. CARD ROOM   10. ROOM

1. LOUNGE   5. LINEN ROOM   9. ROOM
2. DINING-ROOM   6. STORE   10. GARAGE
3. BEDROOM   7. SERVERY   11. DRESSING ROOM
4. BATHROOM   8. KITCHEN

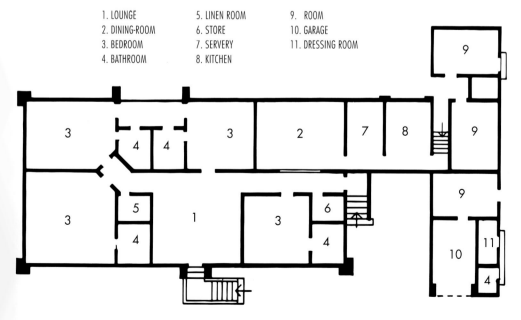

Above *Ground-floor plan of a house for L W Geddes, Ridout Road (1934).*

Below *Ground-floor plan of a house for W Russell, Lady Hill Road (1936).*

Both plans show the clear separation between the areas for the servants and areas for the family.

From the Street to the House

❖

The significance of cultural values in the internal arrangement of the pre-World War II house began with the way entrance was admitted. Common to all communities was the concern to separate a more public domain at the front from a more private one at the back. Attitudes to privacy and external appearances were two sides of the same coin. Both were related to the succession of spaces and images which, in its most elaborate form, began at the front wall or hedge facing the street and extended through the front garden, via the porch and entrance steps, on to the veranda. From here, depending upon who was being admitted, access was allowed further into the house.

For the English, the inherited middle-class concern with formal, proper appearance took on an additional dimension, the need to communicate their social and political position, as in India. This began at the street. In wealthier areas, high walls and hedges and elaborate gates and gateposts signalled the status of the owner and the line of demarcation between public and private territory. Derived as it was from the country estates of 18th-century England and emulated in 19th-century English suburbia, the walled and gated enclosure was quickly adopted by the rich among the Chinese and other races. Indeed, eventually, upper-class Chinese houses were more likely to have their walls or hedges and gates than European ones.

Among the Chinese élite, the impulse to take on the trappings of English high society, such as the high wall, may have been linked also to recollections of the walled residential spaces of southern China. Conversely, for the English, despite some apprehension about being too open to the indigenous population, there was less fear of intrusion than there had been in India. Even so, as in India and suburban England, distance was an effective substitute for the use of barriers in the concern for security and the desire for privacy: hence the removal of the European upper crust in their own enclaves in houses set well back from the street.

Class was a significant factor. The more established, educated Straits Chinese were more likely to have their hedges than those Chinese who had achieved their position through a rapid accumulation of wealth. In the latter case, there was more concern with 'conspicuous consumption': the house was more likely to be on a main thoroughfare and to be visible to passers-by. As for the less wealthy Eurasians, Chinese, Indians, Europeans and others who were in the majority, the possession of a smaller allotment in a less exclusive area usually meant low front fences or none at all. This became more generally the case as houses became smaller towards the 1920s and 1930s. The concern for appearance and privacy, however, was still there; the front garden provided some measure of privacy to the house even if the garden itself was not private.

The lack of walls did not necessarily mean sacrificing security. In wealthier areas, dogs, such as alsatians and dobermanns, were often employed to guard entrances from the street. In the case of the Straits Chinese, though, there was another reason for having dogs—the association that this had with the English, who regarded dogs primarily as pets.

Alternatively, *jaga* or guards could be employed. In the more exclusive areas, the desire for security was not the only reason for employing *jaga*, however. Quite apart from their symbolic value, they performed the function of intermediate contact between the visitor and the owner of the house. Strangers, hawkers, tradesmen and others entered the grounds only with the *jaga*'s permission. The use of 'calling cards', introduced by the English from India and taken up by a small number of well-to-do Chinese, performed a similar function. This practice, which diminished toward the 1920s and 1930s, consisted of a minor social ritual: the newcomer would deposit his card in a private box at the street entrance and, even if seen to do so by members of the household, would then retire and await an invitation at a later date.

For those granted permission to enter the grounds, whether by vehicle—carriage or car—or on foot, a long, curved driveway gave access to a spacious entrance porch, following Palladian precedents. The larger the garden, the longer the driveway and the longer the time it took to reach the front porch, the greater was the impression on the visitor and the higher the apparent status of, and degree of privacy given to, those inside. Although the entrance

Mandalay Villa at Amber Road was built in 1921 for Lee Cheng Yan, a prominent businessman from the Peranakan community. It was well set back from the road.

Singapore. Tanglin Road.

A view of the hilly, well wooded aspect of the Tanglin area which attracted well-to-do Europeans and Chinese in the period between 1900 and 1920. Behind the itinerant pineapple seller, ricskhaw coolie and bullock cart is a flight of stairs leading up to a house set back a fair bit from the road.

approach to many of the houses in the Tanglin area or Spottiswood Park were sufficiently impressive, none was as grand as the large residential estates of colonial India. Most properties in Singapore were rather akin in size and scale to the better-off English suburban estates, such as Turnham Green, and in this sense often strove to follow the precedent set in the Tanglin area but in miniature, as it were. For others—and the number increased with time—the front garden was reduced to something little bigger than that of a Southgate semi-detached.

As to the porch: apart from its psychological function, in the bigger houses it provided shelter for the visitor to disembark and for vehicles and their syces to wait. In larger houses, porches were often of generous dimensions, though none after 1880 was as impressive as the entrance portico of the Residency at Barrackpore in India with its rusticated base, eight Tuscan columns and triangular pediment: three storeys high and nearly 60 feet in length! Even the largest houses in Singapore were of much more modest dimensions, as were their porches, which were usually big enough to accommodate one, or at the most, two vehicles at a time. In two-storey houses, the porch only sometimes took on the architectural significance of the Palladian original or its later derivatives such as Chiswick House or the more local example of Coleman's Maxwell House.

In these earlier examples, the porch was an element in its own right, but by the 1880s, following precedents set in Indian colonial country houses and repeated in the early European residences of Penang and Singapore and in later plantation houses, it had become assimilated into the body of the house through the extension of the upper floor in the form of an upper sitting-room or veranda over it.

In the case of smaller houses in particular, the porch had become merely a projection of the veranda at the same floor level with steps leading up to it in the spirit of the Malayan *serambi*, yet articulated in form and centrally placed, like its Anglo-Indian forebear. Under the influence of the plethora of house designs being circulated from the turn of the century and particularly after 1920, it became even more difficult to distinguish between porch and veranda, particularly with the tendency to partly enclose them. The names used did not help: what were in effect porches were called 'verandas' and vice versa. But, generally, the idea of the porch as a place through which to enter persisted.

With the trend towards smaller houses in the 1930s, it might be expected that entrance porches would be fewer in number, but this was not the case. Whereas fewer than half the houses had porches in 1884, slightly more than half had them in 1939.

Certainly, however, porches became less grand and, particularly in the case of bungalows, began to take a different form. Following the designs set out in the various books on bungalows, such as *The Daily Mail Bungalow Book* (1922) and Cecil Keeley's *A Book of Bungalows and Modern Homes* (1928), porches were often recessed, partly in keeping with the trend toward asymmetry away from the pseudo-Palladian formalism of the early years. But even before the World War I, small porches of this kind were evident, as copies of the *British Architect, Builders' Journal,* and other publications found their way into architects' files. The truly recessed porch with no projecting roof, as in the early Victorian suburban terrace, was less common in Singapore than in England because the competition for land was less intense, allotments were therefore wider and, even if the climate was less severe, protection was needed against the sun and tropical downpours.

View of a proposed bungalow, England, early 1920s, from A Book of Bungalows and Modern Homes *by CJH Keeley (1928).*

Of greater significance was the degree of importance attached to the porch as a visual feature. Under the influence of the Arts and Crafts Movement, which only began to be felt in Singapore towards the 1920s, although the trend now was towards a more vernacular, less pretentious appearance and towards the use of the porch as a minor element, the concern to make an impression was still there. At this time, it was ornament in the form of latticework or carved timber work of Malay or Chinese origin but with Indian colonial influences or pseudo-classical regalia, rather than size and form, that was to attract attention. The exception was the entrance to the Arts and Crafts 'L'- or 'U'-shaped house where the centrally recessed porch was no longer a significant visual element, and as in current English examples, an extension of the roof overhang was sufficient to provide shelter.

Apart from the owners of these everyday bungalows, there were those who could afford a horse-and-trap or two or whose visitors could be expected to travel by carriage and for whom a porch was essential for this reason alone. Although the proportion of new houses with carriages on the premises in 1920 had fallen significantly from that at the turn of the century when half the new houses had them, this was mainly because carriages were being displaced by motor cars. By the early 1920s many of the new suburban residents had cars, and by the late 1930s the number had grown still further. Although many sites were too small or the amount of money spent on the house was too little to accommodate the luxury of a 'car porch', this was becoming a fairly common feature. The possibility of featuring the family's new Austin six-seater or Model-T Ford was an even more interesting idea and it required little excuse to use

Traditional Malay house with steps leading up to an entrance porch. This architectural feature was often incorporated into European-style houses — so the porch was elevated and safe from flooding in a tropical downpour.

the car porch as a permanent car shelter until the fact of leaking oil or the largely unjustified fear of the car exploding led to its relegation to a garage at the rear.

Where porches accommodated cars or carriages, there was necessarily a set of steps leading up to the house itself, in many cases on to the veranda, just as steps led up to the veranda-cum-porch of the ordinary bungalow. Steps were usually not a significant element, but in the case of the expensive or larger houses or those built on land liable to flooding or on sloping ground, or indeed those whose owners or architects were persuaded to do as the Malays had done traditionally, the steps were functionally more important. They allowed the elevation of the main floor of the house to keep it dry and to permit a better flow of air, and furthermore, longer flights of steps could give additional emphasis to the separation of inside and outside and thus to the act of entering. In the houses of the really well-to-do, the steps would play a role in communication between the owner and strangers, hawkers and others, who would be required to wait at the bottom and proceed no further.

Where the veranda existed—which was more frequently the case at the turn of the century when the majority of houses had one—it often performed the function of entrance hall but opened directly on to the main rooms behind. Conversely, by the 1930s, verandas were rather the exception to the rule and this was but part of a more general attitude towards the changing relationship between the inside and the outside of the house, including the entrance and reception of visitors. ❖

The Sandilands Buttery House, designed by Frank Brewer in 1923, combines features from the Black-and-White house (ie half-timbered gable) with Arts and Crafts influences.

Reception

❧❦❧

Although the Chinese were earnestly following European ideas in regard to the manner of planning and furnishing their houses, including the way visitors were to be received, their own traditions were not altogether forgotten. It all depended on whether they were first-, second- or third-generation Straits-born Chinese or from the mainland, whether they were very rich or only moderately so, and on other factors.

For their part, the Europeans, while inclined towards the traditions of their colonial forebears, were on the other hand not entirely unaffected by Chinese customs. For both groups, there was the influence of current fashions from Victorian England. Despite these cultural cross-currents and those engendered by other races—the Arabs, the Jews, and the Indians—with the general trend towards European ways, it became more and more difficult to tell from the layout of the house whether the owner was European, Chinese or some other race. And yet there were differences, for example in the way the houses were furnished.

The overall trend, however, was towards greater informality. This was despite the fact that the attitudes underlying the layout of the colonial house were originally quite formal, for example, with regard to the segregation of different members of the household and decisions on who could go where. Less familiar acquaintances were traditionally kept further at bay at the front of the house, perhaps being confined to the veranda or the entrance hall. Closer acquaintances, though, could penetrate into the more private parts upstairs or along various halls or passages on to the back veranda and hence outside or along an open passage to the servants' area and kitchen, well segregated from the main house in outbuildings at the back. This was the working domain involving 'messy' activities and the smell of food, and in order to achieve an acceptable social and physical environment within the house and to present an appropriate formal 'face' to the world, it was important that these activities be kept well away and out of sight.

Inner courtyard of gambier planter Seah Song Seah's house, dating from 1896. Based on the Chinese courtyard house form, such houses were long and deep, with a hierarchy of rooms and courts — the further one ventured into the home, the closer one came to the private family domain.

Such an arrangement was not altogether foreign to the Chinese. The house of mainland southern China was based on a hierarchical arrangement of courtyards, halls and pavilions extending from the formal reception hall to the most private family area at the back. This was also the principle of the Chinese urban terrace-house which had a deep, narrow planning arrangement of halls and courtyards, beginning at the street and extending to the family cooking and dining area at the rear. In mainland China, the rule had been to reserve the front of the house for public use and for 'subordinates' and the rear of the house for private activities and senior members of the family.

Johnson Tan's terrace-house on River Valley Road, built in 1929–30, has been decorated in the Peranakan style. Here we see an altar dedicated to the household deity, Guan Yu, along the back wall.

In the case of the southern Chinese house, the reception hall at the front contained a centrally placed shrine dedicated to the penates or household spirits. On either side, formally arranged against the walls, were four chairs and two small tables, and in the centre, in front of the altar, a large sofa for the two household principles. A second place of worship in the form of an ancestral hall was further removed in a more private part of the house.

In the Chinese terrace-house, the first hall into which one entered and into which visitors were formally received also contained a centrally placed altar dedicated to the Goddess of Mercy, Kwan Yin, and the God of Wealth. Set behind the altar was a wall or screen to deflect the path of evil spirits and to demarcate the first hall from the second, immediately behind. Views beyond this screen of the interior of the house—its succession of courts and interior spaces—were only admitted gradually and under privilege. Distant acquaintances and visitors were allowed into the first hall only. Friends and closer colleagues were taken into the second hall. In the truly traditional Peranakan household, close relatives and other members of the family and lifelong friends were granted admission to the third or the fourth halls.

For the Chinese, it was somewhat of a jump from this arrangement to that of the Anglo-Indian house which, although traditionally hierarchical in layout, in its more simplified form, as was usual in Singapore, had a large open central living area extending from the front of the house to the back and flanked by bedrooms. On the face of it, this would seem to represent a significant departure from traditional Chinese domestic arrangements and customs; however, this was only partly true. For reasons referred to below, the central living area was generally divided into a drawing-room and a dining-room, originally side-by-side but now more commonly one behind the other. At least until the 1920s, most suburban houses were deep rather than wide, whether through choice or circumstance, and the existence of two or three rooms in depth was sufficient to simulate the arrangement of the front portion of the Singaporean terrace-house—from which most Chinese had just come—which had fewer halls and courtyards than its Malaccan counterpart.

Either the space occupied by the drawing-room could be used as the entrance hall and as the space for the altar, or a room could be added in front, or the veranda could be enclosed for this purpose. Alternatively, it was possible to have the main central area without walls at all and to add a screen or two to establish the correct set of relationships for worship and entrance.

In all such cases, it was customary to incorporate a centrally placed altar to some household deity such as the Goddess of Mercy. Almost as common was the tendency to place the ancestral altar, which traditionally had been confined to a more private part of the house, here as well, together with photographs of the deceased. Whatever the arrangement, the formal placement of the most expensive blackwood or rosewood furniture in the form of straight-backed chairs set against the walls on either side was symbolically appropriate and in keeping with the tone of formality with which visitors to Chinese houses had been received. Alternatively, for those with more Western inclinations—and this gradually became more common—the furniture might well be more European in style and placed away from the walls in a more informal manner.

Not all Chinese subscribed to the beliefs reflected in the arrangement of a deity or ancestral hall, many being adherents to the Christian faith. For those who did subscribe, the form of the ancestral altar or household shrine and its location, whether in the entrance hall, or elsewhere in the house, depended upon the level of commitment to traditional Chinese ways. It was not uncommon, for example, for the shrine to be relegated to one of the private family rooms. A typical arrangement in Peranakan families was for the ancestral altar to be placed in a room to one side of the entrance hall and to use this space for other family purposes as well. In such a case, the household and other deities would be worshipped on appropriate occasions either in the entrance hall or elsewhere, such as in the dining-room.

Altar dedicated to Kuan Yin in a terrace-house built in the Katong area in the inter-war years. Rosewood furniture with marble insets is lined along the wall in the traditional manner.

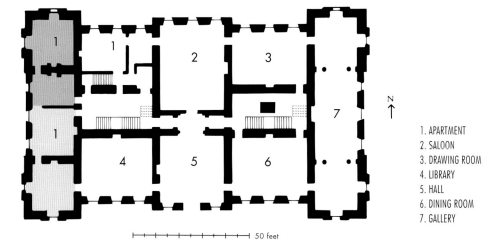

Plan of the ground floor of Hagley Hall, Worcestershire (1753–9) illustrates the complex hierarchy of spaces in the Georgian home.

1. APARTMENT
2. SALOON
3. DRAWING ROOM
4. LIBRARY
5. HALL
6. DINING ROOM
7. GALLERY

50 feet

Adherence to traditional beliefs did not, however, prevent Chinese house interiors becoming more European in character. European houses of the time, for their part, owed much to Anglo-Indian predelictions and increasingly to current English Victorian fashions, both of which had their roots in Georgian high society and even before.

The entrance to the Georgian house, and indeed the layout of Georgian houses in general, were originally part of a complex series of changes in the manner with which the 15th-century Georgian social hierarchy had perceived itself. Decisions regarding the manner of entering and how best to arrange halls, saloons, vestibules, drawing-rooms and dining-rooms to each other were bound up with complex and subtle questions of social protocol: where the gentry stood in relation to the non gentry, the tenantry and so on. In the beginning, the stately centrally placed two-storey hall with its grand staircase celebrated the ascent of the nobility to the great formal dining-room above and the great parlour below. Later, following continental precedents, came the arrangement of the saloon and its formal vestibule in front and then the vestibule–hall which combined the function of entry, waiting and dining on special occasions. By the beginning of the 18th century, the prominence of the vestibule–hall in relation to the more private rooms on either side had been replaced by a more dynamic arrangement of rooms, including the vestibule and reception rooms in processional sequence.

Amidst all these variations, the idea of the formal plan with its symmetrical hierarchies and juxtaposition of axial vistas remained dominant. This was as much in evidence in the compact square plan of the Georgian town house as in the spread-out country Palladian villa. The common theme was that of larger central spaces of a more public kind flanked by small private spaces—withdrawing rooms, chambers and bedrooms—on either side. It was this house arrangement that, with or without the assimilation of the veranda, was introduced into India and the Straits Settlements to appear in residences such as Suffolk House in Penang or the Maxwell House in Singapore.

The faint echo of this form in the ordinary Singapore bungalow or even the larger two-storey house of the pre-1920s was quite a far cry from the stateliness and grandeur of the noble Georgian or pre-Georgian English mansion, but it was still there. It had been as much the motivation for the transformation of the Indian native hut with its veranda as the porticoed town house of the Indian colonial élite.

And so, at least up to the 1930s, most houses were entered via the porch, on to the veranda, and then into some form of entrance area, be it a separate hall, drawing-room or an equivalent space for reception purposes. This usually led to the formal dining-room. On either side, following Georgian precedents, were the bedrooms.

Within this arrangement, there were all sorts of variations and terminologies. The larger two-storey houses were often much more elaborately arranged, as were the more expensive bungalows. Until the 1920s, bungalows of whatever persuasion featured the 'sitting-room' instead of the 'drawing-room', as was common in India. It is probable that the difference between the two was mainly in the name. The 'drawing-room' became more common in the larger bungalows and more expensive two-storey European houses.

In the case of the bungalow, the drawing-room was either a separate room off the central hall or the central room into which one entered directly off the veranda in the Anglo-Indian manner. In two-storey houses, it was usually on the first floor in the form of an enclosed veranda over the porch and reached by the main staircase which, before the early 1900s, was set to one side of the entrance area.

Whatever the drawing-room meant to either the European or the Chinese—often the term seems to have been used more for its name than any more considered reason—in some way it performed the function of receiving and entertaining visitors. To varying degrees, it was used also for family purposes. Intentions regarding its use had been complicated enough even in early colonial days, in Georgian England and even well before. From medieval times, the drawing-room had been a place off the main bedchamber to which one retired to dress, a place to which to withdraw for private meals or to which guests were invited to dine or to retire to after meals. By the 1700s the room had attracted considerable status as a formal reception room, of equal importance to that of its counterpart, the dining-room, to which it was related via a series of intermediate rooms in sequence, as part of an elaborate, social ritual.

Elevation of a house for R Pustan, Tanglin Road, 1894.

Formal drawing room in a English Georgian house in St James' Square: Homes in Singapore tried to emulate such elegance.

By the 18th century, the drawing- and dining-rooms had been brought much closer together, to the point where, as in colonial India, their respective functions were far less exclusive. With these changes and the informality of much of colonial domestic life, the function of the drawing-room changed yet again to that of a semi-formal sitting-room.

Meanwhile, the influence of English Victorian suburban attitudes on the colonial community would ensure that even for the Europeans, the drawing-room would retain some semblance of formality. Victorian customs required that this room, next to the front entrance hall, be reserved for 'best', apart from its occasional use for family gatherings on special occasions such as birthdays; so, too, with the Victorian entrance hall through which one entered the drawing-room. No matter how small, it was essential that the entrance hall be furnished with the family's most expensive chair and side-table, and a portrait or landscape or hunting scene or two, to create the right 'first impression'.

In this, there were parallels with the formal entrance hall of the traditional Chinese house. Here the family's best furniture and most valuable belongings were put on display, yet, like the Victorian entrance hall, it was the least used room of all, being reserved for the formal receiving of guests and, of course, in the case of the Chinese, for worship. In these and other ways there were parallels between the Victorian concern for propriety, including the visual separation of the visitors' area from the rest of the house, and that of the Chinese. Yet in the case of the colonial Europeans, the situation, in the end, was rather more casual. The house of the colonial European was usually more open to view from the veranda or from the entrance and the front rooms furnished more informally with rattan or camp chairs and sofas, although items such as chests and sideboards were often of substantial dimensions, as in India. This was the setting, not only for the way one entered the house, but for something very important in the life of the European community, as for the Chinese: parties and other forms of social entertainment. ❖

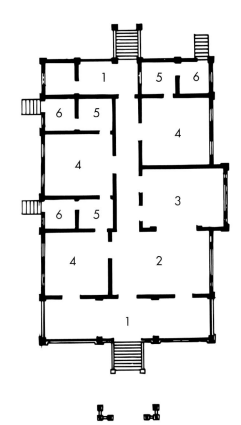

1. VERANDA
2. DRAWING ROOM
3. DINING ROOM
4. BEDROOM
5. DRESSING ROOM
6. BATHROOM

Left *Plan of a house for JA Elias on Scotts Road (1912). The more public rooms are at the front; the private domain is towards the back.*

Below *In the colonial home in the tropics, the formal drawing-room inside was often kept for 'best', and most socialising took place on the veranda, as seen here. Note the informal style of the cane furniture and the drinks tray on the low table.*

Entertaining

❦

"We had," said Jack Tan, a second-generation descendant of the prosperous Tan family, "fantastic parties at Chuville. There was dancing and eating and drinking and the whole place used to be lit up with coloured Chinese lamps."

"The Chinese," said Mr Kee Yeap, whose forebears were also residents in Singapore before World War II, "rarely entertained at home."

For the Chinese, it seemed to be very much one way or the other. For some, entertaining at home was quite customary and, as in the case of the Tan family and other well-to-do Chinese who had the space and the necessary support staff, often lavish in scale. For others, it was something that was just not done, the preference being to entertain outside. If anything, the tendency, certainly up to the 1930s, was towards the former. However, from this time on, the trend was towards entertaining outside, partly because of a shortage of servants and because of increasing opportunities to emulate the Europeans, who up till then had had the run of the good hotels and the best clubs.

Although the Chinese kept their own traditions in their manner of entertaining, their inclinations were increasingly towards European, in particular English, ways. The English, for their part, did as their forebears had done in India, but were also persuaded by the fashions and habits of Victorian England. These still seemed appropriate some 20 to 30 years after the Victorian chapter had officially come to a close. Neither the Chinese nor the English were disposed to entertain each other, particularly at home. As in India, intermingling was definitely frowned upon by the English as being detrimental to their position as rulers. In any case, the Chinese, who understood very well their own position, preferred it that way. It was only after World War II that the Europeans would condescend to invite Chinese home for cocktails, though definitely not for dinner.

As far as the Chinese were concerned, entertainment to a large extent was centred on the family, which, it must be remembered, usually included dozens of relatives of several generations.

There was less family entertainment in European households despite the importance of this in English Victorian middle-class society. European families were smaller and more transient and the children were often at boarding school in England. Amongst the Europeans, entertaining at home was related more to social and business life outside the family. Dinner and garden parties were regular occasions, as were afternoon teas and bridge mornings amongst the *memsahibs*.

Indoor and outdoor luncheon and dinner parties and tea parties were also popular with the well-to-do Chinese, Indians and others. For all races, these were occasions to offer hospitality to existing friends and establish new ones, to keep up one's social and business connections, or to celebrate some event, such as the birthday or engagement of a son or daughter or the launching of a business venture.

In such ways, there was much in common between the various communities, but there were also differences. Amongst the Chinese, birthdays, for example, were not celebrated on a grand scale every year but more rarely, such as when a grandparent or the patriarch had reached 60, 70 or 80 years of age. On such occasions, the number of friends and others invited from outside the family was usually outweighed by the large number of relatives. Celebrations such as these were possible because of the availability of numerous servants but equally, it was usual for the female members of the family, such as nieces and aunts, to assist in laying the table and in serving the guests. Such occasions demanded space and enough helping hands. The same was true for the European who, however, depended almost entirely on servants.

In the case of outdoor or garden parties, the main table was often set up on the tennis-court, if the house were big enough to have one. As this could well be at the front of the house or some distance to the side, a small army of helpers was needed simply to convey the food, drinks and tableware a distance of some 200 feet or so from the kitchen at the back. On such

The grounds of Government House saw an auspicious event in 1918. Mrs Lee Choon Guan was conferred a Member of the British Empire by Governor Sir Authur Henderson Young, the first Chinese woman to receive the award. Afterwards, tea was taken on the lawn.

occasions, temporary marquees were often erected to shelter the assembled company just as solid silver covers were used to keep the food warm during its journey from the kitchen to the table. Outdoor dinner parties would usually spill over into other parts of the garden, which, in the case of birthdays and other such functions, became the setting for children's games and adult social intercourse or organized entertainment in the form of a hired military band, a Chinese Western-style orchestra, a Baba minstrel group or a troupe of Indian *yogi* performers.

With the aid of six or seven servants, the European top brass, who, until the 1930s, had many of the largest properties, were able to conduct such events in style. So, too, were the well-to-do Chinese in their spacious seaside bungalows in Katong and elsewhere. Of course, two to three acres of ground, as in Tanglin, was ideal, but one could do with a lot less. The Jumabhoy family, for instance, used to entertain as many as 200 or 300 guests regularly on the tennis-court in the front garden of their Scotts Road property of a third of an acre.

Whatever the ethnic group, space was needed also for indoor dinner parties to accommodate anything from 20 to 60 or more guests. The need for space was a matter of functional necessity and in order to make a good impression. The length of the dining-room might well be about 30 feet to accommodate a long rectangular table usually to seat about 24, plus a commodious sideboard and serving tables, all in the European manner. As in Victorian England, dining-room furniture was often quite massive.

For the more educated and privileged Straits Chinese, the desire to be European applied not only to the furniture. It influenced the choice of Victorian-style tableware, including dinner sets—often embroidered with a family crest—cutlery, and other appurtenances, such

The capacious dining-room at Panglima Prang was kept cool with tall windows and plentiful ceiling fans. The quality of the furniture indicates this room was used for formal entertaining, not everyday meals

An early advertisement for silver tableware in the John Little catalogue, Singapore.

as silver cruet sets, tureens and candelabra. It extended naturally enough to the provision of a European as well as a Chinese menu which, in turn, had its implications for space as cooking of both kinds often had to be undertaken simultaneously. Few families, however, went so far as to have two separate kitchens as was frequently the case in India. Even so, extra space was needed in the form of store-rooms and pantries, and in some cases serveries, including equipment such as ovens, sinks, tables and benches.

In such a European-style setting, it was also appropriate for the Chinese to wear European attire, but Chinese dress was almost as common. For the Straits Chinese, it was perfectly appropriate to combine Western and traditional customs in this way.

The same families, for instance, were quite capable of hosting a Western-style dinner party one weekend and a *Tok Panjang* or traditional Peranakan luncheon party the following week. The *Tok Panjang*, like its Western counterpart, was set out on a long table. This was very much a family affair involving anything up to 30 or 40 relatives. The female members of the family would lay the table, cook and serve the food, and generally wait in attendance on the older members, who were usually served first and in general given priority. Apart from its significance as a family gathering, the *Tok Panjang* was an occasion to demonstrate and savour the art of Nonya cooking, in combination with Indian, Thai and Malay dishes. Traditional attire was worn. Relatives would be served at the table and, after eating, would adjourn, and other relatives would take their place. All of this meant that other rooms were necessary for entertainment and social intercourse. This applied, too, in the case of

A group of Englishmen and servants in the 1890s. Note that the Europeans habitually donned a cool sarong *while relaxing at home.*

Western-style dinners, when cocktails would be served in the downstairs drawing-room or, more commonly, in a sitting-room or on the veranda.

The *Tok Panjang* was mainly a lunchtime event but other functions held by the Straits Chinese might well involve sittings at both lunch and dinner. All such functions depended on the availability of female relatives in addition to house staff to wait on tables and do the necessary serving of drinks and clearing away. On occasions such as these, it was not unusual for the female and male members of the family to eat at different times, just as there was a tendency for them to be separated spatially. The women tended to gravitate toward the rear of the house and the men to the front. On principle, the Peranakan menfolk would abstain from any involvement in back-room activities and so, quite naturally, it was understood that the patriarchal territory was at the front of the house, whether downstairs or upstairs.

All of this had implications for the way the house was laid out and furnished. In the most expensive of the Chinese houses, the father of the family would have his own study or office, whether or not business was conducted from the home. In other cases, one of the rooms near the entrance was made available for uninterrupted use by the head of the house when desired, either on his own or to conduct meetings with or entertain his male friends in privacy. The allocation of the front of the house to the adult male is well illustrated in the example of Mrs Betty Lim's elder brother, who admittedly saw himself as somewhat of a lady's man and, as such, held frequent dinner parties during which the women of the family were banished to the back of the house.

Such a situation could hardly apply in European families. The front part of the house was as much the wife's territory as the husband's. An example of this was in the use of the drawing-room and the veranda, separately or together, as the setting for ladies' tea or coffee mornings or bridge parties in European houses. These were mainly occasions for female chit-chat yet not devoid of the pretensions that one would expect of the European upper set. Tea mornings and such events were strictly the province of the *memsahib* who came to the fore in a much more visible way than her non-European counterpart. Whatever her middle-class English upbringing, it was important that she convey the right image, in speech, demeanour and dress, in the furniture and decor, and in the degree to which her guests were to be outdone, just a trifle, by the quality and presentation of the morning repast—cakes, pastries and sandwiches—all on the best China and served by the *amah* from an elaborate silver trolley. It was important, at the same time, that her guests be from a similar social level; thus the wife of a Division II government official would hardly be seen at the home of an officer of more senior rank.

The exception to the tendency for non-European women to remain in the background was the trend for the wives of some of the more senior Chinese businessmen to emulate the European habit of bridge parties and tea mornings. Mostly, however, the Chinese mode of entertaining guests was less staid, less formal, more gregarious in nature. It was also more likely to involve the man of the house rather than the lady in the leading role. Mrs Betty

Entertainment in the home often included local dance or musical troupes, such as the Chinese cast of a drama as seen here.

Lim and Mrs Gracia Tay Chee had fathers who, like Jack Tan's family, frequently threw parties at which much of the entertainment was put on by members of the family in the form of children's concerts or musical events and there was much eating and merrymaking. In Peranakan households, it was common to have performances of Malay songs, plays, poems, and dancing to the accompaniment of traditional instruments, including gongs. For all such activities space was needed. In very exceptional cases, there was a ballroom especially for dancing in the European manner, complete with orchestra, but more commonly, one of the main living areas, such as the drawing-room or the hall or the veranda, was used for this purpose.

In such ways, there was much overlapping of entertaining and family life in the way the house was used, the Chinese tending to regard the front of the house as more formal and visitor-oriented and the back as more informal and the place for family activities, a situation which applied also to the Europeans, but to a lesser degree. ❖

Family Activities

⁂

Although there were differences between family activities in European and in non-European households, there were also similarities. Many European—and particularly English—habits were copied by the Chinese and other races. For the English, there was the influence of British colonial life as practised in India. And all races, including the English, were subject to the cultural transfer from Europe, in particular that from Victorian England.

The Victorian emphasis on family life at home had its counterpart in the value placed by the Chinese themselves on the importance of the family. The life of the Chinese at home was bound up with the notion of the extended family. Large families had also been characteristic of Victorian suburban England, but by the late 1800s the trend was towards the nuclear family of parents and two or three children. British colonial families in Singapore, being very much a product of late Victorian attitudes and being transient, were also small and, despite the continuing importance of family life in Victorian households, were less inclined this way than were the Chinese.

The Chinese, while taking on new, Western habits, maintained many of their own traditions. In plan and form, their houses were European but were Chinese in the way they were furnished and decorated and in the choice of objects and artefacts such as pictures, screens, chinaware and plant-stands.

The sitting-room, drawing-room, or lounge of the typical European house echoed that of the Indian colonial house in the simple, basic form of its wood and cane furniture. It also included, as in India, and as a reflection of the Victorian passion for collecting things, a variety of memorabilia and artefacts. Depending upon tastes and interests, there were spyglasses and telescopes, mirrors in mahogany frames, a mantle or grandfather clock or two, and portraits, landscapes or war and hunting scenes in gilt frames.

This taste for Victoriana was more evident before the 1920s; by the 1930s, the vogue was for a less cluttered, more streamlined appearance along Art Deco lines.

Even with this change of fashion, furniture throughout the period tended, as in Victorian England, to be bulky. It was mainly imported from England through one of the big mercantile houses such as John Little, Robinsons or Whiteaways, or made by them to order. Lighter cane or rattan furniture purchased from one of the shops along Victoria Street was, nevertheless, also popular. For the managers of private companies, there was the opportunity to choose one's own furniture or to have it custom-made. For government civil servants of all ranks, though, everything down to the Sanderson fabrics on the sofas and armchairs was supplied from government stocks.

As the Chinese and Indian owners of suburban houses followed European fashions, so the interiors of their houses also reflected Victorian and later Art Deco influences. The Indian Jumabhoy family, for instance, had the most up-to-date lounge settings in Art Deco style in their Scotts Road house in the 1930s. Their enthusiasm for Art Deco work extended to find renditions of that style in the form of china, crystal and silver dinner settings for special occasions.

The inclinations of the Straits Chinese towards Western fashions often took the form of European furniture of a more elaborate style than that favoured by the Europeans themselves. Furniture of this kind was interspersed with that of traditional Chinese character, including settees, high-backed chairs, sofas, and at least one *kerusi sandar* ('*krosisandah*') or reclining armchair. These were usually in solid blackwood, teak or rosewood. For the well-to-do, furniture would generally be in complete sets; but even for poorer families with the smallest of living-rooms, there would be one or two pieces of traditional furniture.

In most Peranakan homes, of whatever class, there were three porcelain statuettes, or *datuk anak-anak*, in bright colours. They represented the Gods of Longevity, Wealth and Fertility. In some cases, there would be a fourth statuette symbolizing Knowledge. There were also porcelain or ceramic plant-stands and Chinese paintings or calligraphic scrolls and these were intermingled with family portraits and paintings of English landscapes or sporting scenes.

One piece of furniture common to the more privileged Straits Chinese and European houses was the piano. For both the wealthier Chinese and the Europeans, piano lessons were considered an essential part of the proper unbringing of children. The Chinese did not, however, have the same enthusiasm for the European habit of violin instruction; singing lessons, though, were considered desirable for young girls, for whom private, respectable female tutors were

An early advertisement for rattan and other furniture in the John Little catalogue.

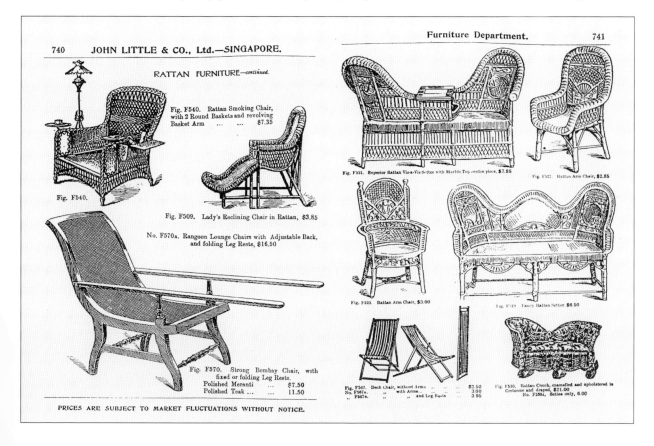

Two views of an enclosed veranda of a European home, circa *1930s.*

engaged to teach at home. It was essential that instruction be at home; to allow young ladies, particularly young Nonya girls, to go outside for lessons would be quite improper.

As in Victorian England, the conscientious nature of piano practice in the quieter atmosphere of one of the front rooms of the Peranakan house was in complete contrast to the use of the piano for family 'sing-songs'. Western songs and music—both modern and classical—were much in favour.

Nevertheless, traditional musical activities were just as popular. The *ronggeng*, an ensemble of Malay songs, poems and dancing, was frequently performed to the accompaniment of Malay musical instruments, including gongs.

Although the Straits Chinese were not at all attracted to Chinese music or to the idea of playing Chinese instruments, their enthusiasm for Malay music such as the *keroncong*, the *setambul* and the *dondang sayang* was unbounded. Indeed, the Straits Chinese often outshone the Malays in the art of *dondang sayang* composition and singing. This called for a particular aptitude in rhythm and imagery and the ability to continue in impromptu vein where the other person had left off.

The playing of Malay instruments in informal family groups or the engagement of a Baba 'minstrel' band on formal or special occasions was matched by the interest of the Straits Chinese in instruments of both Eastern and Western origin. Apart from the piano and the violin, there were the banjo, the mandolin, the piano accordion, and, at a later date, the Hawaiian and electric guitars and the drums.

For all such activities to take place under the same roof required space and suitable furniture and a flexible attitude as to its use. In this and other ways, the sitting-room, the drawing-room, the lounge, the veranda and even the garden served a variety of purposes.

In Jack Tan's family house in Pasir Panjang, the appearance of a hired orchestra to play Chinese or Western music in the garden or on the veranda, was a common occurrence. This house was the setting for the very first orchestra to perform in a private house.

The British also had their 'sing-songs' around the piano, just as they had had in Victorian England, when their children were back from boarding school. Piano-playing and singing were also commonly a part of the evening's entertainment following a dinner party. So, too, was dancing, to the accompaniment of the piano and the violin or a small orchestra. Mostly this took place in the drawing-room or lounge, which would be cleared for the purpose, or on the veranda. Here, to the strict ballroom tempo of Victor Silvester or the more swinging style of Joe Loss, dancing would take place often until the wee hours of the morning. In a few exceptional cases, in the grandeur of the European houses, it would be possible to hold a full-scale ball in the hall which was made big enough for the purpose, or in a specially designed ballroom.

In most of these ways, the Straits Chinese followed suit. They also emulated the Europeans, as did other ethnic groups, in their enthusiasm for the wireless and the gramophone, when these came in the 1930s. With the arrival of recorded music, dance parties became more popular than ever.

In general, the gramophone and the wireless had the effect of encouraging even greater informality in family life. This was true for both the Europeans and the Chinese. Children became a more integrated part of the family as it gathered in the sitting-room or the lounge to listen to the music of Loss or, later, Benny Goodman, Artie Shaw or Jimmy Dorsey on the latest HMV or Parlorphone recordings.

An early advertisement for gramophones in the John Little catalogue.

European men catching up on the news. Note the billiards table in the area of the veranda behind.

Children were hardly to be left out either as the family huddled around its wireless set to be entertained with the latest popular, classical or traditional music, or to be informed as to the latest local or overseas news. Straits Chinese families were most likely to tune in to the Netherland Indies radio station NIROM to hear its regular news broadcasts or programmes of *keroncong* music, of which they were particularly fond. For the Europeans, there was the BBC which was inaugurated in 1922 and started regular overseas broadcasts shortly after. Like the piano, the wireless and the gramophone were equivalent to the television set of today in commanding group attention and thus affecting the way rooms were used and furnished.

All of these activities served to bring guests into a closer relationship with the family. Gramophone recordings, being light and portable, were frequently brought by guests to be played together with those owned by the family.

Indoor games, too, served to draw members of the family together and into a closer relationship to guests in parts of the house traditionally reserved for family use. The Western game of bridge was one game played *ad infinitum* by the Europeans and Chinese as well as other communities. It was particularly popular with European womenfolk, so that parts of the house, such as the veranda, the drawing-room, the sitting-room or the lounge, were used at various times of the day for bridge parties. They were also used by the family for bridge and other card-games.

Unlike bridge, which was played by people of all income levels, the game of billiards was strictly for the rich and played only by the male members of the family. The presence of a billiard room was thus an exception to the general trend toward desegregation. Billiard rooms first made their appearance in the 1890s in houses such as the Tanjong Katong mansion of the wealthy Jewish entrepreneur, Manasseh Meyer. Ownership of a billiard room, though undoubtedly a status symbol as much as an expression of genuine enthusiasm for the game, was something on which the Chinese did not place much value.

Chess was also considered a pastime mainly for adult males in European and some non-European families. In the Jumabhoy family, for instance, young Assat was permitted to play only when he was 12 and had reached an acceptable level of competence. Meanwhile, his grandfather, deciding that nobody in the family was good enough for the game, played by himself in a corner of the living-room set aside for the purpose. While few European families would take the game so seriously, it was generally understood that Father could retire to one of the front rooms of the house downstairs or to an upstairs drawing-room with one of his elder offspring to play the game in solitude.

Chess, like bridge and in common with other European parlour games such as dominoes, also found favour with the Straits Chinese because it was a convenient vehicle for gambling. The gambling instinct found an outlet also in such traditional Western games as poker, 'twenty-one' (blackjack), gin rummy and draughts.

These games, however, paled into insignificance by comparison with that of mahjong, with which the Chinese of all classes and both sexes had an absolute fetish. Other forms of gambling, particularly within Straits Chinese families, were *fantan*, a game involving numbers and dice, *sisik*, played with cards of four colours, and *cheki*, another card-game, played mainly by the older members of the family. Amongst the Straits Chinese, *cheki* was preferred to *sisik*.

Such games meant that Chinese families entertained themselves at home as much as, if not more than, they did outside. This was true even of games involving syndicates such as *chapjiki*, which involved armies of collectors doing the rounds of the Chinese houses every day to collect the stakes in lieu of centralized betting offices, which were a later development. Enthusiasm for such traditional indoor games did not lessen with the arrival of the gramophone and the wireless, which also, of course, served to keep families at home.

Indoor games also brought outsiders into a closer relationship with the family at home as traditional attitudes to such relationships relaxed towards the 1920s and 1930s. All of this had its implications for the way the house was used and arranged, as reflected, for example, in the greater use in these later years of English Victorian names such as 'sitting-room' or 'sitting-hall' or 'parlour'. While indoor table games generally had the effect of uniting the family, certain games were favoured by the different sexes or by different age groups. *Congkak*, a game in-volving a long punctuated wooden board, was played mainly by children whereas *cheki* and *wha whay*, a card-game involving bets on different colours, were special favourites amongst the women.

Despite the tendency towards a more liberal attitude to women, traditional attitudes to the relationship of males or females in the house died hard in Chinese, Indian and Malay middle-class families. In many Arab and Malay houses, women were designated their own territory at the rear of the house.

Originating in the Middle East, the game of congkak *was probably brought to Asia by Arab or African traders en route to China.*

In these houses, the arrangement of rooms was influenced by the subjugation of women in the family hierarchy, whereas in the Straits Chinese family, for the grandmother, it was rather the other way round. Unlike the young Nonya granddaughters who were expected to be meek and submissive, in general the elder lady was accorded considerable authority in running the household, which she was expected to do with a firm hand and in a strict, even fierce, uncompromising manner. Such authority was recognized in the setting aside of part of the house as her territory. More often than not, this took the form of her own lounge–dining-room and sleeping quarters and, as in the case of Hock Gwee Thian's house in Prinsep Street, the provision of her very own reclining armchair.

The congregation of the Chinese family in the sitting-room for activities such as table games or 'sing-songs' did not mean that certain traditional attitudes to the relationship between men and women within the family were entirely forgotten. Undoubtedly, the rigorous separation of the husband and wife from each other—the wife taking her meals with the children in a separate room—as was common in the 1800s, had been considerably modified by the 1920s, but in many families, women were still expected to occupy themselves with domestic matters and, in their spare time, to make things for the house. Meanwhile, the man of the house would concern himself almost entirely with outside affairs. Having this background role, even with servants at her elbow, the woman was naturally less conspicuous in physical terms than her European counterpart, the *memsahib*, who took more of a leading position in family and social affairs.

The privileges accorded the male head of the household, while most evident in Indian, Malay and Arabic households and only slightly less so in the case of the Chinese, also applied to European families, though to a lesser degree. In just a few cases, the European master might have his own study and office. Offices, though, were more common in Chinese houses, partly because of the tendency of the head of the family to run some aspect of his business from home.

The provision of an office for the Chinese man of the house was less of an overt sign of his position in the domestic hierarchy than the fact that he was allowed to have as many mistresses as he could afford. Nevertheless, by the 1900s, some discretion was usual, so that the mistresses were no longer under the same roof, nor was he likely any longer to have several wives, although it was still a matter of pride to keep a large establishment. Large families, many servants, and a house of impressive dimensions meant success.

Success in worldly affairs, however, had to be balanced with the right amount of attention to spiritual matters. The importance of ancestor-worship and reverence for household and other deities in Chinese family life was only slightly affected by the fact that the physical arrangement was often a complete departure from the traditional one of a deity hall at the front and an ancestral hall at the back. Quite commonly, the family altar was set up in one of the rooms for everyday use, such as the dining-room, on religious occasions. That was the case in the house of Jack Tan's family in Pasir Panjang, as in Grace Tan's house, in which the drawing-room was the place where all of the family portraits were hung. Not to be left out in the family's concern with spiritual affairs was the special God who held sway over all matters to do with that most important province of the Chinese house: the kitchen. Hardly to be ignored either in family affairs, including all matters to do with food, were the servants. ❖

In smaller terrace-houses occupied by the Chinese, the altar was often placed in an upstairs room against the back wall.

Servants

❧❊❊❊❧

Servants were an essential ingredient of family life in Victorian suburban England at least until the 1920s. This was even more firmly the case for the British in India, where cheap native labour was readily available. So, too, in Singapore, servants were taken for granted by the British and other Europeans. The Chinese and other communities who aspired to the suburban lifestyle also followed suit.

Servants were not only the prerogative of the rich; even suburban households of modest means had one or two. As in England and India, servants were employed for two reasons. The first was to do the housework; in the largest houses, there were many duties to perform. This was certainly the case before the introduction of domestic labour-saving devices and restrictions on the importation of female labour in the late 1920s. For the European *memsahib* in particular, who had difficulty in adjusting to the tropical climate, many hands were needed. But even for the middle-income Indian or Eurasian family, there was housework to be done which could be taken care of by one or two servants for a modest wage.

The second reason for engaging servants was to signal the status of those who employed them. To the British, it was quite out of the question that the lady of the house should do the housework. Even in Chinese and other non-European households, where the matriarch was traditionally quite involved in domestic tasks, servants were common. For the majority of Chinese, for whom wealth was the main indicator of social standing, servants were an index of monetary status, quite apart from practical considerations. For the British, there were political as well as social implications.

In larger households, whatever the race, six or seven servants were common. The arrangement in Mrs Gracia Tay Chee's family was typical. There was a cook, a cook's boy, a cook's helper, a syce (driver), a *kebun* (gardener) and two domestic servants. In her case, there was no *jaga* (guard) although many wealthier families, such as Mrs Grace Tan's, had one. The arrangement in Mrs Tan's house was exceptionally generous in that there was a servant and a syce for every member of the family. But Mrs Tay Chee's retinue of servants was more representative of that in European households. The Sinclairs had a cook, a cook's boy, a syce, a *kebun*, a *jaga* and three domestic servants. With all communities, the number of purely domestic servants could extend to five or six. The richer the family, the more domestic helpers were employed.

Domestic servants came in several categories. Those considered most important were the so-called 'black-and-white' *amahs*, the name derived from the customary uniform of immaculate white jackets and black trousers which they wore. Amongst the 'black-and-white' *amahs*, who had different duties, the one responsible for the children, including the baby, was the most highly respected. In most Chinese households, the child *amah* or nanny was considered as much a permanent member of the family as any relative. Usually she worked for the one family for the whole of her adult life. Between the child *amah* and her Chinese employers there was often a common bond of loyalty and trust; this was less strongly the case with European employers, who were more transient and with whom there was not so much cultural affinity, for 'black-and-white' *amahs* were Chinese, many from Canton.

The devotion of the child *amah* and the family to each other was characteristic of other non-European households. Asad Jumabhoy recalls the closeness of his relationship to Tuah, the family *amah*, when he was a child. But Tuah had also nursed Asad's uncle who, as a young boy, needed the special protection that she could provide because he was the smallest of three. So far as she was concerned, the young lad could do no wrong. Tuah, in common with most 'black-and-white' *amahs*, saved diligently not only for her old age, but also in order to leave, at the end of her long life with the family, something for Asad's uncle and a gold ring for Asad himself.

Tuah, like most 'black-and-white' *amahs*, had her own living quarters. But unlike the syce

A 'black-and-white' amah with her employer and child: such amahs came from Guangdong province in China and always wore the same uniform: white blouse and black trousers.

or the *kebun* or the cook who were confined to the outhouse or rooms in a separate out-building, she lived under the same roof as the Jumabhoy family, usually in the rear part of the house. In terms of her responsibility for the children, this was a convenient arrangement. It meant that the children could be put in her charge in her part of the house, separate from the rest of the family, when required. At other times, she would amuse the children in the garden or, with the parents' consent, take them out.

In the wealthiest households, such as that of Hock Gwee Thian, there were several child *amahs*, depending upon the number of children. In Hock's house there were four. Like young Asad, Hock found his nanny seemingly indistinguishable from his own grandmother as they both doted on him. Hock speaks of there being five or six nannies in the house in all.

The accommodation of several nannies under one roof at any particular time had its implications for the layout and size of the house. However, houses of such large size with such elaborate provisions were in the minority in relation to the total number of houses built before the war. 'Black-and-white' *amahs* were essentially for the well-to-do.

Other *amahs* necessary for the smooth running of the large house, but carrying less status than the child *amah*, were those required to take care of the general housework. In Chinese families, housework duties would be specified very clearly. Cleaning, washing, drying and airing of clothes and linen, ironing and sewing were the responsibility of different *amahs*.

Most *amahs* did not marry, which simplified accommodation arrangements. Along with their room and keep, *amahs* were paid a salary of about $12 per month although the child *amahs* would earn somewhat more than this. The loyalty that existed between the general household *amahs* and their Chinese employers went hand in hand with a general understanding that duties were to be performed to the letter. If they were not, the grandmother of the house would have something to say. As the person responsible for the conduct and performance of all household duties, she would exercise her authority strictly and with little compassion if work was not up to standard. Such authority, however, served if anything to command respect and loyalty. Partly this was due to the care and attention which the old lady would give to the *amahs'* welfare, including their accommodation, meals and general social life.

The exactitude with which duties were specified and seen to be carried out in Chinese house-holds was not characteristic of all European employers, whose attitudes tended to be more tolerant and flexible. *Amahs* were generally treated kindly by Europeans and were often referred for further employment to other European families at the end of the employer's contract. Europeans were also less pedantic than the Chinese as to the race of the household *amahs* hired by them. The *amahs* of many Europeans were Indian, but this was very rarely the case in Chinese families.

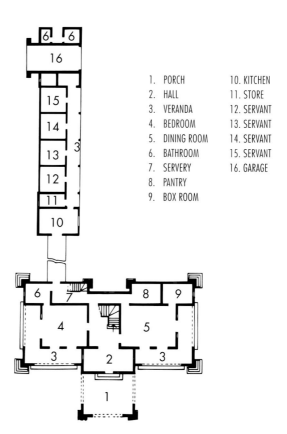

1. PORCH
2. HALL
3. VERANDA
4. BEDROOM
5. DINING ROOM
6. BATHROOM
7. SERVERY
8. PANTRY
9. BOX ROOM
10. KITCHEN
11. STORE
12. SERVANT
13. SERVANT
14. SERVANT
15. SERVANT
16. GARAGE

Plan of a house built for an employee of the EEA & C Telegraph Co on Chatsworth Road, 1924. It clearly shows the divide between the 'served' and 'service' areas.

In addition to the cast of *amahs* present in the largest houses, in the houses of the really rich there were several domestic helpers and *mui tsai*, usually local Chinese girls. This was the case in the parental home of Mrs Betty Lim where there were two or three, who were taken on by Mrs Lim's grandmother. Others came into the house with the blessing of the family through adoption by one of the 'black-and-white' *amahs*. In many cases, these girls were delinquents or from disadvantaged homes. Common in Peranakan families, they were really little more than slaves. Some were Hainanese bought directly off the ship from China for a sum of about $400.

Mui tsai were given sundry minor duties such as sweeping the stairs or outside drains, but at all times were required to be at the beck and call of the grandmother. This meant that the small rooms given to them to sleep in might be close at hand, buried somewhere in the main house. But this was the exception rather than the rule. Most of the bigger houses had no more than one or two rooms for the *amahs* and additional domestic servants were engaged on a daily or part-time basis, and did not live in.

Amahs and servants were mainly single, but the syce and the *kebun* were usually married and separate accommodation was provided for their families. This usually consisted of only one room even if there were three or four children in the family. However, there was usually an adjacent shared toilet, just as the *amahs* were given a toilet between them. The syce, who had higher status, was usually provided with his own shower.

Above left: *Two house boys (Chinese/Malay).*

Above right *Indians from southern India often found work in Singapore as drivers, cattle keepers or laundry men and women.*

The syce and the *kebun* were usually Malay and this was another reason for separating them from the Chinese servants. When it came to food, the servants in Chinese households would normally take what was left of the main meal. But the syce would prepare his own Malay cuisine separately on his own small *dapur* and have his own pots and pans, and the *kebun* would normally have access to these facilities as well.

The syce was usually given a room next to the carriage room and the stable if the family kept a horse on the premises, and the *kebun* was close by. The importance of the syce did not diminish with the decline in importance of the horse-and-carriage in the late 1920s. By the early 1920s, nearly half of all the houses had a motor-car garage, and by the 1930s the proportion had increased still further.

Accommodation for an Indian *jaga* or a Malay guard, if the family was wealthy enough to have one, was much more simple. Usually he slept on the front veranda or in some equivalent sheltered area near the front of the house, such as the porch. So, too, did the *punkah-wallah* until his displacement by the electric fan in the 1920s. He needed no special room but simply operated the *punkah* inside the house by means of a rope attached to his foot, from a position somewhere on the veranda.

A family of four with horse and carriage with driver, probably just before World War II.

Generally, however, servants needed space, both for their accommodation and in terms of the particular functions they were required to perform. A number of these functions—for example, the washing of clothes and tasks associated with the kitchen such as washing-up after

Many syces and kebun *were Malay; here we see two in the shade of a magnificent traveller's palm, a familiar sight in Singapore then, as now.*

meals—were carried out on one of the rear open passages or verandas connecting the outhouse to the main house or in the outbuilding itself. In the beginning, clothes were washed over open sumps using earthenware basins. Later, raised concrete tubs were simply set on one of the verandas. Self-contained laundries were rare, even in the largest houses. Sometimes, clothes were washed in the kitchen.

To dry the clothes, yard space was provided at the back of the house for lines, even in the smallest bungalow. Clothes were also hung out to dry on open verandas at the back of the house, in some cases upstairs. In the bigger households, table-cloths and bed-linen and other such items were usually collected by the Indian *dhobi* or laundryman and washed elsewhere. In wealthier households, an Indian *dhobi* was employed on the premises.

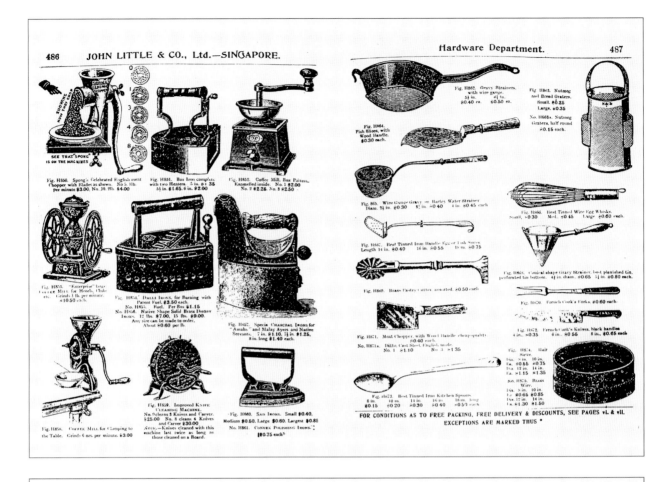

Fig. H850. Spong's Celebrated English meat Chopper with Blades as shewn. No 5. 1lb. per minute $3.00. No. 10. 7lb. $4.00

Fig. H851. Box Iron complete with two Heaters. 5 in. $1.35 5½ in. $1.65, 6 in. $2.00

Fig. H852. Coffee Mill. Box Pattern. Enamelled inside. No. 1 $2.00 No. 2 $2.25. No. 3 $2.50

Fig. H853. "Enterprise" Large Coffee Mill, for Hotels, Clubs etc. Grinds 1 lb. per minute. $10.50 each.

Fig. H854. 'DALLI' IRONS, for Burning with Patent Fuel, $3.50 each. No. H855. Fuel. Per Box $1.15 No. H856. Native Shape Solid Brass DHOBY IRONS. 12 lbs. $7.00, 15 lbs. $9.00 Any size can be made to order. About $0.60 per lb.

Fig. H857. Special CHARCOAL IRONS for "Amahs" and Malay Ayers and Native Servants. 7 in. $1.10, 7½ in. $1.25, 8 in. long $1.40 each.

Fig. H858. COFFEE MILL for Clamping to the Table. Grinds 6 ozs. per minute. $3.00

Fig. H859. Improved KNIFE CLEANING MACHINE. No. 9 cleans 3 Knives and Carver. $25.00 No. 8 cleans 4 Knives and Carver $30.00 NOTE.—Knives cleaned with this machine last twice as long as those cleaned on a Board.

Fig. H860. SAD IRONS. Small $0.40, Medium $0.50, Large $0.60, Largest $0.85 No. H861. CONVEX POLISHING IRONS. *$0.75 each*

Fig. H862. Gravy Strainers, with wire gauge. 5½ in. 6½ in. $0.40 ea. $0.50 ea.

Fig. H863. Nutmeg and Bread Graters. Small, $0.25 Large, $0.35 No. H863a. Nutmeg Graters, half round $0.15 each.

Fig. H864. Fish Slices, with Wood Handle. $0.30 each.

Fig. 865. Wire Gauge Gravy or Barley Water Strainer. Diam. 2½ in. $0.30 3½ in. $0.40 4 in. $0.45 each.

Fig. H866. Best Tinned Wire Egg Whisks. Small, $0.30 Med. $0.45 Large $0.60 each.

Fig. H867. Best Tinned Iron Handle Egg or Fish Slices. Length 14 in. $0.40 16 in. $0.55 18 in. $0.75

Fig. H868. Conical shape Gravy Strainer, best planished tin, perforated tin bottom. 4½ in. diam. $0.65 5½ in. $0.80 each.

Fig. H869. Brass Pastry Cutter assorted, $0.50 each.

Fig. H870. French Cook's Forks. $0.60 each.

Fig. H871. Meat Chopper, with Wood Handle cheap quality $0.40 each. No. H871a. Ditto, Cast Iron, English made. No. 1 $1.10 No. 2 $1.35

Fig. H872. French Cook's Knives, black handles. 4 in. $0.35, 6 in. $0.55 8 in. $0.65 each.

Fig. H874. Hair Sieve. Dia. 8 in. 10 in. $0.55 $0.75 Dia. 12 in. 14 in. $1.15 $1.35 No. H875. Brass Wire Dia. 8 in. 10 in. $0.65 $0.85 Dia. 12 in. 14 in. $1.30 $1.50

Fig. H873. Best Tinned Iron Kitchen Spoons. 8 in. 10 in. 11 in. 16 in. 18 in. long $0.15 $0.20 $0.30 $0.40 $0.50 each.

SEWING MACHINES.

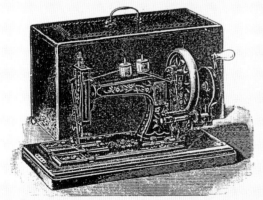

SPECIAL VALUE.

*Fig. D517. Lock-stitch Hand Sewing Machine. High Arm, made of good hardened Steel, on strong wooden base, with all the latest improvements to aid the operator and thirty extra parts, extra needles, etc. With Strong Walnut Wood Cover, complete.

Price, $21.00 each.

This Machine is specially manufactured for JOHN LITTLE & CO., Ltd., each one marked with our name and fully guaranteed.

. Sewing Machine Section—*continued.*

THE "STRAITS."

An English made machine manufactured expressly for Messrs. JOHN LITTLE & CO.

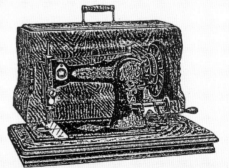

*Fig. D518. THE "STRAITS" Hand Sewing Machine is manufactured expressly for us. It has few parts, and is the simplest, quietest, and lightest running machine on the market. Suitable for either light or heavy work. Complete with cover. Patent microscopic winders. Price $33.50.

The following Machine Accessories are kept in stock, but any part for any of our machines can be obtained to order :—

Sewing Machine Needles for Singers, "Wertheim," or "Straits" Machines, per doz.								$0.60
" " Oil, specially prepared	...		...	...	...	...per bottle		0.30
Rufflers ...	...	...	...	...	...	...	each	2.00
Shuttles ...	...	...	...	...	...	...	"	1.20
Oil-cans ...	...	...	...	...	...	...	"	0.25
Rubber Rings	...	...	...	...	...	...	"	0.10

Sewing Machines Cleaned and Repaired.

Ironing was also normally done outside under shelter or in one of the rooms belonging to an *amah* responsible for this task. It was necessary to be near the cooking range in the kitchen to obtain the charcoal to heat the iron, at least before the advent of the electric iron in the 1930s. By then it was possible for ironing to be done inside the house, as was the case in the Jumabhoy household.

The mending of clothes, sewing or embroidery would also be done by one of the *amahs* or a domestic servant in her room in the main house, perhaps where the ironing was done or in a corner of the back veranda.

Such activities were but part of the general effect that servants had on the form of the house before World War II. One of the more obvious effects was in the size and arrangement of the outhouse. Outhouses grew, rather than diminished, in relative size towards the 1930s, despite advances in domestic technology and restrictions on the importation of domestic labour.

This was partly due to the tendency for certain commercial services such as dressmaking to be conducted from rooms in the outhouse. These were often rented out during the years of economic depression when there were fewer available external economic opportunities. Servants none the less were an important component of domestic life right up to the war, certainly for the British civil servants and those with higher incomes. One aspect of domestic life which would ensure the need for servants was the various activities to do with the preparation of food. ❖

Opposite *Early advertisements for domestic equipment in the John Little catalogue.*

Above *Turn-of-the-century scene—a family on a veranda being served by a house boy.*

The Kitchen

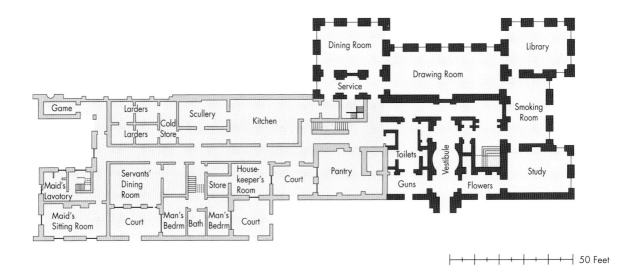

Dining Room   Library

Drawing Room

Service

Smoking Room

Game   Larders   Scullery   Kitchen

Cold Store

Larders

Toilets

Vestibule

Maid's Lavatory   Servants' Dining Room   Store   House-keeper's Room   Court   Pantry   Study

Guns   Flowers

Maid's Sitting Room   Court   Man's Bedrm   Bath   Man's Bedrm   Court

50 Feet

Ground-floor plan of one of England's last grand manor houses to be built (1935–38), Middleton Park in Oxfordshire. There is clear delineation between the main house and the area housing the servants and kitchens.

In the larger manor houses of 18th-century England and the Victorian suburban houses of the 1800s, the kitchen and the rest of the service domain had been separated well away from public view and the house proper, Initially this took the form of an extended and elaborately planned service wing, the entrance to which was marked by the 'green baize door'. In the Georgian town house, the kitchen and servants' quarters were relegated to the basement. In the later Victorian suburban house, they became a somewhat watered-down version of the country-house wing in the form of a two-or three-room rear extension. In colonial India, as in Singapore, the kitchen and servants' quarters were in a separate building at the rear, connected to the main house by a covered passage.

The desire for separation was not only to do with the smell of food or the sight of it being prepared. It was part of a deeply ingrained attitude which would have the servantry and all of their affairs clearly identified at the lower end of the family social hierarchy. But the servants also had their own hierarchy. This was as true in Singapore or India as in England. In Singapore, the cook carried as much prestige as the child *amah*, in his own way. This was because food was given a high priority, particularly by the Chinese.

In Chinese households, the cook was selected with the greatest care. He was given as much scrutiny as he himself would be expected to give to the food before purchasing it. This was not so much the case with European families, partly because they were less permanent. European families often had to settle for the cook who had been passed on to them by their predecessors or choose from amongst those who happened to be available. For civil servants, there was often no choice at all; the cook came with the house.

Even so, the European *memsahib* tended to retain as much authority in the kitchen, particularly in the purchase of food, as her Chinese counterpart. Subject to this, the cook, once appointed, was given dominion over all matters to do with the kitchen. Certainly in Chinese households there was little interference in this area by the family matriarch. There were of course exceptions, as in the case of Mrs Gracia Tay Chee's mother, who simply liked to know what was going on and was often seen visiting the cook. And Mrs Betty Lim's grandmother, being herself a good cook, took a supervisory role, but like the senior matriarch in Gwee Thian Hock's household, was careful not to cross the path of the cook when he was out of sorts.

Visits to the kitchen were, in any case, customary in Peranakan households because cooking was seen as an essential skill for young Nonya ladies to acquire. It was necessary that they spend some time with the cook to be taught and to learn the culinary arts, including what food to buy and how to serve it. The grandmother would see to that.

Most cooks in Chinese households were Hainanese; those employed in Peranakan houses were expected to cook either Chinese or European food. Cantonese cooks, who were considered superior, were found in wealthier households. Cooks in European and Eurasian houses were of either dialect. Indian cooks were preferred by Indian families who, though in other things inclined towards Western ways, retained their preference for Indian food.

Traditional Chinese-style kitchen with charcoal-burning brick hearth. In Peranakan households the kitchen was known as the perut rumah *or 'stomach of the house'.*

Typical market place in Singapore dating from the late 19th century.

The purchase of food was very much the cook's responsibility but in this he had the assistance of the head boy, who also had other duties to perform, such as helping with the cooking, serving the food and waiting at the table. Food was normally bought every day at one of the large wet markets. In many families, the need for fresh food was considered sufficiently important to warrant two visits each day. Trips to the market were normally made early in the morning. For those who had the means, the man of the house or his syce would drop the cook or his boy off at the market on his way to work. Or the European *memsahib* would accompany him there to supervise the various purchases, as would the Chinese housewife if she were fastidious. Otherwise, it was possible for the servant to cycle to the market or go there by rickshaw and be back again within the hour, for there were markets in most areas. In the early 1930s there were six: in Tanglin Road, Orchard Road, Beach Road, Serangoon Road, Market Street and Maxwell Road.

Fresh food—vegetables, meat, and fish such as *ikan parang*, a special favourite with Peranakan families—could be supplemented by dry goods from the provision shops, so that the daily shopping trip might combine visits to both. For those who could afford it, particularly the Europeans, there were specially imported items—biscuits, cheese and wines—to be had at the Cold Storage, who would also deliver to the house if required. It was thanks to this company that the range of food items, in particular groceries, improved so much from the late 1920s. Cold Storage had already produced the first ice-cream in

1920. In 1926 the company started a pig farm, followed three years later by the colony's first dairy farm. By 1930 the firm was making its own bread.

Food bought at the shops or market could always be supplemented by fresh food and other items supplied by hawkers who came to the house every day or two. Condiments— herbs and spices—could be bought from the hawkers, or else the cook could pick them from his own small plot ouside the kitchen door.

The need to buy food every day was partly to do with the problem of keeping it fresh. Until the 1930s, food was kept in large, bench-height wooden ice-chests. These were big enough for one or two days' supply. The custom was to have two chests, one for food and one for drinks, near the kitchen. They were kept on one of the verandas or open passages and it was here that food was left when it was delivered by hawkers.

Ice was delivered to the house from one of the few ice warehouses such as the Atlas Ice House or Whampoa's Ice Warehouse on River Valley Road. For many years, thanks to Whampoa's initiative, ice, remarkably, was imported by ship from America. In 1926, the Cold Storage Company began to manufacture it locally. Several blocks of ice, each weighing about 100 lbs, were needed for the ice-chests every week. The ice, as it melted, was channelled into a tray, then drained through a ceramic filter and used for drinking purposes.

From the early 1930s, refrigeration gradually displaced ice-chests in wealthier homes. Initially these were powered by kerosene or oil and then by electricity in the late 1930s. Electricity was charged under a 'social' or 'domestic' rate. One had to be careful to connect the refrigerator to the domestic outlet, which was two or three times cheaper than the social supply, which was used for lighting.

Hawkers plied their goods around Singapore's well-to-do neighbourhoods. These chickens in baskets would be sold from house to house.

Early signage and buildings of the Cold Storage Company whose headquarters were in Borneo Warf, Singapore.

Before the days of refrigeration, food was often cooked, cooled and left for three or four days before eating. It was then periodically warmed up as it was needed. In any event, the cook was kept continuously busy preparing two or three meals a day. Cooking for Chinese families was particularly demanding because they were bigger than European ones. Demands on the cook were accentuated because of the need to prepare for celebrations and dinner parties, which were frequent. If the amount of work was too much for one cook, or if both Chinese and European food was needed in large quantities at the same time, a second cook would be engaged.

Much of the work involved the preparation of the food before cooking. This was generally done outside or on the veranda of the outhouse. Apart from the preparation of food, this intermediate area between the outhouse and the main house was the scene of much activity and served a variety of purposes. This was where the clothes were washed, or sewing and mending carried out, where food was received and stored, and dishes and pans washed after meals. It was the working area of the kitchen equivalent to the English Victorian scullery, where fish was scraped, chillies pounded, vegetables cut and birds defeathered. For such tasks there were simple utensils such as a mortar and pestle, a granite cutting or chopping block, metal knives and scrapers.

Hock Gwee Thian gives an example of the work involved in preparing food in the case of the *pek kway*, or the gingko nut, used in soups:

"The first step was [to] crack open the hard outer shell with a pestle to get to the kernel. These kernels are covered with a thin papery membrane which has to be peeled off with the aid of a knife. In the centre, running; the length of each kernel is a fibrous rind-like substance, which is bitter and therefore must be discarded. It would have been so simple to just split the kernel and to pull off the fibrous strip. However, this would not be acceptable to any true-blue Nonya who valued presentation above being practical. Each kernel must remain whole. So in order to remove the

fibrous strip a toothpick or matchstick was employed to slowly push it out. The technique was to insert the toothpick into one end of each kernel and push the fibrous material out the other end."[1]

All such preparations took place under the watchful eye of the cook. The heart of his territory was, of course, the kitchen. It was usually large, and high, although no higher than the servants' and other rooms on either side. Unlike the sophisticated developments in cooking equipment that had taken place in England by the early 1900s, the facilities in most pre-war kitchens were extraordinarily primitive, even in the 1930s. Until the introduction of gas, almost all cooking was done over an open stove. It was made of brick, usually with a stone slab or concrete top at bench height in which there were two round holes for metal or clay pots and, later, *wok*. The food in these vessels was heated over burning wood or charcoal in the space beneath. Under the fire, below a second slab, there was space for the storage of the fuel. Although more expensive than wood, charcoal was preferred because of the importance attached to the 'taste of the fire', which had also been a matter of some importance to Victorian cooks.

Charcoal was delivered in bundles of 5 or 10 *kati*; one bundle was enough for a large family for about two days. *Bakau* wood, obtained from neighbouring islands, was brought to the house in chopped lengths of about 15 inches, strapped in wire.

Although the burning charcoal itself did not produce much smoke, it came from the oil used in cooking and from the food dropped on to the fire. Even so, it was only in the more expensive houses that provision was made to take away the smoke.

If the basement kitchens of early Victorian suburban houses were hot and stuffy, the kitchens of pre-war Singapore were often unbearable. But unlike those earlier subterranean chambers, the kitchen in Singapore at least had the advantage of being above ground in a separate wing, so that there was some opportunity for cross-ventilation when there was a

151. An early advertisement for filters in the John Little Catalogue, Singapore.

An early advertisement for laundry equipment and more in the John Little catalogue.

1 Hock Gwee Thian, *A Nonya Mosaic: My Mother's Childhood*, Singapore, Times Books International, 1985, page 27

window on one side and a door on the other. Good ventilation was all the more necessary in Singapore, where the climate was much hotter than that of England.

In many Chinese kitchens, the stove was in the middle of the room as an island fixture, but in the better-class houses, particularly those of the Europeans, it was set against the wall with a brick or metal flue connected to a zinc hood over it, to remove the smoke. With the stove in the middle, the cook stood at one end and the cook's boy at the other, to feed and stoke the fire.

In England by the late 1800s, there were already specially designed fixtures and devices for roasting, boiling and steaming, and compartments for baking, but baking in the pre-war Singapore house was done in cut-out kerosene tins, covered in sand. Such tins were also used for boiling water.

Water, apart from that obtained from melted ice, was obtained either from a well in the back yard or from a tank fed from a roof gutter before the introduction of piped water in the 1920s. Well water was drawn and carried to the kitchen by the *tukang air*. In Peranakan Chinese households, it was customary to store water in an *air kamcheng* or larger clay vessel set on a wooden base; in Peranakan houses, these were elaborately carved. The only other equipment in the kitchen were shelves, a safe, or, in better-off houses, cabinets for bottles of sauce, urns for rice and such like.

In most Chinese houses, cooked food was put into earthenware pots and containers in the kitchen and carried to the table. The procedure in European families, however, was for the food to be carried from the kitchen on trays, already served. Covers were used to keep the food hot and these were removed just before it was taken into the dining-room. Such preparatory work was done on the veranda or in a small annex or at one end of a passage or, in the better-class houses, in a special servery or a pantry.

Few houses had both a servery and a pantry. Mr Mundell's house of 1934 (see right) was an exception in having a servery, a pantry and a scullery. Usually, a single room fulfilled several functions, whatever name it was given. As a pantry it was fitted with shelves for table linen, crockery, and silverware, and as a servery it had a table or a built-in bench. In bigger, wealthier households, it also performed some of the functions of a scullery in having a table, benches with wooden tops for chopping vegetables and a sink. With advances in domestic equipment in the 1930s, there might also have been an additional oven for reheating the food or keeping it warm while salads were being prepared and served.

In all such arrangements, the Straits Chinese followed suit, not only because of their enthusiasm for European fare; the preparation and serving of Malay and Chinese dishes was also facilitated by the inclusion of a servery inside the house, near the dining-room.

By the 1930s there were more tasks being performed inside the house than previously. This was partly due to the availability of more modern equipment such as ovens and refrigerators. It was also due to restrictions on the importation of female labour, which meant fewer servants and, despite the effects of the recession, higher wages to those still in employ.

It was necessary therefore to plan the kitchen area more economically. In many houses, particularly those of middle-income families, the kitchen, the servants' rooms and other

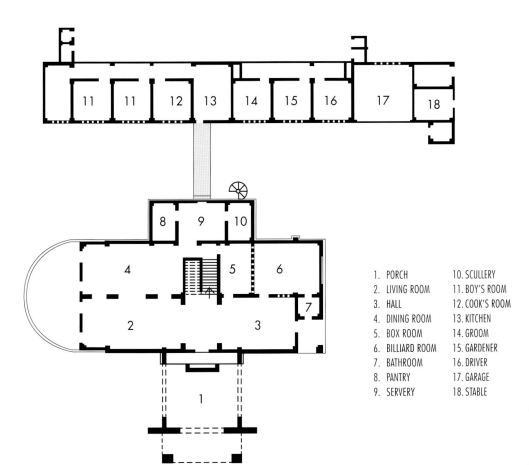

1. PORCH
2. LIVING ROOM
3. HALL
4. DINING ROOM
5. BOX ROOM
6. BILLIARD ROOM
7. BATHROOM
8. PANTRY
9. SERVERY
10. SCULLERY
11. BOY'S ROOM
12. COOK'S ROOM
13. KITCHEN
14. GROOM
15. GARDENER
16. DRIVER
17. GARAGE
18. STABLE

Ground-floor plan of the house for HD Mundel, Pierce Road, 1934. The servants' quarters were linked to the main house by a covered walkway.

service functions had become part of the main house, but in the form of a rear appendage, as in Victorian suburban houses. There was no longer the means to accommodate a separate arrangement of servants' rooms and kitchen but the semblance was maintained: all such functions were still set apart, behind the green baize door. As far as possible it was still felt desirable, as in the 18th-century English country houses, to have two right-angled bends and at least one intermediate space such as a servery or pantry between the kitchen and dining-room, even if the service functions were close by.

In England at this time, servants were even harder to obtain than in Singapore. One result of this was the streamlined compact kitchen, operated by the housewife herself and conveniently located next to the breakfast, morning-room or dining-room, within the house proper. This development did not go unnoticed in Singapore and more and more houses began to incorporate the kitchen attached to the back of the house in an extension, or in the house itself. As in England, these were usually planned, laboratory-like, in the form of a U-or L-shape with fixtures such as the sink, stove and refrigerator built in. But unlike England, these were the exception rather than the rule. The majority of houses still continued to have their outhouses, even if they were now in a much closer relationship with the main house. This general trend to compactness was due also to the fact that allotment sizes were smaller with the general relative rise in land prices. The effect of these developments would be evident in changes in the form and style of the house as a whole. ❖

Materials and Methods

Early Timber Buildings

Quick decisions were needed to get the materials and men with sufficient skills to put up the first buildings when Raffles landed in 1819. The dwellings occupied by the indigenous Malays were primitive timber frame structures raised on stilts. Their floors and walls were covered in plaited bamboo and they were roofed with atap or woven palm leaf. Such buildings seemed unsuitable to the requirements of the European settlers. The natural inclination for them was to build the type of house with which they had been familiar in Europe and colonial India. In due course, the Europeans would adopt some of the principles of the Malay dwelling, such as its elevation above ground in order to catch the breeze, provide extra space, and to avoid floods, rising damp and termites. For the present, at least, the materials of which these dwellings were made was at hand in the surrounding jungle, as was the native manpower to extract it. This could be put to use while more durable materials were being sent for.

By February, barely two months after landing, a cargo of bricks had been brought by Raffles from Penang. This was followed three months later by the arrival of '5000 planks, 5000 flooring tiles and a great quantity of nails for building'.[1]

Timber, machine-sawn and put together using up-to-date Western methods and not native ones, was necessary for floors and ceilings and roofs if they were to be pitched. It would also have to do for walls, pending the arrival of bricks in sufficient quantity and the tradesmen to lay them.

Meanwhile, Chinese carpenters could be brought in from Penang and Malacca. These men were well able to do what was required of them because of their experience in helping to put up most of the buildings there for the colonial administration. Carpentry, in any case, had been a highly developed traditional skill in mainland China. Such skill was reflected in the range of specialized tools that these carpenters brought with them.

When Raffles arrived in Singapore, the only dwellings were kampong-style homes built from timber. This one in Kampong Amber is—unusually—not elevated on stilts.

1 H F Pearson, *Singapore, A Popular History*, Singapore, 1961, pages 15–16

Having the necessary skills and being quick workers, these men were paid a salary well in excess of Malay or Indian carpenters. The speed with which jobs were finished, however, often resulted in carelessness and a good supervisor was therefore necessary.

Most of the buildings put up during these first few years were of timber. These included the residence for Major William Farquhar and that for John Crawfurd, the Police Station and the Master Attendant's house. Unlike the indigenous atap huts, they were set on the ground in the European manner, their floors paved with Malaccan floor tiles brought in by Raffles in 1819.

Timber buildings would suffice for a time, but brick buildings were more appropriate to the nature of a permanent settlement. Further supplies of bricks could be obtained from Malacca and Chinese bricklayers brought in from Penang. Most of the buildings put up in Penang by the British had been built by Chinese bricklayers.

The use of brick, of course, was not entirely a British innovation. Bricks had been made and used by the Chinese from very early times. Ordinary houses, though, were traditionally in timber. In Malacca, although the Chinese lived in timber houses from the 15th to the 18th centuries, they had developed expertise in making bricks for the Portuguese and, especially, for the Dutch. They used simple techniques such as the burning of straw to fire the clay which was readily available in the surrounding area. From the clay they also made half-round roof tiles which were used as much on timber buildings as on brick ones as protection against fire.

Brick had also been a traditional material in England since times past. For the new British settlers in Penang, the motivation to build in brick, as in Singapore, was given additional impetus by the desire to build in the Palladian style as in Georgian England and in modified form, in colonial India. In England, the buildings of John Nash at Regent's Park and much of Regency London were in white stucco over brick, in imitation of the earlier Georgian stone buildings of Bath; so, too, in Bengali India, where all of the European buildings were in brick and mortar and covered in white or yellow ochre stucco.

An old postcard showing the General Post Office building designed by Major McCallum and completed in 1883. It was one of the early buildings in the settlement that used Madras chunam *as an exterior coating. In 1923 the building was demolished and the Fullerton Building was constructed in its place.*

Singapore. General Post Office.

In Singapore, the house built by G D Coleman for John Maxwell in 1827 was also of this character. It was the first substantial brick residence and set the scene for the architectural character of the European settlement in the years to follow.

To build in brick and stucco, it was necessary to have lime and sand: for the stucco itself, for the mortar, and for the concrete foundations to support the walls. Although lime could be shipped from Penang, where it had been manufactured since 1878, it could also be made locally. The need for lime had been anticipated in the establishment of lime kilns at the foot of Telok Ayer Street, using materials obtained from nearby coral atolls and reefs. White sand was readily available on the island.

An alternative to the use of lime to make plaster stucco for both external and internal walls was Madras *chunam*. A product of colonial India, this consisted of lime from burnt shells, egg-white, milk, hair and other ingredients. It was extremely hard-wearing, dazzling white in appearance, and marble-like in its surface quality when polished with a rounded soapstone, as was the custom. It was used also to produce the two-tone effect of yellow-ochre walls and white trimmings in the Georgian manner.

Polishing Madras *chunam* surfaces was a labour-intensive and painstaking process and for this purpose, Indian Tamil convicts were employed. Convicts were brought in for a variety of other tasks involved in building. One of these was the making of bricks at the government kilns set up in the Serangoon Road area in the 1830s. Later, convicts were trained to make bricks of special shapes as a base for the formation of mouldings, capitals and architraves in plaster as part of the Palladian vocabulary. The execution of such plasterwork by convicts was assisted by the fabrication on the ground of wooden models of classical profiles which were then copied, all under the watchful eye of the Superintendent of Convicts.

Like Madras *chunam*, the custom in colonial India of using flat roofs concealed by balustrades in the Georgian mode was repeated in a number of residences put up in the 1830s and 1840s. In India, the 'Madras Flat-top' or *Pukka*-style had become part of the colonial residential vernacular of Bangalore and was well established in the form of the Madras Garden House.

However, flat roofs were not as suitable to the climate of Singapore as to that of the drier Indian interior. They were less likely to remain waterproof in wet tropical conditions and indeed it is surprising that flat roofs were as prevalent as they were in coastal Madras and Calcutta which was described as a 'damp hollow'. Like the traditional Chinese farmer's hat, the widely overhanging pitched roof gave better protection from rain and sun, and from heat, by virtue of the airspace beneath it.

For this reason, a number of houses built with flat roofs were completely re-roofed during the 1830s and 1840s. The roof of the house Coleman built for himself in 1827, which was originally partly flat and included a flat-topped three-storey tower, was completely changed some time during the 1840s into a broad, two-tiered pitched roof with wide overhangs. This was but one of a number of changes to the original Coleman house in response to the tropical climate. Deep verandas were built on and Venetian shutters added to the window openings. Similar changes were made at the same time to several of Coleman's houses nearby, including that of William Montgomerie, the Colonial Surgeon.

In houses bakau *wood piles were used in the early days. These were replaced by masonry piers as seen in this still extant home in Alexandra Park.*

Pitched roofs were not only sensible climatically but also more simple to construct and cheaper. Flat roofs, as in India and Penang, had been excessive in their use of timber. They consisted of very large, closely spaced timber beams, usually of teak imported from Burma, covered in an elaborate arrangement of terracotta tiles on edge, set in lime screed in several layers.

The pitched roof, on the other hand, relied as much on its form as on the size of its members for its strength and was more familiar to the Chinese and other native workmen and therefore easier for them to erect. Clay half-round Chinese tiles were easily laid and readily obtainable from Malacca or Penang. If the shape of the Chinese tile was not completely efficient in keeping out the water, this could be taken care of by overlapping the tiles several times. Although this meant slightly heavier timbers to support the extra load, it provided better insulation against heat.

Protection against heat was also provided by brick walls. Interiors were made even more comfortable by swinging *punkah* fans, high ceilings, deep shaded verandas, wide openings and external rattan 'chicks' or blinds.

With the spreading of the settlement inland after the 1840s, most of the houses built on outlying hilltops were of this character. Many of them, however, eschewed the Palladian trimmings of the earlier buildings. They tended to be more straightforward in appearance in keeping with their function as plantation houses. There was more use of timber to form open verandas. Many houses, being sited on undulating land, were now built on sturdy brick piers with the main floor raised above the ground in the Malay manner.

From the 1860s, the methods used to build houses were partly affected by technical advances encouraged by the need for public buildings such as the Tan Tock Seng Hospital, St Joseph's Institution and the Anglican Cathedral. The gradual introduction of Portland cement meant stronger foundations and its use in combination with iron bars and girders meant that brickwork could be supported over wider openings. 'Portland cement' was a name initially used to refer to a particular brand of hydraulic lime invented in England in 1824 and used as stucco to simulate Portland stone. The product was first used in Singapore in J T Thomson's Horsburgh Lighthouse of 1848–51, which also made use of imported iron bars.

It was not until the 1880s and 1890s, however, that Portland cement and structural ironwork were used to any extent in house-building by foreign architects and engineers. A number of houses built by Swan & Lermit in the 1880s had Portland cement specified for them and De Souza & Son used iron girders in the form of tram rails in combination with concrete made of Portland cement as a flat roof and terrace over the dining-room of the Pragure House of 1894.

Problems encountered with the foundations of certain public buildings led in the 1880s to municipal requirements for piling and this had its effect on the way houses were constructed. In large buildings, reinforced concrete piles were soon to come into use, but for houses, piles made of *bakau* wood were common. The usual practice was to have a cluster of piles at regular intervals, each supporting a masonry pier usually of bricks, occasionally of granite, and increasingly of concrete. These piers were set on timber bearers or concrete pads on top of the piles and in turn supported timber beams, usually of teak, to hold up the walls, whether of bricks or timber, or as part of the floor construction.

The capacity of the piles to do this depended upon the friction exerted on the ground into which they were driven, and for this reason they had to be 20 feet or more in length. In theory, their length, size and spacing should have been a matter of calculation according to the load being supported and the capacity of the soil to hold them in place, but in practice it was a matter of rule-and-thumb and guesswork, according to a prominent engineer of the day.

The mid 19th-century Horsburgh Lighthouse, which marked the eastern entrance to the Singapore Strait, was one of the first buildings in the settlement to use Portland cement.

Early plantation house built on brick piers, thereby elevated above the ground, to facilitate ventilation and prevent ingress of water.

The attention given to foundations was part of a general trend from the 1880s toward higher standards of construction through municipal control and as a result of the increased availability of qualified engineers and architects. Although this applied more to public and commercial buildings than residential ones, many of the houses designed for the European companies, managers and civil servants by foreign firms were now of superior quality as a result of improved specifications and standards of supervision. The Municipality, for its part, began to demand, as a standard condition of every building approval, that 'all materials and workmanship … be of good quality'. This requirement applied as much to the more substantial brick residences of the well-to-do as to the more common, modest brick or timber bungalow.

Timber houses were almost always raised off the ground to keep them dry and well ventilated, but not, as the Malays had done, to keep animals and poultry under them. The Malay dwellings were built three or four feet above ground level but many houses were now fully raised and the space beneath put to use, even if only to accommodate an office, a store room or two or as a covered play area for the children. Houses built of timber were almost always clad, internally and externally, in vertical wooden planks, fixed to a timber frame and treated with preservative and stained or painted. Until 1920 there were as many timber bungalows as brick ones, but by 1939 there were only one-tenth the number.

Timber houses were displaced not only by brick ones but increasingly by those made of reinforced concrete. The vogue for modernism, which had found its way into England in the 1930s as a result of the work of avant-garde architects in Germany and elsewhere on the Continent, came also to Singapore through the pages of the latest architectural and building journals and as a result of trips to Europe by architects and their wealthy clients. The modern style was a language of white-painted, flat-roofed forms with large horizontal areas of glass set in fine steel frames. This appearance could be achieved by using brick or poured concrete walls and plastering and painting them. Floors and flat roofs were generally of reinforced concrete because this was seen as a modern material and because of its capacity to span larger distances than timber or even timber and steel together. This would allow a more spacious and freer arrangement of internal areas, which was also part of the modernist vocabulary.

Despite the claims of the modernists that theirs was a universal, functional style, the flat-roofed box did not function climatically, either in Europe or in Singapore. In Singapore, it provided no shielding against the penetration of heat and rain through its external walls. The flat roof was likely to leak, particularly in heavy downpours. It did not drain properly and water would penetrate through the joints of the tiles used to cover the slab, through the cement screed on which they were laid, and through the concrete itself. Like the walls, it also encouraged the penetration of heat by acting as a conductor and through the lack of an insulating airspace.

To compensate for this and other building deficiencies, a spate of new products came on to the market. These were designed to insulate, cover, preserve, protect or prevent deterioration due to sun, rain, wind, fire or termites. Other products came in competition with traditional ones. Advertisements in the *Malayan Architect* in the early 1930s included products such as:

Roofing	Ruberoid Roofing Malthoid Roofing Cement and other Roofing Tiles
Insulation	Insulating Boards Cork Insulation
Structural	Structural Steel Steel Reinforcement Concrete Mixers Reinforced Concrete Prefabricated Houses Concrete Tiles

EXTERIOR	
Finishes	Anti-corrosive Paint Wood Preservatives Waterproofing Materials
INTERIOR	
Finishes	Italian Marble Cork Tiling
Windows:	Steel Windows

Other advertisements reflected the technical changes that had progressively taken place in domestic buildings during the previous several decades. Air-conditioning systems were now available in the wake of mechanically ventilated ducts which had been introduced in the early 1920s. There were electric lighting fixtures of all shapes and sizes as a result of the displacement of gas by electricity beginning at the turn of the century.

New and modern sanitary fixtures reflected the value now placed on being as up-to-date in this area as the suburban *nouveau riche* in England. Changes in England towards more modern, efficient and compact kitchens were also mirrored in advertisements for the latest-model electric stoves, refrigerators, sinks and ancilliary fixtures.

The effect of these innovations in materials and products was to help change the pre-World War II house from being essentially conservative in form and style into something more radical. This was all part of a development which began in the early 1800s but would now have to wait for its fulfilment until World War II had run its course. ❖

Professionalism and Classicism

❧⸙❧

In the 60 years from the time of Raffles' landing to that of the rapid burgeoning of the economy and the beginning of suburbanization in the 1870s, the style of residential building had been relatively consistent, certainly by comparison with later developments. In the hands of G D Coleman and the anonymous amateur designers of the later plantation villas, the Palladian style of Georgian England and of colonial India had begun to be transformed into something which held the promise of being special, and appropriate, to Singapore's colonial lifestyle and climate.

However, this was not to last in the context of the rapid social and economic changes in the years to follow. The opportunity for a rising and increasingly multi-cultural middle class to follow in the wake of the colonial élite in occupying a detached house, however small, in the suburbs was matched by an increased awareness of foreign ideas and fashions. Accordingly, it would become progressively less clear as to whether there was a single style which could be described as uniquely Singaporean. Cultural cosmopolitanism was an inevitable trend as a part of Singapore's developing role in the international market-place. The implications of this for the form and appearance of the Singaporean house was also to a large extent tied up with the emergence and increasing influence of the professional architect.

In one sense, the first architects—and arguably the best-accomplished—were the native Malays and Chinese who, without formal training, had for generations been building the type of timber atap-roofed hut that Raffles saw when he landed in 1819. The appearance of these simple, vernacular buildings was the outcome of a direct and appropriate response to the native way of life, climate and available resources. The techniques used followed long-established practices based on knowledge handed down from generation to generation.

For these people, there was no artificial separation of the act of designing and building. The idea of aesthetics as something distinct from construction or use was part of the cultural revolution known as the Renaissance which had swept Europe from the 1400s. It had led to the emergence of the architect as an independent designer as distinct from his earlier role as chief builder. By the early years of the 19th century, it had led further to the establishment of architecture as a design profession. John Nash, quite capable of designing in the Palladian or any other style, was one of the first professional architects in Europe at the time of Raffles' landing. As a practising, professional architect, Nash had offices in London and Edinburgh. From this time, architectural firms began to proliferate in England and elsewhere in Europe.

In Singapore at this stage, there were none. Apart from the exceptional figure of Coleman and a few other early architects of official standing, it was not until the 1880s that the professional architect arrived on the scene. Up till then, most buildings were designed by anonymous builders and tradesmen and a handful of military and civil engineers, surveyors and draughtsmen. They were responsible for the succession of large country houses such as Killiney House, Whampoa's house, and those built at Telok Blangah and elsewhere in the 1830s. Other notable examples were Cairnhill House and the residences put up by Thomas Oxley on his plantation in the 1840s and 1850s. Although few of the draughtsmen who designed these buildings had had any formal training and relied instead on the availability of pattern books, a number of houses—such as that built in the Botanic Gardens and Panglima Prang, both of the 1860s—were of superior architectural quality.

Other, more architecturally substantial buildings of the time were the various official residences, but even their authorship is not known. Some claim has been made that the Istana Kampung Glam of 1845 may have been designed by Coleman although there is no proof of this. It is also not known whether J T Thomson, the Government Surveyor-turned-architect, had a hand in the design of the second Istana at Telok Blangah, although there is some suggestion that he did.

The situation was rather more clear in the case of the third Istana built as the official residence for Governor Sir Harry Ord in 1869, for Captain John McNair, the Executive Engineer and Superintendent of Convicts, was officially appointed as architect. Public buildings such as the new Government House were generally undertaken by official engineers

Istana Kampung Glam, built in 1845, is a combination of Palladian style and traditional Malay motifs. It was commissioned by Sultan Ali Iskandar Shah and may have been designed by Coleman.

Dating from 1925, the HongKong and Shanghai Banking Corporation building in Fullerton Square was designed by RAJ Bidwell of Swan & Maclaren.

such as Captain McNair before the establishment of the Public Works Department in 1873, and even then, engineers did most of the design work.

Thomson and Captain Charles Faber, for example, both did architectural work on the side. Officially, though, there were no architects before the 1860s. The 1846 edition of the *Straits Times Almanack, Calendar and Directory* listed only a few private draughtsmen. Few names appeared on the building plans of this period. Plans were mostly poorly drawn and specifications, if any, were scribbled in the margins.

The position began to change with the passing of the 1856 Act. Building plans were expected to be submitted to the Municipal Commission and those who drew them were required to have more expertise than before.

The first architect to receive formal mention was one William Edwards whose name appeared in the 1860 Directory. By 1866 there were three engineers and surveyors listed. During the next decade, the number of new buildings rose dramatically. The acceleration of building activity and the need for official control of the design of buildings of a public nature led to the establishment of the Public Works Department in 1873. The near collapse of several buildings gave additional impetus to the need for building regulations and professional expertise. Regulations governing drainage and waste were promulgated in the 1880s. A series of other ordinances based on the 1856 Act were introduced and more were to follow.

From this time on, the number of architects increased, as did the number of architectural firms. The first firm was that of Lermit & Annamalai, both in fact engineers, who came together in 1884. Lermit subsequently left Annamalai and joined Swan and this was to be the foundation of the most important architectural practice in Singapore for the next 20 to 30 years. The firm became known as Swan & Maclaren.

Swan and Maclaren were both surveyor–engineers. Maclaren had moved in with Swan in 1893. Lermit had left three years earlier to join forces with Westerhout; this firm would also be responsible for many buildings in the years to follow.

But it was Swan & Maclaren which went on to become the largest office in Singapore in the early 1900s and, in terms of the standard of architectural work, probably the best. Much of the credit for this was due to R A J Bidwell, who joined the firm in 1895 and became a partner in 1900. Seventy years earlier, Coleman, who came to the colony as a surveyor, became the first professional architect in the proper meaning of the word and Bidwell was the second.

Bidwell had worked for the London County Council and one or two private firms and was a member of the Architectural Association in London before joining the Public Works Department in Kuala Lumpur. As with Coleman, Bidwell's arrival in Singapore was fortunate because of the opportunity to apply his talent to the design of the many buildings needed at the time. Counted amongst his work were such important landmarks as the Raffles Hotel, the Teutonia Club, the Victoria Memorial Hall, the Chased-el-Synagogue and the HongKong and Shanghai Banking Corporation Building.

It was largely through these buildings, being the more monumental, permanent examples of their work, that Swan & Maclaren established their reputation. But the firm's residential work, much of which was also handled by Bidwell, was no less significant.

As a product of his time, Bidwell was able to design his houses in any style, although he was best known for his classical designs, using elements from the Palladian vocabulary in somewhat eclectic vein. An exception to this was Balaclava, which was rather more in the spirit of the earlier plantation villas and, as such, more rudimentary. At the same time, it was more Palladian than its spirited neighbour, Glencaird, with its tower and asymmetrical entrance, built at about the same time, which Bidwell also designed.

More classical was the mansion that he designed for the rich Jewish merchant, E S Manasseh, on Lady Hill in 1903. For this, he produced several versions before one was chosen. The design was more elaborate than most of his houses, featuring a characteristically Bidwellian arched rusticated base, but transformed into an open veranda. The use of rustications, keystoned arches, balustrades, a central segmental Baroque pediment and two-

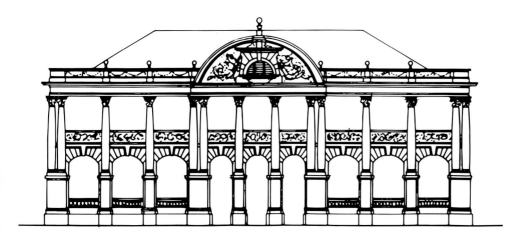

Elevation of a grand classical mansion that RAJ Bidwell designed for E S Manasseh on Lady Hill in 1903.

Elevation of a second house for E S Manasseh on Grange Road, 1907. Although not quite as palatial as the 1903 house, this one is nonetheless characteristic of Bidwell's oeuvre.

storey columns and pilasters reflected the client's wish for a house of monumental, almost public character. Indeed, all of these elements were to appear in the Victoria Memorial Hall that Bidwell designed two years later.

For all of its architectural trappings, the Manasseh house was of the same basic form as other houses by Bidwell. It was of two storeys, symmetrical, with a veranda on three sides with a projecting portico and a simple hipped roof culminating in a ventilated ridge. A more restrained, and as such architecturally more successful, interpretation of this mode was the type of house that he designed for the EEA & C Telegraph Company in 1908. This house, and others by Bidwell, reflect his excellent sense of proportion and scale. It was because of this and his use of simple rather than elaborate detailing that these houses were so successful.

Of similar character, though not quite of the same standard, were houses that in many ways were typical of the time, such as Spring Grove on Grange Road and the house built by Boey Chuan Poh, which later became known as the Sun Yat Sen house. Spring Grove, the latter of the two, was the more successful, being less architecturally fussy and having rather more of the straightforward character of the plantation villa. It is not known who designed these houses, but they are both still extant.

All the houses designed by Swan & Maclaren, at least until the war, were exclusively for the European top brass: senior civil servants and managers of the bigger private firms. Rich Jewish clients, including E S Manasseh, Manasseh Meyer, B N Elias, and N Reuben, figured prominently. Manasseh Meyer had built Joshua, a most palatial residence, in the 1890s at Katong in Renaissance guise. E S Manasseh commissioned Swan & Maclaren to do several houses. The first was a bungalow on Scotts Road in 1901. Then, in 1907, four years after Lady Hill, he had the firm design another substantial and handsome residence on Grange Road. All of these were of high architectural quality—even allowing for the ostentatious flavour of Lady Hill—and of the character of other houses known to be by Bidwell.

Bidwell must also have designed the first Mount Echo for the HongKong and Shanghai Banking Corporation with its characteristic 'nut and bolts' style, heavily rusticated ground floor columns, and its generally good proportions in plan and elevation. Less probably Bidwell was the 1904 house called Hartwell for Maclaren on Mount Alma: not because of its style—Bidwell would have been quite capable of the architecturally witty 80-foot-high tower over the main entrance hall—but because the house was for Bidwell's partner and presumably it was to Maclaren's own design, albeit with some advice from Bidwell, because Maclaren was by training and temperament an engineer.

The spate of residential and other commissions with which the firm was dealing in these early years necessitated many hands. In 1904 there were 23 on the staff, all Europeans. There was also a branch office in Penang. Inevitably the firm spawned a number of other architectural offices such as those of David Craik, at one time a partner of the firm, and Frank Brewer.

Already by 1897, Lermit, Swan's former partner, had gone into partnership with Westerhout. By then there were numerous other small firms which had formed and reformed. It was inevitable that in most cases these firms, not being of the same stature as Swan & Maclaren and lacking their confidence, would turn for guidance to published architectural ideas from abroad and to seek inspiration in particular in the fashions of Victorian and Edwardian England, thus introducing a new and more evident phase of architectural eclecticism. ❖

Junior Mess House for single employees of the HongKong and Shanghai Banking Corporation displays all the features of a Swan & Maclaren house in the tropics.

Eclecticism

❦

Lermit & Westerhout appears as one of the more prominent firms in these early years, partly because of its volume of work and size. There were two architects and five surveyors on a staff of 18 before the firm was dissolved in 1906. Change in the composition of firms was the order of the day; dozens of firms, mostly small, had come and gone by the time of the 1914–18 war. This was true both of firms whose background was European or in some other respect non-Chinese and those whose members were 'local'. 'Local' firms and personalities appeared to have fallen roughly into one camp and 'Western' ones into another, despite the myriad changes up to the 1920s and 1930s. The members of local firms came from the ranks of the Engineers' Department of the Public Works Department in many cases.

Like Swan & Maclaren, the firm of Lermit & Westerhout was also headed up by men whose background training was in surveying or engineering rather than in architecture, *per se*. Even so, the firm purported to refer to itself as 'Architects and Surveyors'.

Alfred William Lermit, an Englishman from Colchester, had practised in London on his own as a Fellow of the Surveyor's Institute before he came to Singapore in 1883. In joining Annamalai, a Tamil Catholic, he signalled a departure from the strict European enclave. However, four years later he had set up with Westerhout at 3 Raffles Place. One of Lermit & Westerhout's more important commissions, done in association with Swan & Maclaren, was the new Adelphi Hotel. Other projects of this scale were carried out by the firm in parallel with a steady volume of residential buildings.

The firm's work reached a peak in 1902 and this was part of a more general trend. Indeed, so voluminous was the amount of building activity in that year that the Municipality, whose function it was to check the plans and the building work on site, must have had a hard time doing justice to the task with its limited staff. Such checking as there was must necessarily have been perfunctory and the standard condition, 'all materials and workmanship to be of good quality' written on the plans, was intended to obviate the worst excesses.

Most of the houses designed by Lermit & Westerhout were built in the Tanglin area for prominent European and Eurasian clients. They were all architecturally competent, but not in the class of those by Swan & Maclaren. However, few firms could be expected to have the talent of a Bidwell on its staff and so these houses were representative of the general standard of residential work produced by the better-known firms of the time. Later houses done by Westerhout, after he separated from Lermit, were of a higher standard; clearly he was the designer in the partnership.

By now, with the gradual appearance of architects from abroad with some type of formal training, most commonly in the form of articleship to established practices in England, there was more than ever the intimation of an architectural self-consciousness in the work of most firms, in contrast to the more restrained mood of earlier years. The work of Lermit & Westerhout was no exception to this.

Their work, however, was less self-conscious, certainly less pretentious, than most. Most of the houses done by the firm were simple rectangular blocks with a single pyramidal roof, more often than not with a jack roof above and the usual projecting portico on two floors. Some were made more 'architectural' through the use of classical elements such as pilasters, columns and half-columns but with the addition of scalloped eaves fascia boards of more Eastern flavour and such idioms as Venetian fanlights and louvred windows. Such houses were not untypical of houses by other firms of the time.

In forming their verandas and window openings, Lermit & Westerhout had a preference for arches so that the encircling veranda of the 1903 house for T Sarkie—of Raffles Hotel fame—on Nassim Hill appeared as an arcade of semi-circular configuration on both floors. By contrast, the house for the distinguished Syed Mohammed Alsagoff of 1901 had no veranda at all, but instead featured symmetrically placed semi-circular windows of generous size and proportion. These were fitted out with elaborately worked timber shutters, panelling and fanlights of Venetian inspiration.

The Sarkie house and others done by the firm during the next few years began to reflect an increasing inclination towards a more eclectic approach, partly associated with the trend toward the picturesque which had already taken place in England half a century earlier. Like the Sarkie

The grand Adelphi Hotel (1926) was an early commission for Lermit & Westerhout.

ADELPHI HOTEL
SINGAPORE

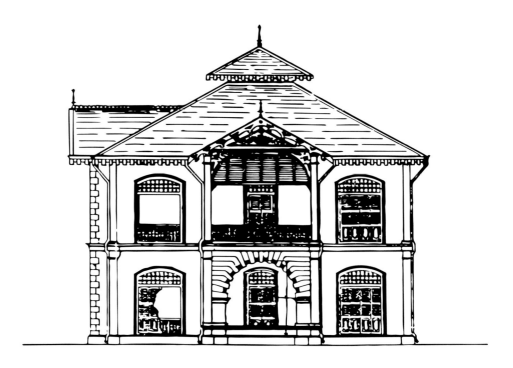

Top *Elevation of house for P Zimmer in Cluny Estate (1902).*

Right *Elevation of a house for G M Preston in the Tanglin area (1903).*

house, the Zimmer house of 1902 on Cluny Road (see top) and the seaside residence at Tanjong Katong of the same year, though still basically Palladian in form, were more decorated and more vertical in overall form and in their parts. Their porticoes were gable-ended rather than hipped and made more entertaining through the use of carved timber barge-boards and valances and suspended trellis work. The house on lower River Valley Road was of this character.

In much of this and in the use of roof finials and ornamental ridge tiles—as with the Preston house of 1903 (see above)—there was an affinity with the architectural treatment of the colonial bungalows of parts of India, such as Bangalore, of about a decade earlier.

Lermit & Westerhout's clients were mainly European, whereas those of an equally prominent firm, d'Almeida & Kassim, were mainly Malay and Chinese. George d'Almeida, CE, MSE, BSc, was a grandson of Sir Jose d'Almeida, a well-known Portuguese doctor and the owner of several large estates in the 1820s. The family into which George was born in 1871 was therefore well connected. The young d'Almeida attended the élite Raffles Institution where he won numerous prizes and scholarships and went on to train as an engineer with the Public Works Department. His first experience in practice was with the Tronoh Gold Mining Company in Kelantan.

Mohamad Kassim, for his part, came from the Malay nobility, from Kelantan. The Kelantan connection must therefore have come to d'Almeida through Kassim when they were working together as engineers with the Public Works Department. D'Almeida must have joined Kassim in 1894 or even earlier, because numerous plans had already been submitted for Municipal approval in that year. The stamp that they put on the plan for a proposed bungalow for Syed Abdullah al Manawar in 1894 identified the firm as 'Commission Agents, Architects and Government Licensed Surveyors'. Like other firms of the time, they were quite at liberty to call themselves 'architects' whether or not they had licensed architects from abroad on their staff, because legal control of this designation was not enforced until 1927.

Typical European home, built circa *1900.*

Although, like other firms, d'Almeida & Kassim were involved in the design of large, elaborate houses, bungalows such as the one they did for Syed Abdullah were modest affairs and representative of the bulk of the firm's residential work. For all of the firm's connections in high places, only a relatively small number of its Malay and Chinese clients were in a position to put up residences of the size and substance of those of the European establishment. As a result, many of the houses done by the firm were confined to peripheral areas in and around Serangoon Road and the areas of Toa Payoh and Kallang or in the predominantly Chinese area to the south of the town centre.

A good deal of this outlying area was swampy and it was because of this that many of the houses designed by d'Almeida & Kassim were raised off the ground, on brick piers. Although this characteristic was typical of many of the houses being put up in outlying suburban areas, it also reflected the firm's particular inclination toward the Malay style of building. Kassim was a Malay and so were most of the draughtsmen employed by the partnership. Much of the firm's detailing and decoration was Malay in character, although the use of carved timber fascia and barge-boards and suspended latticework formed in curved outlines could equally have come from Indian sources. Both sources in fact were influential: idioms such as these were in part a product of Malay–Indian connections.

Of more specifically Malay origin were the entrance steps leading on to the entrance porch or veranda of many of these houses. They were either in timber, with carved balustrading in the Malay manner, or of masonry (or possibly concrete), covered in brightly coloured tiles, the whole stair curved in plan from bottom to top in the tradition of Malaccan houses.

Houses such as that for Syed Abdullah or the one built for Hadjee Eusope at Padang Jiringau, Kallang, in 1897 were even more fundamentally Malay in that their planning arrangements were closer to that of the traditional Malay dwelling than to anything of European descent. There was the front *serambi* or open *rumah anjung*, the large central *rumah tengah* and the *rumah makan* or dining area, often interconnected, and the *dapur* or kitchen separated at the rear, or attached, but set at a slightly lower level. In other respects, these examples, however, did not conform to the Malay original. Their roofs, for example, were shallow, not steeply pitched; indeed the roof of Syed Abdullah's house was extraordinarily low, considering it was in tile rather than in atap.

More generally, the houses done by the firm were, like those of Lermit & Westerhout and others, of symmetrical form in plan and elevation with a projecting central porch, whether rectangular, pentagonal, or more rarely, as in India, single-storeyed with a balustraded flat roof. As a faint echo of the Palladian theme, the symmetrical porticoed form was typical of most houses of the period. This configuration applied also, at the other extreme, to the substantial residence, Adis Lodge, that they designed for a member of the d'Almeida family in 1899. This house was thoroughly Renaissance in flavour with its arcaded ground-floor and columned first-floor porticoes, rusticated piers, roof balustrading, and all of the *cinquecento* classical trimmings characteristic of that style. The firm's facility with the Renaissance could equally well be applied to the façade of a town house of traditional Chinese layout such as the one they did for Cheong Swee Whatt in 1896.

D'Almeida & Kassim's versatility was matched by that of Wee Tek Moh, another locally born, largely self-taught practitioner. Wee Tek Moh and Kassim were together in the Chief Engineer's office as draughtsmen and subsequently entered into partnership. This only lasted one year before Kassim left to join d'Almeida. Wee Tek Moh then started his own practice and became one of the most prolific architects of the period.

In general, these were years of intense building activity, notwithstanding a recession in 1908. But the level of skill involved in the design and construction of residential and, particularly, public and commercial buildings was often of a doubtful standard. Further ordinances were introduced as extensions to the 1856 Act to give the Municipality greater control. These measures, however, were only partly successful so long as there was no legal requirement for the registration of those responsible for preparing the plans and other documents necessary for building. It would be some time before there was sufficient agitation to enforce appropriate legislation.

In spite of this situation and in the absence of adequate architectural tutorship, a number of firms, such as that of Wee Tek Moh, were able to achieve a relatively high standard of professional performance. The house that Wee designed in 1906 for Mrs A B Leicester on Thomson Road (see below) was well executed and quite of the calibre of anything that Bidwell might have done. At a time when architectural fashions were becoming more flamboyant, the Leicester house showed that restraint, good proportions and careful detailing meant more than artistic licence.

This house and that on Geylang Road for Pakir Malden, though really unalike—the one being of substantial dimensions, two-storeyed and of brick, and the other a timber structure raised full floor above ground level on brick piers—were still in the tradition of formal symmetry in elevation and plan, despite the early trend toward the picturesque that was already evident in 1892 in houses such as Bwethow House on Mount Sophia. Bwethow House was emulated precisely in a house on the beachfront at Tanjong Pagar; both were symptomatic of the general trend toward romanticism. ❖

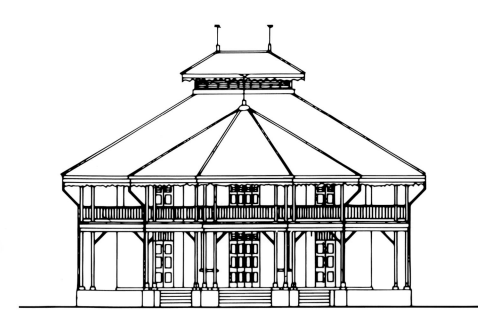

Elevation of house for Mrs A B Leicester, Thomson Road, 1906. It was designed by one of the early local architects, Wee Tek Moh.

Romanticism

⟨ꞏ⟩

There was considerable overlap of the classical style and the vogue for romanticism from the 1880s right up to the war. The two approaches were combined in the house built by the Tanjong Pagar Dock Company on Mount Sophia in 1891. There was the same marriage of styles in a second house on Mount Sophia, for the Singapore Land Company, in the following year. Both company houses were designed by the Crane brothers at the time that they were working with Lermit & Westerhout. All of these houses featured a juxtaposition of horizontal and vertical elements, the latter in the form of square towers with pyramidal roofs. In Bwethow House, a single such tower was used to celebrate the main staircase, just as Bidwell was to do, but using a cylindrical form, at Glencaird some five years later. In the Tanjong Pagar house, it was the four corner dressing-rooms, in the Anglo-Indian manner, each leading via a staircase to a bathroom beneath, that justified a square tower in each corner in Jacobean vein. If the original Jacobean had been a transition from the Gothic to the classical revival, the Jacobean references in the Tanjong Pagar house were symptomatic of the general change from the classical Palladian to the romantic revival style.

The Hill Street Central Fire Station building features bands of red brick interspersed with white stucco. It was completed in 1908 and also has a central watch tower.

These themes were brought together in Golden Bell, the house on Mount Faber that Wee Tek Moh designed in 1909. The fact that Golden Bell was the English translation of the name 'Kim Cheng', the father of Tan Boon Liat who built the house, probably only gave additional incentive to the desire to have a tower which could then be capped with a roof shaped like a bell. The gesture was even wittier in that the shape of the bell, even if it echoed the Jacobean, also made a vague reference to a Thai *stupa* and thus to the fact that Tan Kim Cheng was at one time the Governor of a southern province of Thailand, had extensive trade dealings with that country and, according to one of his descendants,[1] was responsible for the despatch of a young lady, Anna, subsequently of *The King and I* fame, to be a tutor of the King of Siam.

In Golden Bell, with its round tower, its pseudo-Renaissance portico, its application of white rustication or bands to exposed red brickwork—another Jacobean reference, as in the Central Fire Station building of the same year—and its stone quoins, Wee appeared to have done a complete about-face as far as the Leicester house was concerned. That work had shown commendable constraint. Golden Bell, by contrast, showed that Wee could be as eclectic as the best of his contemporaries. But it was eclecticism disciplined by a sense of the proper arrangement of parts and good proportions, as was the case with the house

Golden Bell, Mount Faber, built in 1909, is characteristic of the move towards a more romantic style at the turn of the century.

1 Dr Eu Jin Seow. However, in her book *The English Governess at the Siamese Court*, Mrs Anna Leonowens says that she was strongly recommended by Tan Kim Cheng, the Siamese Consul at Singapore, when the King of Siam had sent for 'an English lady to undertake the education of his children'.

Located on Mount Sophia, the flamboyant Eu Villa, the residence of Eu Tong Sen, was designed by Swan & Maclaren in 1913. It was a typical 'statement residence' for the Chinese nouveau riche.

that Wee designed on Emerald Hill Road for the Seow family at about the same time. The Seow house was of the same quality as the Leicester house. It was another essay in the Malay–Indian–Palladian theme using the vocabulary of Wee's predecessors such as Lermit & Westerhout: projecting lateral and front porticoes, a double pyramidal jack roof and, in the Malay mode, carved fascia boards and suspended eaves fretwork, carved timber window shutters and balustrading.

The control exercised by Wee in the manipulation of elements of diverse sources in Golden Bell was not present in Eu Villa, designed by Swan & Maclaren for Eu Tong Sen on Mount Sophia in 1913. For all of Swan & Maclaren's earlier mastery of the classical plantation villa mode and for all the promise that this held for the development of something unique and appropriate to the local climate and colonial lifestyle, it was inevitable that this firm, too, would succumb to current fashions.

The trend toward greater flamboyance was a belated version of late English Victorianism of some 30 years before. This style was also a convenient vehicle for the display of the fortunes amassed by the Chinese *nouveau riche*, who wanted to appear European, but at the same time were less conservative in their tastes than their British overlords.

Eu Villa, poised on the heights of Mount Sophia, was an extraordinary concoction. It was an assemblage, none too well organized, of a centrally placed tower capped with a cupola of late Renaissance inspiration, a rotunda with pointed roof of quasi-Elizabethan vintage, references to the Jacobean in a central three-storey bay complete with white stone pediment, and other diverse elements from the vocabulary of the classical revival. The house was no less of a mélange internally. There were expensive items of furniture especially supplied by the fashion houses of Paris and London, chandeliers and, in the words of the owner, 'fine examples of Florentine art' in the form of marble statues.

The acquisition of fortunes by men such as Eu Tong Sen was due to the substantial increase in the colony's trade and the boost given to this by the improvement of shipping and port facilities, despite the interruption caused by the war. The establishment of port authorities such as the Tanjong Pagar Dock Company and the Singapore Harbour Board gave rise to new buildings, including staff housing. For the Harbour Board, individual houses, designed by European architects, were built on the slopes of Mount Faber in a style which adapted the vogue for mock-Tudor—an offshoot of the Arts and Crafts Movement—then fashionable in the stockbroker belt of suburban London, to the basic plantation house form. Here, then, a few years after Eu Villa, was another, but much milder, essay in eclecticism by European architects but leading, in the manner of Bidwell, to the possibility of something much more uniquely Singaporean.

In general, though, the discernment necessary to the development of architectural forms appropriate to the local context was far less evident than the tendency to ape European, particularly English, fashions. A number of local architects had by now travelled abroad, but even if they had not, were aware of the latest trends as they appeared in the pages of various architectural and building journals. Local European practitioners, for their part, were now increasingly being trained in English schools such as the Architectural Association rather than merely as articled draughtsmen to English firms. But, in the main,

A house on Scotts Road, built circa *1920.*

Two views of a bungalow that illustrates the move toward the 'picturesque'. Built on a single floor, it nonetheless features a porte-cochère *and two six-sided turrets.*

this only served to make them more conservative and to reinforce the view of architectural design as being dependent on purely Western antecedents.

To appear European was, in any case, what the clients, many of whom were well-to-do and well-travelled Chinese, wanted. Chinese clients, at the same time, tended to choose local rather than European architects. Only two out of 93 of Chung & Wong's residential clients were European, judging from the plans submitted for Municipal approval during the period of their practice, 1920–40. Conversely, of the 20 residential clients who commissioned J M Jackson, a European, as architect during a similar period, eight were non-European: of these, four were Chinese.

The work of the Chung & Wong association in many ways epitomized the stylistic developments that were to take place during the 1920s and 1930s. In general, although large houses were still being built and the preference for the classical, either in its tropical Palladian or some more eclectic form, did not disappear, the tendency was now increasingly toward the picturesque, though mostly in the form of smaller suburban houses as the pressure for land, even well removed from the town centre, increased.

Many houses of picturesque character, however, did contain the ingredients of eclecticism and thus were of a different interpretation to that in England. There, the movement to a bungalow in the suburbs had been associated with a concern for simplicity, away from the ostentatious display of earlier years. It referred, too, to ideas about comfort and cosiness. Novelty, yes, but one's little country house, as Briggs[2] described it, should also be modest.

Such ideals were not what the magnate Aw Boon Haw had in mind when he commissioned Chung & Wong to design his house on Nassim Road in 1924. Though hardly as elaborate as Eu Villa, Aw Boon Haw clearly wanted to make an impression. For one thing, it is said that he wanted this house to look like the American White House, though if this were true, there must have been a change of heart. The only vestige of similarity with that building was in the central balustraded colonnade of Ionic columns; in every other respect, it was High Victorian rather than neo-classical Georgian.

Indeed, houses of the flamboyance of the late Victorian style, against which the adherents of the aesthetic movement in England were to react, was something with which the rich Chinese *towkays* were far more likely to identify than the modesty of the ordinary English bungalow. The Aw house, for one thing, illustrated the desire of the Victorians to make their buildings seem bigger and more important than they were. The result was a distortion of scale and of proportion. Aw's house did indeed look rather odd. With its axial juxtaposition of rotunda on one side and overblown rectangular bay on the other and its central colonnade, there appeared to be no unifying concept, nor was it possible to tell how big it was. Either the columns were miniscule or the Jacobean-style bay window was gigantic.

Nevertheless, this was all at least more fun than the sobriety of the Palladian villa and more in keeping with the ebullient personality of Aw Boon Haw and the spirit of self-confidence, almost bravado, that pervaded Chinese high society at this time of unusual economic prosperity. ❖

Elevation of a house for Chee Soon Keng, Tanglin Road, 1925. Exoticism is provided by the round turret at one corner.

2 R A Briggs, *Bungalows and Country Residences*, London, Batsford, 1891 (and later editions, 1894, 1895, 1901)

The Vernacular House

⊰⊹⊱

Not all of Chung & Wong's houses were of the character of the Aw Boon Haw house on Nassim Road. Like most firms of the time, the partnership was able to produce houses in any style and for clients of various dispositions. Lim Han Hoe was a doctor who sought something far more unassuming and was given a bungalow of the character of those appearing at the time in California and Australia. By now the crosscurrents of architectural fashion, as far as Singapore was concerned, were not confined to Europe and the Far East. Other houses by Chung & Wong, such as that for Dr S C Yin, were 'American Georgian' in character, as Aw Boon Haw had originally wanted.

However, the general trend was not to be in the stylistic excursions of a Dr Yin house or an Aw Boon Haw residence or in the exuberance of an architectural folly on Mount Sophia. In the end, it was to be the ordinary bungalow that was to be significant. This was not only because of the tendency for a greater number of smaller houses to be built by those on middle incomes. Despite the continuing fad for the exotic in houses large and small, the desire for the unpretentious and the vernacular that had begun in England with the Arts and Crafts Movement 40 years before was, after all, to find its way on to the drawing boards of an increasing number of architectural offices in Singapore.

At heart, the Arts and Crafts Movement had been a commitment to ordinary, non-architect-designed forms of building which, in Singapore, would have been the indigenous dwellings of

The Red House of William Morris and Philip Webb (1851), built to exemplify 'ordinary styles and materials'.

the Malay *kampongs* or the atap-roofed huts of the Chinese farmers. In England, it was at first exemplified in the now-famous Red House of William Morris and Philip Webb of 1851 which was a poke-in-the-nose for architectural élitism. This was a house for the ordinary man, using local materials—in this case, exposed red brick and shingles—built for its purpose without any self-conscious concern for stylistic precedents. Underlying this was an ideology which embraced Gothic truthfulness as it was imagined to be, and from this a belief in 'fitness as a basis for beauty'.

By the 1870s this had led, through Norman Shaw and others, to a highly original interpretation which happened to include elements of the so-called 17th-century Queen Anne style. This was characterized by Dutch gables, dominant tiled roofs, dormer windows, large areas of tile-hanging and of brickwork defined by dressings of white stonework, white-painted woodwork and small-paned windows. Because architecture was now seen as a craft, there was also an interest in the resolution of intricate details such as the joinery of bay windows, inglenooks and bracketed roofs over porches and all of the internal elements of the house, including the furniture.

The new mood was revealed in a variety of ways during the next several decades. One was the simulation of Tudor half-timbering, walls and carved barge-boards, and roof finials in gable ends. Gables of this kind became a cliché in the bungalow designs of the 1920s and 1930s in England, as they did in Singapore in houses such as that for Lim Han Hoe.

With the influence of the Arts and Crafts Movement came vernacular detailing in architecture in Singapore — as evidenced by this window and chimney.

'Tudorbethan' cottage style—with timbers painted black and the rendered surfaces white—was an inspiration for the Black-and-White houses of Singapore.

Tudor half-timbering became much more meaningful and original, however, in the Black-and-White houses of the Singapore Harbour Board and of the various estates designed and built by the Public Works Department for civil servants in Mount Pleasant, Malcolm Road and Seton Close in the 1920s. Other estates built for the British army, such as Ridley Park and Goodwood Hill, also consisted of Black-and-White houses. The design calibre of such houses was not merely in their visual novelty; it was in the skilful reinterpretation of the plantation villa as a form of building appropriate to the Singaporean environment.

This innovation, however, was to lead no further. Instead, the appearance of the Arts and Crafts Movement in Singapore was, if anything, a denial of the local context, certainly as far as the climate was concerned. The 1920s and 1930s saw a reversal of the sensible approach adopted in the 19th-century plantation villas and the later Black-and-White houses. Instead of high ceilings, broad verandas, wide roof overhangs and large shuttered openings—a logical response to the tropical climate—the trend was increasingly towards the character of the contemporary English bungalow which, coming as it did from the desire for cosiness and warmth, was compact and had small windows.

The trend toward compactness, of course, was not simply to do with fashion. Plot sizes were now on average smaller and, associated with this, the lifestyle of the average suburban dweller was well removed from that of the colonial élite with a retinue of servants and the time and space for private leisure.

Meanwhile, in England, the Arts and Crafts designers were beginning to move away from the more fussy character of the previous period with its Queen Anne details, to something much simpler. It was C F A Voysey, a significant exponent of the Arts and Crafts Movement but one of its more radical figures, who led the change. Voysey's houses of the 1890s were long and low, with plain white stuccoed walls and dominant barn-like roofs which swept low to the ground or formed a strong, horizontal eaves line over horizontal bands of small-paned windows.

Such houses were characterized also by massive sloping buttresses and dominant chimneys but it was mainly their ground-hugging horizontal forms, white walls and clean-cut character

In the 1930s, houses such as this one on Ewe Boon Road, took their stylistic influences from the English country cottage. They were less well adapted to the tropics than earlier plantation homes and the Black-and-White residences.

that suggested to later historians an early development toward the Modern Movement to follow. Voysey's work considerably influenced bungalow designs of the 1920s except that the windows of these houses were still holes in the wall rather than grouped horizontally and, as such, more part of the 19th-century picturesque tradition than of 20th-century modernism. Designs of this more picturesque kind were not popular in Singapore, but houses of stronger Voysey-esque character began to make their appearance by the 1930s.

Indeed, there was one architect in Singapore who was already influenced by Voysey's more radical approach. This was J M Jackson, whose practice coincided with that of Chung & Wong from about 1920 until World War II. Houses designed by Jackson, such as those for Alkaff & Company in 1921, Seah Eng Kwang and H A Hoeden, both in 1925, and T K S Dawood in 1932, were closer to Voysey than most of the English bungalow designs of the time. In the case of the two houses of 1925, there was the same dominant horizontal form in the broad, simple, overhanging hipped roof, the banding of the windows and the sharp definition of openings in plain white walls.

The only departure from Voysey was in the ventilated gable of the Seah house and the raising of the main floor of both houses above the ground, whether simply to achieve under-floor ventilation as in the local vernacular, or because the sites were subject to flooding, which was more likely in the case of the Seah house at Tanjong Katong than the Hoeden house, which was on higher ground on Barker Road. However, this elevation of the floor was handled, not as a series of piers or columns as was traditional, and as Jackson had been accustomed to do in his work on the Black-and-White houses with the Public Works Department, but as a series of horizontally proportioned openings integral with the body of the house.

Jackson's knowledge of and interest in the work of the avant-garde architects in Europe and elsewhere at the beginning of the 1920s—no doubt he knew of the work of Frank Lloyd Wright,

Elegant Black-and-White house built circa *1920 is well positioned to encourage cross flow of air on the first floor.*

which had some connection with that of Voysey but was far more radical—was part of an increase in the interchange of ideas and personal experiences of work abroad amongst architects in general.

Greater sophistication and maturity brought greater self-confidence and further concern for architectural standards, both in design and construction. Twenty years previously, Robert Pierce, the Singapore Municipal Engineer, had voiced concern about standards, referring in particular to the matter of inadequate supervision. However, it was 1926 before any action was taken. Three years prior to this, the Singapore Society of Architects had been formed. Its newly elected president, William Oman, also drew attention to the mass of building work being undertaken by 'tracers, draughtsmen, overseers, inspectors, land surveyors and brokers who were mainly uneducated and untrained, of every nationality and varying degrees of

J M Jackson, building in the inter-war years, was heavily influenced by CFA Voysey, as seen in these three elevations for (top) house for Seah Eng Kwang, Tanjong Katong, 1925; (middle) house for H A Hoeden, Barker Road, 1925; (below) house for Mr Wakeford, Swettenham Road, 1927.

Grand East Coast house built in the early 1930s.

incompetence'.[1] He also pointed to various malpractices by architects including the receipt of commissions or 'kick-backs', involvement in real estate speculations through the submission of plans for bogus clients, and the use of the architect's signature on plans without the necessary contractual obligations.

By 1926 sufficient lobbying had taken place by the newly formed society and, in particular, one Oscar Wilson, to push through the Architects' Ordinance, and in the following year, 1927, registration of architects commenced. The title of 'architect' was conferred on 31 Asian and 39 British and other European practitioners. Of the latter group, about half were members of the Royal Institute of British Architects (RIBA). It was a quarter of a century earlier that the first associate of the RIBA, D M Craik, had arrived in Singapore. In this sense, progress had been slow. On the other hand, the new ordinance, which gave protection to the title 'architect', governed standards of professional practice and established a legal scale of fees, was well in advance of similar moves in Britain.

Craik had been a partner with Swan & Maclaren between 1913 and 1928. The younger Jackson became a member of the firm in 1921, but prior to this, Jackson had designed several houses under his own name. In 1923 he left Swan & Maclaren, and in the next year, started his own practice, catering mainly to European clients.

Not all of his houses were as radical as those referred to earlier. His own house of 1928 was an interesting amalgam of ideas gleaned, it would seem, from the plans of Frank Lloyd Wright, the forms of Voysey and elements from the earlier Arts and Crafts Movement and the plantation villa, the latter undoubtedly reinforced in Jackson's mind by his experience in documenting the Black-and-White houses for the PWD. As in those houses, there were brick piers of Tuscan form supporting a timber superstructure at first-floor level, in this case an encircling veranda. There were also tiled roofed canopies on timber brackets in the Arts and Crafts manner as in Jackson's Wakeford house of 1927, although in that house they were used rather more consistently. The Wakeford house in other respects also relied for its effect more on the purity of its geometry than did Jackson's own house and, in this respect, was more symptomatic of future trends. ❖

1 *Journal of the Singapore Society of Architects*, 1924, pages 33–34

Towards Modernism

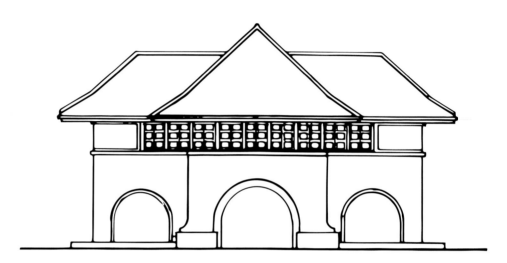

Elevation of house for T K S Dawood, 1932. Simplicity had become the name of the game.

By the late 1920s, there began to appear a number of houses, the aesthetic quality of which came from the simplicity of their form and the abstract relationship of solid surfaces and large, clean-cut openings rather than from applied ornament or decoration. This was true of the Wakeford house. The house for the National City Bank of New York of 1928 and the Dawood house of 1932 (see above), which were similar, were also of this character.

So, too, was Belmont House designed by Frank Brewer. Like Jackson, Brewer was instrumental in moving residential design away from the quaint and craftsmanlike version of the English vernacular into something closer to modernism. Brewer's role in bringing the Modern Movement to Singapore extended beyond the boundaries of residential work. Singapore's first high-rise building, the Cathay Building, a particularly fine essay in modernism, was designed by him. As a graduate of London University, Brewer was the first university-trained architect to practise in Singapore. He arrived in 1919 and began designing houses in the same year. In 1922, like other aspiring young European architects, he joined Swan & Maclaren and remained there as an architectural assistant for 10 years. He then joined H R Arbenz, but these being depression years or perhaps for other reasons, the partnership lasted just a year, and in 1933 he started his own practice.

Belmont House was characteristic of Brewer's work but the house at Number 1, Dalvey Estate was perhaps a better example. There is Voysey here in the buttresses, the bold form of the hipped roof, the strong horizontal lines of the eaves, and the grouping of windows as voids defined by the roof soffit and the clear-cut line of white stuccoed wall beneath. But the flavour of this is also partly Dutch, in the sense that the houses often favoured by Dutch colonial immigrants in Indonesia had broad roofs sweeping out at the eaves, stucco surfaces, battered walls and large arched openings outlined in patterned brickwork.

These and other characteristics—the occasional Flemish gable as a vertical feature or the way adjacent ground-floor arches were made to be interconnected through the use of continuous brick banding, or the fish-scale texture of the stucco work—clearly identified such houses as being the work of Brewer. Typical Arts and Crafts features, on the other hand, were not altogether absent, and indeed other houses by Brewer, such as that for the E E A & C Telegraph Company on Chatsworth Road, were much less radical with their smaller square window panes, Venetian fanlights and rectangular or small 'bull's-eye' windows. Even the Dalvey Estate house had its square-paned oriel and bay windows. After all, Brewer was a member of the English Art Workers' Guild.

With Arbenz, Brewer produced several houses, such as those for the Managers of the Tiger and Anchor Breweries and the house on Holland Hill. The strong hipped-roof theme

I Dalvey Estate, still extant, a masterpiece by Frank Brewer (1927).

in these houses would suggest the dominance of Brewer in the partnership except that houses such as the Wallace house, which Arbenz designed on his own in 1931, also had a roof of this type. The house at the Tiger Brewery featured Arts and Crafts details such as tiled canopies and casement windows with diagonal glazing bars, but overall it was of the uncomplicated character of Brewer's other houses.

Arbenz, who had an engineering background, was engaged to design the main buildings at the Anchor Brewery, which he did with consummate skill, producing some innovative structural forms in the process, but in his residential work he could be more of a romantic than Brewer. Thus, although he was capable of a Brewer-like house—for example, the one that he did for the Archipelago Brewery in 1931—he could also do something as picturesque as Chamonix on Grange Road or, for that matter, the Dutch Club or the Swiss Club, which were much more early Arts and Crafts with their gables and turrets and internal exposed timber beams.

Less romantic and more masculine in form were the houses built as part of the British military estates as Alexandra Park and Portsdown Road by the Public Works Department. Apart from the reference to the plantation villa formula of a raised ground floor on rectangular brick piers, and except for the vertical rectangular window openings, the 'stripped' appearance of these houses and their lack of personality was more symptomatic of future trends than the work of Brewer or Arbenz or even Jackson.

In houses by other architects, such as the Bailey residence of 1920 by Booty & Edwards, there was a merging of the reductive character of the Alexandra Park houses and the style of

Single-storey building on Orange Grove Road, (1928). It was the first Dutch School building in Singapore. It now stands within the grounds of the Shangri-La Hotel and is used for various events.

Brewer and Arbenz. Booty & Edwards, however, became better known rather for their 'Dutch-style cottages' which could have been straight out of one of the European design journals of the 1920s. These harked back to the picturesque phase of the Arts and Crafts Movement with their quaint imagery and asymmetrical massing but they were more simple, more economical than the earlier examples. The small-paned casement and bull's-eye windows were still there, but not much besides. A few of these houses featured half-timbering work and there were canopies over the windows but now these were just as likely to be in the form of thin reinforced concrete slabs as timber and tile. If this was a little too severe, there was a characteristically Booty & Edwards picturesque touch in the downward sweep of the roof over a decorated brick arch to the carport within the extended wall of the front elevation.

Houses like these often formed part of speculative housing estates such as the Bukit Tunggal Estate on Chancery Lane, which was designed and laid out by Booty & Edwards between 1930 and 1934. Speculative housing estates had been a significant component of suburbanization in England and had their origins in the 19th-century philanthropic 'model' villages of Copley and Saltaire and later, Port Sunlight. Such villages had individual houses of 'medieval' character, each with its own front garden arranged around a village green and a cluster of community buildings. The ideology which gave rise to this led, in due course, to the middle-class 'garden-city' new towns of Letchworth and Welwyn.

In Singapore, housing estates such as Bukit Tunggal and Tudor Close, with which the architect Ng Kheng Siang was involved, echoed these concepts though on a much smaller scale, usually consisting of no more than a few streets of houses.

The village imagery of Booty & Edwards' Dutch-style cottages may have been less appropriate to the Singaporean tropical climate than the quasi-Mediterranean character of Brewer's large houses, but the several houses that the firm designed in the style of the Modern Movement were hardly appropriate either.

By this time, the influence of this flat-roofed, sleek, glazed, white, box-like and geometrically abstract aesthetic was beginning to find its way into Singapore. Although the philosophical roots of this style lay in the same social and moralistic theories which gave birth to the English Arts and Crafts Movement, it was an essentially continental, German development which did not find a great response in England where, by the 1930s, the mood was conservative rather than avant-garde. None the less, English propagandists, like F R S Yorke who took up the cause of modernism in his book, *The Modern House*, began to stimulate some interest, as did the popular and professional journals, and as a result, modernist imagery became steadily more fashionable, along with the vogue for Art Deco.

For all of its functionalist rhetoric, the Modern Movement became in the end, however, just another style, even if the original premises remained important. The new aesthetic was seen to be universal, applicable to buildings of all kinds and to climates and cultures as dissimilar as those of England and Singapore. The result was the appearance in England of houses, albeit with an occasional leaking roof and stained exterior surface, by avant-garde architects such as Yorke or Maxwell Fry, cast in the same streamlined mould as that of Singapore's new Kallang Airport or the Chee Guan Chang house on Grange Road by Ho Kwong Yew.

The new aesthetic made references to modern ships and airliners and fast travel and the Bohemian lifestyle, metaphors put forward by two of its principal exponents, Le Corbusier and Walter Gropius. The Ho Kwong Yew Grange Road house and Kallang Airport (both built in the same year, 1938) had cantilevered ships' decks and railings, large areas of horizontally proportioned glazing in metal frames, curved glass surfaces analogous of ships' bridges or the control towers of modern airports, an overall sleek, streamlined appearance, and both were of white painted reinforced concrete. Brewer's Singapore Swimming Club of 1935 was also of this character.

Such imagery appeared also in the public housing project of Tiong Bahru, designed and built, under the supervision of European architects, by the Public Works Department, and of Everton Estate by the Singapore Harbour Board. Projects like Tiong Bahru were the result of efforts by the colonial government to remedy the rapidly deteriorating housing situation, reflected in slums of the worst kind. The application of the Modern Movement vocabulary to such housing projects appeared to have more legitimacy, in view of the movement's socialist origins, than to private houses for rich Chinese nabobs like Aw Boon Haw and Aw Boon Par.

The Kallang Airport terminal building (1937) is a wonderful example of the streamlined Modern Movement.

Nevertheless, such houses were bound to appear, and to appear the way they did, for precisely the same reasons as Aw Boon Haw had built his original eclectic-style villa on Nassim Road in 1926. The motive were still to signal position, status and worldliness; only the language was different. The fact that Aw Boon Haw could commission Chung

& Wong to design a second house in the modernist concrete-and-glass style immediately next door and only four years later, proved the point.

By the time of the second house, the modernist idiom had already become a stereotype. It was repeated right through the 1930s in houses such as the Chee house by Ho Kwong Yew, who was a former employee of Chung & Wong, and in those by Chan & Tan and Wong & Lee, the latter mainly for European clients in the Tanglin area and for Eurasian clients in the developing areas of Geylang and Tanjong Katong.

Less stereotyped was the house that Aw Boon Haw and Aw Boon Par (the 'Tiger Balm Kings') had Ho Kwong Yew design for them at Tiger Balm Gardens, which was much more of a personal interpretation of the style and more related to the expressionist approach of an Eric Mendellsohn, who was somewhat of a dissident as far as the mainstream modern theorists were concerned. This house, in any case, was plain good fun, with its concrete shell bubble dome roofs, its cylindrical forms and interior shell-like surfaces, concealed lighting effects and pseudo-classical treatment, all far removed from the intellectualism of the Modern Movement pioneers. It was also well removed from the many other manifestations of the Singapore pre-war house—the work of G D Coleman, the plantation villa, the numerous stylistic excursions from the late 1880s, or the Arts and Crafts experiments of the 1930s. This then was not a more mature phase of earlier developments, but something quite different, and as such, the last of a series of diverse episodes which together made up the complex story of the nature of the Singaporean house before World War II. ❖

Expressionist modern home for the 'Tiger Balm kings' in Pasir Panjang, 1930s. Designed by Ho Kwong Yew, it was unlike any residence built before.

Conclusion

The Singapore house before World War II has been seen as having its roots in the detached house in England, itself a fundamental part of the ideology of the 19th-century suburban movement, which was an important dimension of the culture of the middle classes. The suburban movement, in turn, was indebted to India by virtue of the origin of the detached house in the Indian bungalow. The connection with India was important in that as Singapore and India were both British colonies up until the late 1940s and early 1950s, there were similarities in the political and social circumstances which gave rise to the emergence of the detached house in both places. As in India, the pre-war house in Singapore was an essential ingredient of the process of colonization and thus, in the case of Singapore, the colony's role in the international–regional economy.

Despite the cosmopolitan character of Singapore, embracing as it did other European races and regional cultures—of which the mainland and Straits Chinese were the most predominant—the main influences on the Pre-World War II house were English. Social and political values, attitudes and ideas were extended from colonial India and, increasingly, directly from England to Singapore—and manifested in the lifestyle of the colonial suburb. This was given expression in the form of the detached house including its architectural style, the nature of the domestic interior, the shape and the arrangement of the compound, and the relationship of the house to the street.

Many of the values embodied in the culture of the British colonial community were embraced by the Asian *nouveau riche*, particularly the Chinese, who formed an increasingly substantial portion of those aspiring to a detached house and therefore of those constituting the emerging pre-war residential suburb. Although the private domestic life of the Chinese suburban family remained in many ways traditional—involving as it did fundamental attitudes to the meaning of the home and of the natural and supernatural world—in other respects, it became increasingly difficult to differentiate the Chinese suburban home or, for that matter, that owned by a Jewish or Indian family, from an English one. The emulation of certain English modes of behaviour in private and social life and of English architectural fashions was assisted by an acceleration in the dissemination of ideas from abroad through travel, publications and in other ways. Architecturally, this meant that styles currently fashionable in England were taken on board more immediately by the new colonial suburbanites, whatever their race, and by their architects and draughtsmen.

As in British colonial India, such styles began to be adapted to the conditions of colonial life and climate in Singapore. This was more evident in the earlier period in the work of the influential figure of pioneering architect G D Coleman, and more particularly in the later 19th-century plantation houses by amateur designers. In these buildings, it appeared for a time that a unique style was evolving in Singapore, in part thanks to the lessons learnt from Malay vernacular ways of building. Something special also appeared in the form of the late 19th-century colonial mansion in the hands of the best of the early professional architects. This was an exception to the less innovative work of the architectural profession in general which paid little heed to the indigenous forms of building of the Chinese and Malays. However, the work of the largely English-trained government architects was more original, including as it did the Black-and-White house, which was an appropriate response to the Singaporean climate, context and way of life. But the overwhelming trend on the part of the non-Europeans and, ultimately, the English themselves was, rather, to copy English and other European architectural models and movements.

The resulting lack of differentiation between houses built by the wealthier Europeans, Chinese, Malays, Indians and Jews, and those of suburban England, however, belied differences in social life in private and in public. Indeed, one of the significant aspects of the pre-war house in Singapore was the co-existence of Western, mainly English, styles and layouts with certain culturally unique social and domestic customs, including the segregation of men and women and the value placed on ancestor worship. Such customs did not necessarily diminish with time. On the surface, in form, there was an apparent unqualified deference to Western, particularly English, ways. Beneath the surface, in values, customs and behaviour, tradition often prevailed and the change was not necessarily so profound.

In the light of the myriad cultural differences and developments from 1819 to 1939, the nature of the Singaporean house cannot be summarized simply. If anything, its essential character, its very identity, lay in the possibility of co-existence between the form and behaviour, the amalgam of ideas, values and mores of English and Asiatic culture, the reality that the nature of cosmopolitan Singapore, though of the East, would continue to be significantly oriented towards the West. ❖

Glossary

Adamesque English architecture of the mid- to late-18th century of the style of the brothers Adam, who designed on a grand scale and are well known for their decorative work in chimney pieces, ceilings and furniture.

Aesthetic Relating to things perceptible through the senses; of or pertaining to the appreciation or criticism of the beautiful.

Air kamcheng Malayan term for earthenware water vessel or pot.

Amah Originally from the Anglo-Indian and Portuguese word *ama*, meaning a wet-nurse.

Anglo-Indian Person of British birth, resident of India; also, of mixed English and Indian parentage, Eurasian.

Anglo-Indian architecture Colonial style of architecture adapting Palladian principles and used in India in the 17th and 18th centuries and in other parts of South East Asia in the late 19th and early 20th centuries; characterized by high ceilings, neo-Classical ornamentation, and white stucco on walls.

Arcade Series of arches supported on piers or columns.

Arch Curved structure of wedge-shaped blocks, over an opening, so arranged as to hold together when supported only from the sides.

Architrave Moulded frame around a door or window; also, the lowest division of the entablature, spanning between columns.

Art Deco Decorative style of design stimulated by the Paris Exposition Internationale des Arts Decoratifs et Industrielles Moderne, which was held in Paris in 1925. The style was widely used in the architecture of the 1930s.

Arts and Crafts Movement English aesthetic movement of the second half of the 19th century that represented the beginning of a new appreciation of the decorative arts throughout Europe in reaction to the low level to which the quality of design craftsmanship and public taste had sunk, in the wake of the Industrial Revolution. There later developed a controversy as to whether the Arts and Crafts doctrines were practical in the modern world. The progressives claimed that the movement was turning the clock back and was not practical in mass urban and industrial society. In the 1890s, approval of the Arts and Crafts Movement was widened and diffused; its ideas spread to other countries and became identified with growing international interest in design, specifically with the Art Nouveau.

Atap Woven palm leaves, commonly used as a roofing material in traditional Malay houses.

Baba Malay name given to the Chinese–Malay ethnic group living in the former Straits Settlements, unique in their language, clothing, and eating customs, with their origin dating from the mid-15th century; a male Straits-born Chinese.

Bakau Mangrove swamp. A generic name for mangroves.

Baluster Pillar or column supporting a handrail or coping, a series of which is called a balustrade.

Balustrade Row of balusters with rail or coping as ornamental parapet to terrace or balcony, etc.

Barge-board Timber member placed at the sides of rafters to conceal the ends and sides of gable roof timbers; often decorated with local motifs to give a building a cultural identity.

Battered Term used for the inclination of a wall which recedes from bottom to top.

Bauhaus School of design, building and craftsmanship founded by Walter Gropius in Weimar in 1919. It was transferred to Dessau in 1925 to a new building designed by Gropius and to Berlin in 1928, where it closed in 1933. As the most significant school of art of the 1920s, a major goal was to promote the collaboration of the artist, craftsman and architect in the design of the total physical environment.

Baweanese Indian Muslim.

Bay window A window or series of windows forming a bay or recess in a room and projecting outward from the wall in a rectangular, polygonal or curved form.

Bencoolen Area in Sumatra where Raffles was once Governor; the British exchanged it for Malacca from the Dutch.

Bengali Native or language of Bengal. Local term (incorrect) for all Sikhs.

'Black-and-white' *amah* Chinese female servant, usually from Guangdong province, who traditionally wore immaculate white jacket and black trousers. The 'black-and-white' *amah* held a senior place amongst the servants, a position reflected in the responsibility given to some 'black-and-white' *amahs* to take care of and tend to the needs of the children.

Black-and-White house Term used to describe some of the colonial houses of Singapore, mostly built in the 1920s and 1930s, designed by British architects and engineers. Although responding to the equatorial requirements, these houses also appealed to nostalgic inclinations in reflecting a Tudor style of architecture. Such Tudor buildings were originally made of 'wattle and daub', consisting of interwoven twigs plastered with clay or mud.

Boria Wandering minstrels.

Buddhism Religious system based on the assumption that suffering is inherent in life and that one can be liberated from it by mental and moral self-purification. It was founded by Buddha (Sakyamuni, Gautama or Siddhartha). Buddhism flourished in Northern India in the 5th century BC (Sakyamuni is regarded as only the latest of a series of Buddhas, which is to be continued indefinitely). Hinayana Buddhism stresses individualistic faith and simple iconography. Mahayana Buddhism started in the 2nd century AD from the teachings of Nagayana and stresses a complex understanding of the five aeons of time, the four levels of creation and the role of saints or Bodhisattvas.

Bugis Bugis or Buginese are an Indonesian people of the southern part of the Celebes Islands, now called Sulawesi.

Bungalow Single-storey house, lightly built, usually with a tiled or thatched roof and encircling veranda; the word is derived from the Hindi word *bangla*, meaning 'belonging to Bengal'. In Singapore, the term is used to describe almost any detached house irrespective of its height or form.

Campong See *Kampong.*

Cantilever Any part of a structure which projects beyond its supporting element.

Cantonese Derived from or associated with the Chinese city of Canton (Guangzhou) in South Kwangtung (Guangdong) province or the delta of the West River, hence also the language spoken by its inhabitants. Canton was the major southern port for the extensive trade between England and China from the 17th to the 19th centuries. The Cantonese are among the early migrants to Singapore and were traditionally goldsmiths.

Cantonment To 'canton' or 'cantoon' means to quarter soldiers; thus a cantonment is a place of lodging assigned to a section of a force when cantoned out.

Capital The top member of a column or pilaster.

Chapjiki Chinese betting game.

Cheki Chinese name for the game involving Chinese playing cards, 'chicky-cards' and the card themselves.

Chettiar *Thaipusam* The participants of the Chettiar, or Hindu caste of money-lenders from the Coromandel Coast of Southeast India, in the *Thaipusam* Festival. See *Thaipusam.*

Chick From the Hindi word *chik*, meaning a screen blind made of finely split bamboo laced with twine.

Chinese New Year The first day of the Lunar New Year, which is the most important in the whole of the Chinese festive calendar, in preparation for which all debts are paid, houses cleaned and sometimes redecorated, delicacies are bought (oranges and kumquats for good luck), and new clothes and shoes purchased. Filial piety is the order of the day, visits are made to relatives and friends, *angpow*—red packets or red envelopes containing money—are distributed, and there is much feasting, especially on the eve, the first day, and the last (fifteenth) day.

Chinese tiles See *Tongwa.*

Chingay Parade Annual procession staged by the waterfront. Long bamboo poles, 20–40 feet high, serve as tapering masts for huge triangular flags carried by Chinese amidst a cacophony of drums and gongs. Acrobatics and balancing acts are also performed.

Chunam From the Tamil word for lime, *chunnam*; a cement or plaster made of shell lime and sea sand, originating in Madras.

Cinquecento A 16th-century Italian art style characterized by a reversion to Classical forms.

Classic Literally, of the first rank or authority; the term used to describe the art of Hellenic Greece and Imperial Rome (*circa* 500 BC–395 AD) on which the Italian Renaissance (*circa* 1300–1500) movement and Neo-classical revivals were based; the five Orders of architecture are a characteristic feature.

Clerestory Upper section of a wall (especially in some church designs) with windows or openings above adjacent roofs, for light and/or ventilation; also called 'clear-storey'.

Colonial architecture Style of architecture transplanted to a colony from the governing country but which usually adapts the chosen style to suit the particular climatic conditions.

Colonnade Row of columns.

Column Vertical support usually consisting of a base, a circular shaft and a capital.

Compound In the Far East, an enclosure containing residences, business offices or other establishments of Europeans. In Africa, the term traditionally referred to a similar enclosure for native labourers. Generally, the term can refer to any enclosure, especially for prisoners of war, or to any cluster of houses, often owned by members of the same family.

Confucianism Doctrines or system of social interaction of Confucius or his followers which stress order and loyalty, personal virtue, justice, and devotion to family and the ancestral spirits; 'Confucius' is the Latinized form of K'ung Fu-tsze (Kong-zi), the Chinese scholar and teacher (551–479 BC) who advocated reform of Chinese society under the Chou (Zhou) Dynasty. 'K'ung' means 'Master' or 'Philosopher'.

Congkak Generic name for cowrie shells and, mainly in the case of the Malays, a game played with these shells. Also refers to the board used for playing this game.

Cornice Any crowning projection, but more usually referring to the uppermost portion of the entablature in Classic or Renaissance architecture.

Court Area open to the sky and mostly or entirely surrounded by buildings, walls, etc. Also a high interior space usually having a glass roof and surrounded by several storeys of galleries.

Courtyard A court open to the sky, especially one enclosed on four sides.

Cupola Spherical roof over a circular, square or polygonal space; it can be segmental, semi-circular or pointed, and it may be constructed on an elevated drum.

Datuk Anak-anak An idol or image of a senior person or a person of distinction, including that of a god or spirit.

Dapur A Malay kitchen; an oven; a brick kiln. The word is used as slang for 'pipe' or 'flue'.

Deepavali Hindu Festival of Lights denoting the return of Rama from exile; it takes place in November of each year, represents the victory of light over dark and good over evil, and is associated with many and varied legends. One legend relates to the defeat by Lord Krishna of a tyrant king who forbade the use of lights, hence light symbolizes freedom from tyranny or captivity. In Singapore, homes are brightly lit, new clothes worn, delicacies eaten, and shrines and altars decorated with flowers and fruit.

Detached Separated, unattached, standing apart, isolated; used to describe a free-standing house.

Dhobi From the Hindi *dhobi*, meaning a native washerman.

Dondang Sayang A lullaby or song expressing regret, pity, love or affectionate pining, especially associated with Malacca.

Doric order The first and simplest order of Greek architecture which was also used by the Romans in a simplified form and with a base.

Eaves Lower part of a roof which projects beyond the supporting structure.

Eclectic In architectural terms, a style derived from the borrowing of a selection of elements from other styles and motifs, usually diverse and often unrelated.

Edwardian Of the reign of King Edward VII of England (1901–10).

Elevation Literally, a drawing of a building made in projection on a vertical plane but now more commonly used to describe the vertical face of a building itself.

Entablature Upper part of an order of architecture which consists of an architrave, frieze and cornice, supported by a colonnade.

Entrepôt French for a commercial centre or place to which goods are brought for temporary deposit or distribution.

Eurasian Person of mixed European and Asian blood. In Singapore, the Europeans were: first, the Portuguese, then the Dutch, and then the British; the Asians were predominantly Malays.

Façade Face or elevation of a building, usually referring to the front elevation which contains the main entrance and faces on to a courtyard or thoroughfare.

Fanlight Semi-circular window with sash bars arranged like the ribs of a fan.

Fantan A game of chance, popular amongst the Straits Chinese, involving numbers and dice.

Fascia A flat horizontal member of an order or building having the forms of a flat band or broad fillet. It is also the term used to refer to a horizontal board at the edge of the eaves, often carved and painted symbolically.

Festival of the Nine Emperor Gods On the ninth day of the ninth lunar month, the nine Emperor gods, who are believed by the Chinese to cure ailments and bring luck, wealth, and longevity, are worshipped. In Singapore, *wayang* and processions are held and, at night, devotees, carrying yellow flags and images of the gods, parade to the accompaniment of cymbals and drums.

Finial Ornament placed upon the apex of a roof, spire, pediment or at each corner of a tower.

Fret, fretwork In Classical and Renaissance architecture, this term referred to an ornament consisting of straight lines intersecting at right angles and of various patterns, but now it also refers to timber work which has been decorated by cutting patterns with a fretsaw.

Feng shui Literally 'wind and water', this is a system of geomancy employed in China and elsewhere to bring practice into harmony with natural forces (as in the determining of the site or orientation of a city, grave or house). It also refers to the good and bad luck of individuals, families and communities resulting from advantageous siting in harmony with the cosmic elements.

Gable Triangular or shaped portion of an end wall enclosed by the sloping lines of a roof. In Classic architecture, it is called a pediment.

Gambier Astringent resinous extract prepared from the leaves and young shoots of the *Uncaria gambir* tree and used largely in medicine and for tanning and dyeing. Together with betel-nut, tobacco and limestone, it is used in *paan* by the Indians.

Georgian style A term applied to English late Renaissance architecture of the period 1702–1830.

Gharry Derived from the Hindi word *gari*, and used to describe a horse-drawn cart, often resembling a bathing machine.

Glam, *Gelam* Properly named *Melaleucaleuca dendron*, this tree is a native of Malaya and Australia. It has spirally arranged, narrow leaves and white flowers, and grows to a height of 20 metres.

Gothic Revival Movement which originated in the late 18th century and reached its peak in the early 19th century with the intention of reviving the forms, if not the spirit, of Gothic architecture.

Gothic style Style of pointed medieval architecture which developed in Western Europe between the 13th and 15th centuries and was succeeded by the Classic forms of the Renaissance.

Gropius, Walter (1883–1969) Gropius of Germany was one of the main founders of the International Modern Style usually associated with functional designs using glass curtain walling, unrelieved cubic blocks and corners left free of visible supports. He re-established the School of Arts and Crafts at Weimar in 1919, renaming it the Bauhaus, and became a proponent of the intelligent application of standardization and prefabrication. Above all, he regarded teamwork as essential to the design of the total physical environment.

Gutta-percha Corruption of the Malay word *getah perca*: getah means 'gum' and *perca* refers to the tree yielding the juice, especially the *Isonanda gutta* or *Dichopsia gutta*. *Gutta* is Latin for 'drop'.

Hainanese Native inhabitant or the language of the Chinese island of Hainan, off the coast of southern Guangdong.

Half-timbered Structure formed with timber posts, rails and struts, the walls of which are filled in with plaster, wattle and daub, or masonry such as brickwork.

Hari Raya Puasa In Malay, *hari* means 'day', *raya* means 'festive, big or great', and *puasa* means 'a fast', hence a day of celebration for Muslims at the end of Ramadan, the fasting month. It always falls on the sighting of the new moon of Syawal. It is the day when, dressed in new clothes, Muslims offer prayers at mosques and spend the rest of the day visiting friends and relatives and feasting.

Hawker Man who goes from place to place selling his wares and usually crying them in the street.

Hindu Aryan of Hindustan in northern India who retains the native religion of Hinduism; hence anyone who professes that religion, which is a development of Brahmanism.

Hipped roof Roof which slopes upwards from all four sides of a building.

Hokkien Chinese group originally from Fukien (Fujian) province in China. Many inhabitants of Taiwan are also Hokkien.

Hungry Ghosts' Festival The origin of this festival begins with Ti Kuan, who surveys the human world to record the merit and demerit of each person. Subsequently, all Taoist saints are assembled in the Taoist Palace to inspect records of men and the registers of hungry ghosts and prisoners in Purgatory. A grand offering of vegetarian food, flowers and fruits must be made to these saints while the 'Canon of Lao Tzu' and the 'Chapter on Souls' are chanted and recited. Only then would the hungry ghosts and prisoners in Purgatory be fully fed and permitted to return to the human world. The event is celebrated with zeal and pomp during the seventh lunar month by the fishing fraternity and traders of marine products and other goods; these goods are displayed in all market places and the Chinese *wayang* and puppet show are performed.

Ikan parang In Malay, a sea-fish.

Inglenook Chimney corner. From 'ingle' (or fire burning on the hearth) and 'nook' (a secluded or obscure corner).

International style Style of architecture created in Western Europe and the USA during the early 20th century, devoid of local, regional or national characteristics, based on so-called functional responses. The style is often asymmetrical with large windows and cubist façades, and is applied throughout the world irrespective of nationality.

Ionic order Second order of Ionian Greek architecture with slender columns and having a capital made up of volutes (spiral scrolls) and a simplified entablature.

Istana Malay for 'palace'.

Jack roof Gabled or pyramidical roof separated from the main roof by a clerestory opening.

Jacobean style Style of architecture and furniture named after King James I of England (1603–25), prevalent during the early 17th century. The style was an adaptation of the Elizabethan style to continental Renaissance influences.

Jaga Malay for 'guard' or 'watch', hence *penjaga* means 'watchman'. *Jaga* is the shortened version.

Jawi Peranakan 'Mixed' class of people born as the result of a union between an Indian Muslim man and a Malay woman.

Jinricksha A Japanese word (*jin* means 'man', *riki* means 'power', and *sha* means 'vehicle'; a light two-wheeled hooded vehicle drawn by one or more persons. The word is now shortened to *ricksha* or 'rickshaw'.

Joist One of the beams supporting a floor or ceiling and supported in turn by a larger beam.

Kampong Malay settlement or village, the new Malay spelling of which is *kampung*.

Kati A Malay unit of weight, equivalent to 1 and one third pounds.

Kebun Malay for garden and an abbreviation (from *tukang kebun*) for a gardener.

Keroncong A form of plaintive Malay song. Also refers to a large tinkling anklet; a rough bell or clapper, eg for bullocks.

Kerusi sandar A Malay reclining armchair.

Keystone Central stone of an arch or a ribbed vault which counterbalances the thrust of the sides; it is often sculptured. See Arch.

Le Corbusier, Charles-Edouard Jeanneret (1887–1965) As well as being a well-known abstract painter from Switzerland, Le Corbusier was one of the most influential of all early 20th-century architects. His early works (glass and concrete) were seen as rational ('A house is a machine for living in'); later, he turned to an apparent anti-rational style of more sculptural forms. He invented a new, all-embracing system of proportioning and measurement (The Modular), related to the human body. His town-planning ideas—which included the substitution of tall buildings set in landscaped public parks for the compact city of closely packed low buildings—were very influential in urban developments in many countries before World War II.

Lorong Malay for lane or small street.

Louvre Mostly used in the plural to mean an arrangement of overlapping blades or slats.

Madras *chunam* A particular version of *chunam*, consisting of lime from burnt shells, egg-white, milk, hair and other ingredients.

Mahjong A game of Chinese origin, usually played by four persons with 144 domino-like pieces or tiles marked in suits, counters or dice, the object being to build a winning combination of pieces.

Maidan An open area or space in or near a town, often used as a market-place or parade ground.

Malacca Town on the west coast of the Malay Peninsula which is the capital of a state of the same name. The city was founded *circa* 1400 when Parameswara, ruler of Tumasik (now Singapore), fled from Javanese forces and found refuge at this site of a small fishing village. It developed into a prosperous trading centre under Malay, Portuguese, Dutch and British rule. The name is currently officially spelt as 'Melaka'.

Masonry Stonework, brickwork, or the trade of a mason.

Memsahib A term of respect for a married European woman, as used in colonial India.

Mendellsohn, Eric (1887–1953) A pioneer, through the use of glass, steel and concrete, of modern architecture in Germany. As a result of the Nazi occupation, he emigrated to England where he formed a partnership with Serge Chermayeff. The best-known work of this partnership was the De la Warr Pavilion at Bexhill-on-Sea. This building, with its streamlined curved forms and nautical references, was more 'form for form's sake' than the work of other Modern Movement architects and, like Mendellsohn's Einstein Tower at Potsdam of the early 1920s, became representative of the particular branch of modern architecture known as Expressionism.

Modern Movement Development in Western art and architecture from the end of the 19th century to its pinnacle in the 1920s and 1930s. It actually embraces a wide variety of movements, theories and attitudes whose modernity resides in a common tendency to repudiate past architecture. Le Corbusier, Mies van der Rohe and Walter Gropius were important figures in the general trend towards a radically unornamental, simplified approach to architectural design.

Mooncake Small, round pastry filled with a rich mixture of bean or lotus seed paste and mixed nuts and egg yolk. It is traditionally associated with the Chinese Mid-autumn Festival which is always held on the fifteenth day of the eighth moon of the lunar calendar. At night, children parade with brightly coloured paper lanterns and joss-sticks and candles are lighted.

Mortar Mixture of lime and water used to secure bricks or stones in a wall.

Muslim Describes one who adopts Islam. Derived from the Arabic word *aslama*.

Nanyang Literally meaning 'South Seas', this is the term by which South East Asia was commonly known.

Neo-Classicism Last phase of Classicism of the late 18th and early 19th centuries, characterized by a severe and restrained monumentality, a sparing use of ornament and a strict use of the orders of architecture. The style influenced Anglo-Indian architecture.

Nonya Malay for a girl of a Straits Chinese (ie Peranakan) family. The term is sometimes spelt as *Nyonya*.

Nutmeg Hard, aromatic seed obtained from the fruit of the *Myristica fragrans* or *Myristica officinalis*, indigenous to the East Indian Islands and used as a spice and in medicine. Mace is a spice made from the dried outer covering of the nutmeg.

Orang laut Laut is Malay for 'sea' and *orang* is Malay for 'person'. *Orang laut* are people who live on and off the sea.

Palanquin A passenger conveyance, formerly used in India and other countries of the Far East. Usually for the conveyance of one person, it consisted of a covered or box-like litter carried by means of poles resting on the shoulders of several men.

Palazzo Italian for 'palace' but now applied to an impressive structure.

Palladian Style of architecture strictly using Roman forms as set forth in the publications of Andrea Palladio (1518–80), the Italian architect from Vicenza; the main revival was in England under the influence of Lord Burlington in the 18th century. Palladio actually imitated ancient Roman architecture without regard to Classical principles.

Parapet Portion of a wall above the roof or roof gutter, sometimes battlemented or balustraded.

Pavilion In the context of this book, this means a detached structure used for special activities.

Pediment Term used in Classic architecture for the gable end of a building enclosed by the two sloping lines of a roof and supported by the entablature; pediments were often used above window and door openings in the Neo-Classical style.

Pekkway The gingko nut.

Penates Chinese household spirits, traditionally the subject of worship at home.

Peranakan Straits-born Chinese as distinct from China-born Chinese. It is a Malay word made up from *per* which is a prefix for 'to participate in the action of' and *anak* (child) or *anakan* (to be born); literally, a person who was born here or a person of this place.

Piazza An open square or public space in a city or town, especially in Italy. It can also refer to an arcade or covered walk or gallery, as around a public square or in front of a building.

Pier Mass of masonry as distinct from a column, from which an arch springs, in an arcade or bridge; also, a thickened section of a wall placed at intervals along its length to provide lateral support or to take concentrated vertical loads.

Pilaster Rectangular or semi-circular pier or pillar, engaged with a wall and often with a base and capital in the form of one of the orders of architecture.

Plinth The lowest square member of the base of a column; also, the projecting stepped or moulded base of any building element or the building itself.

Porte-cochère French for a gateway for carriages, usually leading into a courtyard.

Portico Colonnaded space forming an entrance or vestibule, with a roof supported on at least one side by columns.

Portland cement A type of hydraulic cement, usually made by burning a mixture of limestone and clay in a kiln. In colour it is rather like that of Portland Stone, a valuable limestone obtained from the Isle of Portland in Dorsetshire.

Pukka Anglo-Indian term meaning genuine, reliable or good; proper.

Punkah From the Hindi word for fan, *pankha*; a large swinging fan made of cloth stretched on a rectangular frame, suspended from the ceiling or rafters and worked by cord. The word came into use in 1807.

Punkah-wallah A servant whose duty it was to operate the *punkah* by means of a long cord.

Quoin A term generally applied to the corner-stones at the angles of buildings and hence to the angle itself.

Rafter A slanting beam of a roof.

Ramadan The ninth month of the Muslim calendar. A fasting month which occurs each year during which Muslims deprive themselves of all food and drink between the hours of sunrise and sunset. At the sighting of the new moon, the fast is broken by a festival, Hari Raya Puasa.

Regatta Originally a Venetian word for boat races held on the grand canal; now a boat or yacht race or an organized series of such races forming a sporting and social event.

Regency style Style of furniture and architecture prevalent during the Regency (1811–1820) of George, Prince of Wales (later George IV) of Great Britain.

Renaissance French word applied to the 'rebirth' of classic architecture all over Europe in the 15th and 16th centuries; characterized by the use of the Greek Doric, Ionic and Corinthian orders, Tuscan and Roman styles, and the use of the round arch, dome and vault.

Rickshaw See *Jinrikisha*.

Ridge Horizontal line at the junction of the upper edges of two sloping roof surfaces.

Romantic Movement A late 18th- and early 19th-century movement in France, Germany, England and America in art, architecture and literature. Characterized chiefly by a reaction against neo-classicism with its stress on reason and intellect and an emphasis instead on the imagination, emotion, and on freely individualized expression in all spheres of activity. It also embraced exaltation of the primitive and the common man, the worship of and exaltation of nature, interest in the remote in time and space, a predilection for the melancholy, etc.

Ronggeng A Malay form of square dance to the accompaniment of singing, poems, and musical instruments, including gongs.

Rotunda A large and high circular hall or room in a building, especially one surmounted with a dome. It can also refer to a round building, especially one with a dome.

Rumah anjung The open sitting-room at the front of a Malay house similar to the *serambi*, or veranda. Sometimes referred to as *anjung* only.

Rumah makan The dining-room of a Malay house. Usually described as *ruang makan* or *bilik makan*.

Rumah tengah The central family room of a Malay house.

Rustication Method of forming masonry with roughened surfaces and recessed (usually chamfered) joints; principally used in buildings of the Renaissance period to give a feeling of strength and solidarity.

Scale In architecture, the formal, visually appropriate relationship between the dimensions of parts of a building and that of the human figure.

Serambi A Malay open veranda.

Setambul A type of Malay travelling musical performance.

Shophouse Shop with a dwelling above. Shophouses are usually built as part of a terrace, often with their upper floors over-hanging the first storey to form a covered pedestrian arcade. They were characteristic of the 19th- and early 20th-century commercial centres of South East Asian towns and cities.

Shutter Movable screen applied to the inside or outside of a window or door to shut out the light or to ensure privacy or safety.

Sisik A game, popular amongst the Straits Chinese, involving cards of four colours.

Straits Chinese Those Chinese born in the area of the Straits of Malacca, distinct from those who were China-born. Refers more accurately to a cultural group of Chinese who have adopted a unique lifestyle, an integration of Chinese religion and ancestry, and Malay food and costume.

Stucco Exterior finish, usually textured and composed of cement, lime, sand and water.

Stupa Relic based on the Vedic Indian funerary mound and representing the Buddhist cosmic mountain (Mt Meru). It commemorates sacred places, events or people.

Syce From the Hindu and Arabic word for groom (*sais, sayis*); also an attendant who follows on foot a mounted horseman or a carriage. In the Singapore context, it refers to a chauffeur.

Tamil One of a race of people of the Dravidian stock who inhabit southeast India and northern Sri Lanka; also the language spoken.

Taoism System of religion founded on the doctrine set forth in the work of *Tao Te King* (*Book of Reason and Virtue*), attributed to the ancient Chinese philosopher Lao-Tzu (b. 604 BC). It ranks with Confucianism and Buddhism as one of the three religions of China. It stresses an understanding of the mystic forces of nature (especially *yin* and *yang*) and a belief that man need not be active since things will come to a successful conclusion without him.

Temenggong In the traditional Malay States, this word stood for an official responsible for maintaining law and order and for commanding the police and army (something like a grand chamberlain). He was usually someone in the family. This important non-hereditary position became delineated during the development of the 15th-century Malaccan state, which emerged as a trade entrepôt between India, China and South East Asia. The term is now spelt as 'Temenggung'.

Terrace Embankment with a level top, a platform adjoining a building usually used for leisure and an abbreviated expression for a terrace-house which is one of a row of houses sharing common side (party) walls.

Terracotta Fired red earthenware clay or the colour of such ware.

Thaipusam Celebration of the birthday of the Indian god, Murugan, who comes to earth in the form of a boy. Anyone who asks him a favour which is granted must repay by carrying a *kavadi* for a certain time. The person must fast for at least two weeks before the celebration, feeding mostly on milk and abstaining from meat, alcohol and sex. When the day arrives, he will go into a trance when the god enters him and carry a *kavadi*, which can range from a simple jug of milk to a huge metal structure dug into the skin. The festival is held around January to March each year on a date set according to the Tamil–Hindu lunar calendar.

Thatch A material, such as straw, rushes, leaves, etc, used to cover roofs, grain stacks, etc.

Timithi Hindu practice of fire-walking. The most common ritual in Singapore occurs annually at an all-day ceremony at the Sri Mariamman Temple as part of the month's celebrations to Mahabharata.

Tok Panjang Traditional Straits Chinese meal taken at a long table.

Tower Any building characterized by its relatively great height.

Tudor style Style of architecture which was the final development of English perpendicular Gothic architecture during the reigns of Henry VII and Henry VIII (1485–1547), preceding Elizabethan architecture and characterized by four-centred arches, square-headed mullioned windows, gable roofs with high and carved pinnacles, vaulting and half-timbering.

Tukang air An adult male workman or servant.

Tuscan order Classical order similar to Roman Doric but with an unfluted column shaft and a simplified base, capital and entablature.

Valance A short curtain or piece of drapery that is hung from the edge of a canopy, frame of a bed, etc. Also a short ornamental piece of drapery across the top of a window.

Venetian shutters Shutters shaped to fit a Venetian or Palladian window. This is in the form of a round-headed archway with a narrower, lower rectangular window on either side.

Veranda A large, open porch, usually roofed and partly enclosed as by a railing, sometimes with the roof supported on pillars, often extending across the front and sides of a house; a gallery.

Victorian style Style of architecture which was revivalist and eclectic and was produced in the 19th century in Great Britain, named after the reign of Queen Victoria (1837–1901).

Villa Large, elaborate dwelling with outbuildings and gardens of the Roman and Renaissance times; in modern times it refers to a detached urban or suburban house of a superior type and often with some pretension.

Wayang Classical Javanese shadow puppet drama, developed before the 10th century. The form had origins in the leather puppets of southern India. The art of shadow puppetry probably spread to Java with the spread of Hinduism.

Whawhay A card game, popular amongst the Straits Chinese, particularly women, involving bets on different colours.

Wok A Chinese cooking pan. The Malay word is *kuali*.

Wright, Frank Lloyd (1869–1959) A famous American architect whose work reflected his belief in such principles as the integration of a building into its natural setting, the fact that a building's aesthetic quality should arise substantially from the nature of its materials and the fusion of spaces one into the other. Such principles were demonstrated in his series of 'Prairie Houses' built between 1900 and 1910 and later buildings of varied type and form, such as the Imperial Hotel, Tokyo, commenced in 1916, and offices for S C Johnson and Company, Wisconsin, of 1936–9.

Bibliography

Archer, M and Bastin J, *The Raffles Drawings*, Singapore, Oxford University Press, 1968.

Archives and Oral History Department, Singapore, *Singapore Retrospect through Postcards 1900–1930*, Singapore, 1982.

Archives and Oral History Department, Singapore, *The Land Transport of Singapore*, Singapore, 1981.

Archives and Oral History Department, Singapore, *Serangoon Road. A Pictorial History*, Singapore, 1983.

Aslet, C and Powers, A, *The National Trust Book of The English House*, London, Viking in assoc with The National Trust, 1985.

Barrett, H and Phillips, J, *Suburban Style: The British Home, 1840–1960*, London, MacDonald Orbis, 1987.

Beamish, J and Fergusson, J, *A History of Singapore Architecture: The Making of a City*, Singapore, Graham Brash, 1985.

Briggs, R A, *Bungalows & Country Residences*, London, Batsford, 1891.

Buckley, C B, *An Anecdotal History of Old Times in Singapore 1819–1867*, Singapore, Fraser & Neave Ltd, 1902; reprinted Kuala Lumpur, University of Malaya Press, 1965, and Singapore, Oxford University Press, 1984.

Burnett, J, *A Social History of Housing, 1815–1970*, London, Methuen, 1980.

Cook, O, *The English House through Seven Centuries*, London, Penguin, 1968.

Daily Mail, *The Daily Mail Bungalow Book*, London, Associated Newspapers Ltd, 1922.

Davies, P, *Splendours of the Raj: British Architecture in India, 1660 to 1947*, London, John Murray, 1985.

Doggett, M J, *Characters of Light*, Singapore, Times Books International, 1985.

Falconer, J, *A Vision of the Past*, Singapore, Times Editions, 1984.

Fermer-Hesketh, R, *Architecture of the British Empire*, London, Weidenfeld & Nicolson, 1986.

Fletcher, B, *A History of Architecture on the Comparative Method*, London, Batsford, 1954.

Flower, R, *Raffles. The Story of Singapore*, Singapore, Croom Helm Ltd, 1984.

Gibbs, P, *Building a Malay House*, Singapore, Oxford University Press, 1987.

Girouard, M, *Life in the English Country House: A Social and Architectural History*, London, Penguin, 1978.

Hall-Jones, J, *The Thomson Paintings*, Singapore, Oxford University Press, 1983.

Hall-Jones, J and Hooi, C, *An Early Surveyor in Singapore: John Turnbull Thompson in Singapore, 1841–1853*, Singapore, National Museum, 1979.

Hock Gwee Thian, *A Nonya Mosaic: My Mother's Childhood*, Singapore, Times Books International, 1985.

Hancock, T H H, 'George Drumgoole Coleman', *Journal of the Institute of Architects of Malaya*, Vol 1, No 3, 1951.

Hancock, T H H and Gibson-Hill, C A, *Architecture in Singapore*, Singapore, Singapore Art Society and Institute of Architecture of Malaya, 1954.

Institute of Architects of Malaya, *Quarterly Journals*, Singapore, various issues.

Journal of the Malaysian Branch of the Royal Asiatic Society, *Singapore: 150 Years*, Singapore, Times Books International, 1969.

Keeley, C J H, *A Book of Bungalows and Modern Homes*, London, Batsford, 1928.

Keughran, T J, *Picturesque and Busy Singapore*, Singapore, Journal of the Malaysian Branch of the Royal Asiatic Society, 1887.

King, A D, *Colonial Urban Development*, London, Routledge & Kegan Paul, 1976.

King, A D, *The Bungalow: A Product of Several Cultures*, London, Routledge & Kegan Paul, 1984.

Kohl, D G, *Chinese Architecture in the Straits Settlements and Western Malaya: Temples, Kongsis and Houses*, Singapore, Heinemann Asia, 1984.

Makepeace, W E, Braddell, R St J, and Brooke, G S (eds.), *One Hundred Years of Singapore*, Volumes 1 & 2, London, John Murray, 1921.

Moore, D and Moore, J, *The First 150 Years of Singapore*, Singapore, Donald Moore Press, 1969.

Morris, J and Winchester, J, *Stones of Empire: The Buildings of the Raj*, Oxford, Oxford University Press, 1983.

National Archives, Singapore, Building Plans, 1884–1940.

National Archives, Singapore, *Singapore Historical Post Cards*, Singapore, Time Editions, 1986.

National Museum, Singapore, Maps & Prints Collection.

Nilsson, S, *European Architecture in India 1750–1850*, London, Faber & Faber, 1968.

Pearson, H F, *Singapore: A Popular History 1819-1960*, Singapore, Eastern Universities Press, 1961.

Pott, J, *Old Bungalows in Bangalore, South India*, London, published by the author, 1977.

Quaile, Y, *We Remember*, Singapore, Landmark, 1986.

Raffles, S, *Memoir of Sir Stamford Raffles*, London, John Murray, 1830.

Seow E J, 'Architectural Development in Singapore', unpublished PhD thesis, University of Melbourne, 1971.

SIAJ (Journal of The Singapore Institute of Architects), Singapore various issues.

Song Ong Siang, *One Hundred Years' History of the Chinese in Singapore*, London, John Murray, 1923.

Straits Settlements Records, MSS on Microfilm, National Library Holdings, Singapore.

Turnbull, C M, *A History of Singapore 1819–1975*, Kuala Lumpur, Oxford University Press, 1977.

Tyers, R, *Singapore Then and Now*, 2 volumes, Singapore, University Education Press, 1976.

Wright, A and Cartwright, H A (eds.), *Twentieth Century Impressions of British Malaya: Its History, People, Industries and Resources*, London, Lloyds Greater Britain Publishing Company Ltd., 1908.

Picture Credits

All photography, maps, prints, postcards and other archival material belong to the author except where listed below.

The author and publisher would like to thank the following individuals, museums and hotels for their contribution towards the book. Every possible effort has been made to identify, locate and contact owners of copyright and to seek formal permission for reproducing these images.

Acknowledgments

The Author and Publisher would like to thank the following for all their help in the production of this book (the acknowledgments that follow are not in any particular order):

Miss Lucia Ellen Bach, Mrs Cynthia Cook, Mrs Marjorie Doggett, Mr Andrew Gilmour, Mrs Pamela Hickley, Mr R H Ho, Mr Rajabali Jumabhoy, Mr Asad Jumabhoy, Mr Lee Liang Hye, Mrs Betty Lim Koon Teck, Dr Evelyn Lip, Dr Earl Liu, Mrs M Namazie, Mr M J Namazie, Mrs Linda Siddique, the late Mr Sinclair and Mrs Lu Sinclair, Mrs Grace Tan, Mr Jack Tan, Mrs Gracia Tay Chee, Mr Kee Yeap, Mr and Mrs Walter Handmer, Mrs Geraldene Lowe-Ismail, Mrs Elizabeth Brown, Mrs Allison Meares, Mr Andrew Tan, Dr Sharon Siddique, Dr Anthony King, Mr Peter Brown, Beng Mee Nah, Cheong Kok Leong, Ang Boon Keng, Chao Heok Jiang, Ho Fon Yen, Hsia Shih Chiang, Laila Jamali, Lee Aik Lau, Low Wing Kin, Ng Oai Chee, Tan Kay Yong, Tan Lai Kheng, Lim Kheng Chye, Robert Powell, Luca Invernizzi Tettoni, Jacob Termansen, Ong & Ong Architects, Julian Davison.

Special acknowledgments are due to the National Archives, the Oral History Department, the National Museum, the National Library Board, the National University of Singapore Reprographic Service and the support given by the University.

Special thanks are due to Professor Eu Jin Seow, Jon Lim, Peter Keys, Robyn Edwards and other family members in the production of the first edition; and special mention for the second edition goes to Hsien Yoong How, independent collector, and Julie Yeo of Antiques of the Orient, whose unswerving dedication to the preservation of heritage in Singapore has ensured many historical records have not been lost.